LINKING CITIZENS AND PARTIES

COMPARATIVE POLITICS

Comparative Politics is a series for students, teachers, and researchers of political science that deals with contemporary government and politics. Global in scope, books in the series are characterised by a stress on comparative analysis and strong methodological rigour. The series is published in association with the European Consortium for Political Research. For more information visit www.essex.ac.uk/ecpr

The Comparative Politics series is edited by Professor David M. Farrell, School of Politics and International Relations, University College Dublin, Kenneth Carty, Professor of Political Science, University of British Columbia, and Professor Dirk Berg-Schlosser. Institute of Political Science, Philipps University, Marburg.

OTHER TITLES IN THIS SERIES

Democracy within Parties
Candidate Selection Methods and
Their Political Consequences
Reuven Y. Hazan and Gideon Rahat

Party Politics in New Democracies
Edited by Paul Webb and Stephen White

Intergovernmental Cooperation
Rational Choices in Federal System and Beyond
Nicole Bolleyer

The Dynamics of Two-Party Politics
Party Structures and the Management of Competition
Alan Ware

Cabinets and Coalition Bargaining
The Democratic Life Cycle in Western Europe
Edited by Kaare Strøm, Wolfgang C. Müller, and Torbjörn Bergman

Redistricting in Comparative Perspective
Edited by Lisa Handley and Bernard Grofman

Democratic Representation in Europe
Diversity, Change, and Convergence
Edited by Maurizio Cotta and Heinrich Best

Losers' Consent
Elections and Democratic Legitimacy
Christopher J. Anderson, André Blais, Shaun Bowler,
Todd Donovan, and Ola Listhaug

The Presidentialization of Politics
A Comparative Study of Modern Democracies
Edited by Thomas Poguntke and Paul Webb

Environmental Protest in Western Europe
Edited by Christopher Rootes

Democratic Challenges, Democratic Choices
The Erosion of Political Support in Advanced Industrial Democracies
Russell J. Dalton

Citizens, Democracy, and Markets Around the Pacific Rim
Congruence Theory and Political Culture
Edited by Russell J. Dalton and Doh Chull Shin

Extreme Right Parties in Western Europe
Piero Ignazi

Linking Citizens and Parties

How Electoral Systems Matter
for Political Representation

LAWRENCE EZROW

OXFORD

UNIVERSITY PRESS

Great Clarendon Street, Oxford OX2 6DP

Oxford University Press is a department of the University of Oxford.
It furthers the University's objective of excellence in research, scholarship,
and education by publishing worldwide in

Oxford New York

Auckland Cape Town Dar es Salaam Hong Kong Karachi
Kuala Lumpur Madrid Melbourne Mexico City Nairobi
New Delhi Shanghai Taipei Toronto

With offices in

Argentina Austria Brazil Chile Czech Republic France Greece
Guatemala Hungary Italy Japan Poland Portugal Singapore
South Korea Switzerland Thailand Turkey Ukraine Vietnam

Oxford is a registered trade mark of Oxford University Press
in the UK and in certain other countries

Published in the United States
by Oxford University Press Inc., New York

© Lawrence Ezrow 2010

The moral rights of the author have been asserted
Database right Oxford University Press (maker)

First published 2010

British Library Cataloguing in Publication Data

Data available

Library of Congress Cataloging in Publication Data

Library of Congress Control Number: 2010922414

Typeset by SPI Publisher Services, Pondicherry, India
Printed in Great Britain
on acid-free paper by
MPG Books Group, Bodmin and King's Lynn

ISBN 978–0–19–957252–6

1 3 5 7 9 10 8 6 4 2

Preface

This book presents three basic arguments. First, electoral systems do not matter in ways that are commonly accepted (Chapters 2 and 3). Second, electoral systems, however, do influence levels of niche party competition (Chapter 4). Third, citizen-party linkages, that is, channels of political representation, are fundamentally different for niche parties than for mainstream parties (Chapters 5 and 6). Thus, electoral systems matter because they influence the level of niche party competition. Figure 1.2 depicts an overview of these relationships on page 15.

Acknowledgments

Shortly after I arrived at the University of Essex in 2007, Ian Budge remarked to me "your papers are very nice." Then, he demanded "But Lawrence, how do they all fit together?" This project constitutes my response. I thank Ian for pushing me to approach my research with wider scope and for his extensive feedback on the manuscript.

Kai Arzeimer, John Bartle, Royce Carroll, Scott Desposato, Marty Gilens, Garrett Glasgow, Kristian Gleditsch, Tim Hellwig, Ken Kollman, Kent Jennings, Michael McDonald, Tony McGann, Lorelei Moosbrugger, Thomas Plümper, Jesse Russell, Hugh Ward, and Albert Weale have provided valuable comments on earlier versions of the chapters.

I owe gratitude to David Farrell and Kenneth Newton, the current and previous editors of the comparative politics series at Oxford University Press (OUP), for providing me with practical advice and comments throughout the project. In addition, I thank the commissioning editor at OUP, Dominic Byatt, for his remarks on the project and for his flexibility. I am grateful to my colleagues in the Department of Government at the University of Essex for contributing to an innovative research environment for studying citizens, parties, institutions, and elections. When I first arrived, this culture was led by the former Head of Department, David Sanders, and has been sustained by the current Head, Han Dorussen. I also thank the helpful and supportive Administrative team in the Department.

This project has also been assisted by funding from the UK Economic and Social Research Council (ESRC) Grant, RES-000–22–2895, "Subconstituency Representation Across Western Europe." Spyros Kosmidis and Anja Neundorf provided me with excellent research assistance under this grant. I also completed a good portion of the project in July and August 2008 in College Station, Texas, with an award from the European Union Center for Excellence at Texas A&M University. I thank the Director of the Center, Guy Whitten, for his substantive comments on drafts of chapters and for being an excellent host.

Chapter 6 is based on a coauthored project with Catherine de Vries, Erica E. Edwards, and Marco Steenbergen. I am indebted to these scholars for, among many other things, their ideas and for allowing me to use them in the manuscript.

Gary Marks agreed to supervise my undergraduate honors thesis in the fall of 1996 at University of North Carolina, Chapel Hill (thereby starting my professional academic career). Later, I reunited with Gary and Liesbet Hooghe at the Vrije Universiteit, Amsterdam. They have provided me with crucial support, and extremely helpful comments on the manuscript. I am unable to express the gratitude for my former thesis advisor, Jim Adams, who has spent countless hours preparing comments and conferring with me about my work. As Jim's past and current students are already aware, his enthusiasm, encouragement, and ability to inspire are almost as valuable as the substantive feedback he provides.

On a personal note, I thank my parents, brothers, and parents-in-law for their unconditional support. I am also grateful to Erica Frantz and Cliff Williams for "productive breaks" from this project. Lastly, I dedicate the following to Annika, Natasha, and our future.

Contents

List of Figures

List of Tables

List of Abbreviations

CMP	Comparative Manifesto Project
CSES	Comparative Survey of Electoral Systems
ENEP	Effective number of elective parties
ENPP	Effective number of parliamentary parties
OLS	Ordinary least squares
PR	Proportional representation
SMD	Single member districts
UPE	Unweighted measure of the average party policy extremism
WPE	Weighted measure of average party policy extremism

Part I

Introduction

1

Citizen–Party Linkages, Political Institutions, and Type of Party

1.1 TRANSLATING CITIZENS' PREFERENCES: INSTITUTIONS AND PARTIES

Popular democratic beliefs dictate that somehow policy preferences of citizens will translate into the selection of representatives who, in turn, produce policies. These policies then govern the interactions of citizens. How do citizen preferences influence policy? The most straightforward way is through voting in elections. In this sense, democratic ideals imply citizen participation and voting in elections drive the policies that govern citizens.

The *translation* of citizen interests into government policy may be far from smooth or simple, however, and this transmission is also dependent on institutions and parties. For example, the rules that govern the translation of votes into legislative seats directly affect pathways of representation. Writing in Great Britain in the nineteenth century, John Stuart Mill noted that distorted representation was a direct consequence of plurality voting rules, that is, laws that dictate that a candidate with the most votes wins. Although plurality voting systems are likely to produce winning candidates that will represent their supporters' interests, Mill complained that many citizens, who had voted for the loser, would largely be left unrepresented. The discussion over the effects of electoral systems on political representation has continued (Hoag and Hallet 1926; Hermens 1941; Duverger 1954; Rae 1967; Riker 1982; Cox 1990, 1997; however, for dissenting opinions on the overstated impact of electoral systems, see Grumm 1958; Lipset and Rokkan 1967).[1]

---

[1] In addition to electoral systems, institutions that determine how the executive branch is selected and organized also affect the nature of democratic governance. Although the systematic study of constitutions and executive power sharing arrangements is relatively new (Lijphart 1984, 1999; Powell 2000), these authors have underlined a major distinction, between systems where executive power is shared by more than one party, and systems where authority is bestowed upon *only* one party through elections. These power-sharing rules affect the way in which citizens' underlying preferences are translated into representative outcomes. For example, citizens are more likely to vote sincerely where power-sharing is the norm and, strategically, where only one party dominates government decision-making. While the mediating effects of power-sharing are only partially explored in this

Underlying the importance of electoral institutions is the important role of *parties*, which are critical in mobilizing citizen participation, especially during election periods. More importantly, parties are responsible for expressing the ideological preferences of citizens and converting them into public policy. The role of parties has been articulated under the "party government model," which assumes parties compete on the basis of distinct policy platforms, which respond to the ideological interests of their supporters (Dalton 2002).

In this sense then scholars of political representation pay attention to linkages between citizens and parties – and how these linkages may (or may not) be mediated by electoral institutions. In the following chapters, these linkages are analyzed. First, I identify how citizen preferences are translated into election outcomes (Chapter 2), and the policies that parties announce (Chapter 3). This task requires a macro-level approach that employs cross-national analyses of party ideologies, public opinion, election outcomes, and institutions.

The layout and argument of this study is relatively straightforward. Scholars of comparative democracy often identify electoral systems as the prime factor in explaining cross-country variation in patterns of representation. I find that while electoral systems matter for political representation, they do not matter in ways we might expect. For example, there is a fairly common expectation that parties cluster toward the center of the ideological space under plurality-like systems, and that one of the main reasons for doing so is that the electoral incentives for centrist positions are greater in these systems. Yet, the evidence presented in Chapters 2 and 3 suggests that electoral systems do not systematically motivate parties to take divergent or convergent positions. I wish to implore scholars to alter the discourse on citizen–party policy linkages by lowering the level of analysis from the country-level to the party-level. When parties are classified along the lines of two recent studies by James Adams and his colleagues (2006) and Bonnie Meguid (2008; see also Meguid 2005) into "niche" and "mainstream" parties, a powerful narrative emerges that these groupings of party families represent citizens' viewpoints in starkly different ways (in Chapters 5 and 6). Niche parties refer to those parties that occupy the extreme Left, the extreme Right, or a distinctly noncentrist niche; specifically, these parties belong to the Communist, Right-wing Nationalist, and Green party families. Mainstream parties are defined as parties belonging to the Social Democratic, Liberal, Christian Democratic, and Conservative party families.

It is the type of party that is important for policy representation rather than differences between election systems. In several respects democracies operate

study because it is not the main focus, it should be noted that concentrated power-sharing arrangements tend to be associated with plurality electoral rules, and dispersed power-sharing arrangements with proportional systems. To the extent the two are observed hand in hand, the mediating effects of electoral systems will also apply to power-sharing arrangements.

similarly, regardless of particular electoral institutions, and in many ways patterns of representation vary quite drastically by type of party – each type offering different channels of political representation to citizens. If the type of party is so vital in mediating linkages between citizens and parties (as I argue), then the question naturally arises: Under which settings do different types of parties thrive? Unsurprisingly, electoral systems influence levels of niche party success. *My central argument is that electoral systems matter for political representation through their influence on the balance between niche and mainstream party influence.*

The rest of the chapter addresses several issues. Related to this argument, it identifies the core questions behind my analysis, and the limitations to it. Additionally, the chapter identifies several conceptual building blocks that underpin the discussion: these are electoral institutions, two models of electoral outcomes, two models of party responsiveness, and type of party (niche and mainstream groupings). The following sections discuss these concepts, assess the significance of the study, and set the plan for the book.

1.2 CENTRAL QUESTIONS AND THEMES

My central goal is to determine when and how electoral institutions mediate citizen–party linkages on a "Left–Right" dimension that is defined as the level of support for government intervention in the economy (Downs 1957). En route, I aim to produce theoretical and empirical contributions to understanding why parties take the Left–Right ideological positions that they do, and also to explore the subsequent electoral effects of these positions. We will examine the correspondence between citizens' policy preferences and parties' ideological programs – and how this pattern varies across eighteen industrialized and stable democracies from 1973 to 2002. I will address four questions in regard to representational congruence between voters and parties:

1. Do political system variables (i.e., voting rules) affect whether it is electorally advantageous for parties to advocate centrist policy positions, relative to the distribution of voters' policy preferences?
2. Do institutions (in particular, electoral rules) affect the average distinctiveness of policy alternatives that parties offer citizens?
3. Do institutions affect the configuration of niche and mainstream party families that exist or compete within a political system?
4. How do niche and mainstream party families matter for patterns of political representation, with respect to responsiveness and election outcomes?

1.2.1 Which aspects of democratic representation are covered by this study?

Figure 1.1 partially reproduces figure 1.2 from Powell (2000), depicting connections in the democratic process. It is particularly useful for illustrating components of representation that are dealt with directly (and those that are dealt with less directly) in the analyses here. This figure identifies citizen preferences and public policies as the necessary starting and finishing points for democratic theory. The correspondence between A and E is obviously important. However, it is the *process* by which the "connection" is made, which is also critical for democracy. For example, a system would not be considered a democracy where a benevolent dictator implements policies that match the ideological preferences of the citizens, because there is no element of citizen control over policy making. Democracies are identified as such by whether or not institutions, or connections, are in place that establishes a mechanism for citizen preferences to be translated into public policies.[2]

This study focuses primarily on Links A–C in figure 1.1. There are, however, several steps of the representative process that I do *not* systematically explore, such as the *formation of citizen preferences* in the sense of any examination of the socialization processes that shape individual political attitudes (Jennings and Niemi 1981). Scholars have persuasively argued that citizens take cues from political leadership when forming their policy preferences (Przeworski and Sprague 1986; Rabinowitz and Macdonald 1989). Some final aspects of the representative process that will not be addressed are policy making and policy implementation during the postelection bargaining process (for the effects of institutions on policy outputs, see Soroka and Wlezien 2010; Lijphart 1999; McDonald and Budge 2005).

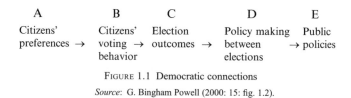

FIGURE 1.1 Democratic connections

Source: G. Bingham Powell (2000: 15: fig. 1.2).

---

[2] This scenario is similar to that raised by Hanna Pitkin (1967: 234) who comments, "An absolute monarch or dictator who chooses, for a reason of his own, to take public opinion polls and do whatever the people seem to want is not yet a representative government. We require functioning institutions that are designed to and really do, secure a government responsive to public interest and opinion (quoted in Powell 2000: 280)."

1.3 DEFINING INSTITUTIONS

It is worth clarifying what is actually meant by the term "institutions." In a comparative analysis of economic performance, Douglas North (1990) presents a concise and reasonable definition:

> Institutions include any form of constraint that human beings devise to shape human interaction. Are institutions formal or informal? They can be either, and I am interested both in formal constraints – such as rules that human beings devise – and in informal constraints – such as conventions and codes of behavior. Institutions may be created, as was the United States Constitution; or they may simply evolve over time, as does the common law. (p. 4)

In what follows, I analyze the effects of *formal institutions* by concentrating on voting rules. One benefit of this decision is that formal institutions are easier to identify, measure, and classify than informal institutions.[3] However, the price paid for this simplification involves losing some information about the cultural context of each country.

1.4 DEFINING ELECTORAL SYSTEMS: PLURALITY VOTING VERSUS PROPORTIONAL REPRESENTATION

By electoral system, I denote the rules that specify how votes are translated into seats for representatives in the main legislation making body. What I particularly want to focus on here is the *outcomes* of these rules. Thus, I focus on the *discrepancies between parties' national vote shares and their parliamentary seat shares*. If the vote and seat shares for a party roughly correspond as in the 1998 Dutch elections where the Labour party (PvdA) won 29% of the popular vote and subsequently received 30% (45/150) of the seats in the lower house (the Tweede Kamer), then this system is considered "proportional." However, systems where votes and seats do not correspond – for example, in the 2002 French elections the National Front received above 11% of the national vote and were subsequently allotted zero seats in the National Assembly – are labeled "disproportional."[4]

---

[3] While there is no systematic analysis presented here of informal institutions, which include cultural factors such as customs, traditions, and codes of conduct, it is worth noting that these factors are relevant because they are crucial in the understanding of how a given political system came to adopt a particular set of formal institutions.

[4] I owe this simplification to an *Electoral Studies* article by Gallagher (1991), where he develops a continuous index of disproportionality (discussed in much greater detail in Chapter 3).

While the literature classifying electoral systems is extensive, and there are many combinations of electoral rules that will yield proportional and disproportional outcomes,[5] in the subsequent discussion the major fault line that is drawn is between systems allocating seats by *plurality voting* and those that determine seat shares via *proportional representation* (PR) electoral formulae. Under single-member district plurality voting, the winning candidate is the one who receives the most votes. For this reason "first past the post" and "winner-take-all" voting are perhaps more common labels for the plurality voting formula. Examples of countries that use plurality voting rules include Britain, Canada, and the United States, and New Zealand prior to 1993. Plurality voting rules generate disproportionate vote-to-seat allocations. More specifically, these voting rules hurt smaller parties and reward larger parties.[6]

As this discussion suggests, the plurality voting formula often manufactures a majority of seats for one party in the legislature, because a party that wins a nationwide plurality will tend to be overrepresented and hold a majority of seats in the legislature. One of the potential benefits of this system of voting is that *accountability* should be clear to voters by the legislation passed. However, the major drawback is uneven, or unfair, representation of citizens' policy preferences, which in turn bars entry for third parties, and it induces voters not to "waste" their votes on third or losing parties. Instead, voters cast their ballots strategically for one of the two contenders as opposed to voting *sincerely* for the parties that best represent their policy preferences.

On the other hand, electoral systems featuring PR are associated with more "proportional" vote-to-seat conversions than in plurality systems. The difference in outcome can be attributed to four differences from plurality systems based on: formula, district magnitude, candidate versus party voting, and effective thresholds. The latter three characteristics are a by-product of the differing voting rules that determine how votes are translated into seats. That is, plurality systems will almost automatically be associated with single-member districts, individual candidates, and high effective electoral thresholds. In contrast, PR systems are associated with multimember districts, party lists, and relatively low effective thresholds.

PR systems are more prevalent in developed democracies than are plurality systems, perhaps because they are more appealing insofar in terms of their "representativeness" than plurality systems. More parties and smaller or minority

---

[5] A comprehensive discussion of electoral systems would also include attention to the effects of district magnitude (i.e., the number of seats awarded per district to the legislature), electoral thresholds (or the minimum percentage of the vote necessary for a party to gain representation in the legislature), and assembly size (Lijphart 1994). Notice too that there are several methods of allocating seats within PR systems that will affect the proportionality of the system; some systems include the Hare, Droop, d'Hondt, Saint Lague, and the Imperiali methods of allocating seats.

[6] In systems employing plurality voting, smaller parties will receive smaller shares of seats than their national vote shares indicate (recall the example of the National Front), while larger parties benefit by receiving larger proportions of the seats than their shares of the votes.

interests can gain representation in the legislature in a way that is commensurate with their level of popular support. However, critics argue that PR allows too many parties to gain power, which affects the efficiency, stability, and accountability of policy making. A more serious objection that is often raised against PR systems is that they present the opportunity for extremist factions to gain too much influence, a claim that is refuted in Chapter 3. Parties that compete in PR and plurality systems are on average equally extreme (or centrist). I return to these normative arguments in the conclusion, arguing that – in addition to the conventional justification for PR that it increases the raw numbers of parties and thereby the number of outlets for representation of citizen interests – PR also enhances niche party competition, which in turn provides fundamentally different channels through which political representation can take place.[7]

1.5 EFFECTS OF INSTITUTIONS

The central goal of this study is to determine how electoral institutions mediate citizen–party linkages. I briefly outline here how institutions, with specific regard to electoral systems (and power-sharing arrangements), play a role in structuring the *number of competitive parties* in the political system; and the role institutions play in *policy making* and the quality of representation (Lijphart 1984, 1999; Powell 2000). Then, I discuss the role institutions play in elections and in influencing *party support*. Additionally, I consider their effects on *positioning incentives* – under which sets of circumstances are centripetal or centrifugal incentives more prevalent for competing parties in a political system (Cox 1997; Dow 2001; Merrill and Adams 2002)?

1.6 INSTITUTIONS, THE NUMBER OF PARTIES, AND POLICY OUTPUTS

In 1954, Maurice Duverger asserted that electoral institutions affect the number of parties that are able to compete in a political system. Specifically, Duverger's Law states that plurality rules are associated with two-party systems. Conversely,

---

[7] The dichotomy between PR and plurality voting, and the subsequent trade-offs that academics acknowledge between the two systems, are disputed by Carey and Hix (2008). In a paper titled "The Electoral Sweetspot," they argue that low district magnitude (approximately 6) PR systems maximize on the conventional strengths of both types of systems (choice, accountability, and stability).

Duverger developed hypotheses claiming that PR is associated with multiparty systems. Two ballot majority systems, which in a certain sense lie between PR and plurality, are associated with "multipartism tempered by alliances."

Duverger identifies *mechanical* and *psychological* effects of "first past the post" electoral rules to support his "Law," that plurality tends toward bipartism. The mechanical effect comes from the fact that smaller parties, that is, third parties, fourth parties, and so on are unable to become significant competitors because of the disproportional vote-to-seat translations that have already been discussed. Plurality systems award seat shares to large parties that exceed their national vote shares, while smaller parties receive seat shares that are significantly less than their national vote shares.[8] For smaller parties, this unfair allocation of seats is a threat to their future viability.

The mechanical effect induces voters to cast their ballots strategically in order to avoid "wasting" their votes on parties that will not gain at least a proportionate influence in the legislature. This effect on voters is referred to as the *psychological effect*. Additionally, William Riker (1986: 40) supposes politicians and party donors are "rational purchasers" of political careers and "influence and access." If this is the case, the psychological effect influences the behavior of more than just voters, as it will indeed also cause leaders and donors to desert marginalized parties.

Plurality rules therefore induce broad interests in society to coalesce *before elections* in order to have any chance of gaining the most votes. Much later research has reinforced Duverger's point that voting institutions are crucial because they influence party systems (Rae 1967; Riker 1982; Taagepera and Shugart 1989; Cox 1997).[9]

---

[8] The British election of 1983 is perhaps the best example of Duverger's mechanical effect. The Liberals and the Social Democrats allied, and gained just over 25% of the votes, and yet they only received 23 of 650 seats (approximately 3.5%) in the House of Commons. Ironically, the competitiveness of what would become the Liberal–Democrats in these elections with plurality voting can also be construed as evidence against Duverger's Law.

Further supporting the presence of the mechanical effect, Sprague (1980) found that in order for parties to gain fair representation in PR systems (that their shares of votes translate into at least the same shares of the seats), they must receive around 12% share of the popular vote. Contrast this with plurality systems where he estimates that parties need to receive approximately a third of the popular vote in order to receive at least a third of the seats in their legislative assembly.

[9] As with many influential theories in the social sciences Duverger's Law has its share of critics. Debates either circulate over its status as a "sociological law" and/or by focusing on endogeneity issues relating to the relationship between voting rules and the party system. Grumm (1958) documents the latter objection by asserting that it is the party systems that affect the adoption of voting rules and not the other way around, that is multiparty systems adopt proportional representation electoral rules.

Alternatively, Lipset and Rokkan (1967) explain party systems in terms of the number of and depth of *cleavages* (e.g., center–periphery, church–state, land–industry, and owners–workers) in society. Hence the structure of these cleavages at the time of mass enfranchisement was established influenced greatly the structure of party competition.

G. Bingham Powell Jr. (2000) and Arend Lijphart (1999) have done important work that analyzes the relationship between institutions and policy making. Powell concludes that the Left–Right positions of the governing parties are significantly closer to the median citizen's position in proportional systems, as opposed to majoritarian systems (see also McDonald et al. 2004).[10] Lijphart (1999) provides additional evidence that consensual systems, which are often associated with PR electoral systems, perform better than majoritarian systems on several dimensions by arguing that "consensus democracies do clearly outperform the majoritarian democracies with regard to the quality of democracy and democratic representation as well as with regard to what I have called the kindness and gentleness of their public policy orientations" (p. 301).[11]

1.7 TYPE OF PARTY: MAINSTREAM AND NICHE

The above arguments support the idea that electoral institutions matter. The central argument of this book is that their main effect is exerted by influencing the ability of the smaller niche parties to exist and compete effectively. This is an extension of the Duvergerian logic sketched out above. PR encourages small party survival, and many of these small parties are niche parties.[12] To my knowledge scholars have not yet made this precise point. While they tend to focus on the electoral success of one type of niche party, like extreme Right-wing parties or Green parties, a survey of the literature actually turns up few studies that analyze niche parties as a bundle.

How are niche and mainstream parties classified? Concretely, "niche" parties refer to those parties that occupy the extreme Left, the extreme Right, or a distinctly noncentrist niche; specifically, these parties belong to the Communist,

An additional study of the relationship is in *Patterns of Democracy* by Arend Lijphart (1999) where he finds the correlation coefficient that estimates the relationship between proportionality and the number of parties is .55 and reaches statistical significance for the thirty-six postwar democracies.

[10] Powell accurately identifies inherent trade-offs that are built into each "vision" of democracy. While majoritarian systems are portrayed in a negative light because there is a weak correspondence between policy makers and the median citizen, the strength of these systems is that citizens should be able to hold their leaders more accountable because the responsibility for policies is clear.

[11] However, McDonald and Budge (2005, chapter 6) present evidence that the median legislative parties across *all democratic systems* dictate policy.

[12] In addition to the communist, extreme Right-wing Nationalist, and Green party families, smaller party families that could emerge under permissive (i.e., PR) electoral rules are the agrarian, regional, ethnic, and liberal party families.

Right-wing Nationalist, and Green party families. Mainstream parties are defined as parties belonging to the Social Democratic, Liberal, Christian Democratic, and Conservative party families.

There are several characteristics particular to niche parties that lead to the distinction made above – one of which is that these parties promote distinctly noncentrist ideologies along the conventional Left–Right dimension. Bonnie Meguid (2005, 2008) has pioneered the study of niche party competition. Meguid attributes three crucial characteristics to niche parties. First, they can be identified as those parties that attempt to introduce new issues to party competition. Second, these issues are noneconomic or do not comfortably fit on the traditional Left–Right dimension. And third, niche parties limit the number of issue appeals to one. Using these criteria, Meguid explores the electoral fortunes of Green, Nationalist, and ethno-territorial parties. For example, the historical goal of Green parties has been to emphasize environmental issues, and accordingly this issue has remained at the center of its programmatic appeals. Similarly, ethno-territorial parties emphasize regional autonomy, and far-Right Nationalist parties make programmatic statements about restricting immigration.

There is a difference between the definition used in this book and that employed by Meguid, which is that Meguid defines niche parties based on their emphasis of additional issue dimensions that run orthogonally to the traditional Left–Right. As noted above, Green parties highlight environmental concerns, and extreme Right-wing Nationalist parties stress immigration and traditional values (Marks et al. 2006). While Meguid emphasizes the additional issue dimensions on which niche parties compete (see also Rovny and Edwards 2009), I make a central departure from her study and others by pointing out that while niche parties do attempt to compete on additional dimensions, this does not preclude them from also competing in traditional Left–Right terms. The strongest example of this is that Communist parties remain within the typology of niche parties, because they clearly do compete on traditional Left–Right issues. However, in Meguid's study, Communist parties are not considered niche parties, because they do not focus on issue appeals on additional dimensions.

Indeed parties that belong to the Nationalist party family are also called "Right-wing" or "extreme Right" parties. The labels themselves connote competition on the far "Right" of the "Left–Right." Environmental parties tend to fall distinctly to the Left. To the extent political trade-offs have existed historically between environmental interests and commercial industry, one would expect environmental parties to lean distinctly to the Left. However, there are smaller parties characterized as neither mainstream nor niche parties. These are the regional, ethnic, and agrarian parties. Several studies have defined these parties as niche parties. Here I do not because I contend that these parties really do not compete on the Left–Right. So, while Meguid emphasizes additional issue dimensions, I emphasize the distinctly noncentrist space on the traditional Left–Right in which these parties compete. I note that practical differences are actually quite slight.[13] The major difference is the analysis of these parties' relevance on the Left–Right dimension.

1.8 TWO MODELS ON THE ELECTORAL CONSEQUENCES OF PARTY PROXIMITY TO THE MEAN VOTER POSITION: THE PARTY PROXIMITY MODEL AND THE PARTY DISTINCTIVENESS MODEL

The logic of the party proximity model suggests that parties increase popular support when their policies are closer to the Center of the distribution of voters' policy preferences, while the party distinctiveness model posits that the opposite holds, namely, that parties are rewarded when they advocate noncentrist or radical policy positions. Traditional spatial theory predicts that parties contesting two-party elections gain votes by converging toward the Center (Downs 1957). Theoretical predictions in multiparty settings are mixed: theoretical models that assume deterministic policy voting predict that noncentrist positioning may be optimal (Cox 1990; Adams 2001), while models that assume probabilistic voting predict that parties will increase their expected votes by moderating their positions (De Palma et al. 1990; Lin et al. 1999).

In future chapters (2 and 5), I conduct such analyses in an effort to clarify expectations about the relevance of the convergence prediction in multiparty systems. *Macro-level* analyses are conducted in these chapters, which examine the effects of party positioning on election outcomes across Western Europe from 1976 to 1998. The dependent variable is the party vote share in real-world elections, and the crucial independent variables are based on *policy distance* between the parties and the mean voter positions in the countries included in the study. For this purpose, Eurobarometer surveys have been gathered from the country election years, which have made it possible to construct a measure of the mean citizen policy preference, as well as measures of the policy distances between the parties' policy positions, and the mean citizen preference.

The findings in the second chapter support the conclusions developed in many of the existing studies of multiparty competition: *proximity to the mean voter position matters*. More specifically, I conclude that parties receive a statistically significant electoral benefit from locating near the mean voter position. This benefit, however, is relatively modest in size, so that parties that advocate noncentrist positions may nonetheless be electorally competitive. Chapter 5 shows

---

[13] The difference is the substitution of ethno-territorial parties with communist parties in the niche party classification. In practice when ethno-territorial parties are included in the niche party classification, it has changed few of the substantive conclusions about niche parties. For example, the conclusions reported in Chapter 6 are robust to a definition of niche parties that includes these parties.

that this finding remains robust in statistical analyses that control for the type of party. This finding is labeled the *general policy centrism result*. However, the major contribution of Chapter 5 is to show that the opposite dynamic holds for niche parties. That is, radical niche parties tend to receive more votes than their moderate niche counterparts. This finding is labeled the *party distinctiveness result*. It provides one of the foundations for the argument of the book that the *type of party* matters for analyzing political representation.

1.9 TWO MODELS OF PARTY RESPONSIVENESS: THE GENERAL ELECTORATE MODEL AND THE PARTISAN CONSTITUENCY MODEL

Do political parties respond to the mean voter position, or to the ideological shifts of their supporters? Several theoretical and empirical studies stress that the mean or the median voter position is the starting point for political representation, and the implication of these studies is that parties would be highly sensitive to shifts in the *mean voter* position (Downs 1957; Huber and Powell 1994; Stimson et al. 1995; Powell 2000; Erikson et al. 2002; Adams et al. 2004, 2006; McDonald and Budge 2005). However, an alternative and equally plausible model of party responsiveness exists. This model emphasizes the policy preference of the mean *party supporter* in explaining party–citizen linkages (Weissberg 1978; Dalton 1985; Wessels 1999). I refer to the first model of party responsiveness as the general electorate model, and to the second model as the partisan constituency model. The general electorate model is defined by the political parties responding to shifts in the mean voter position, and the partisan constituency model posits instead that parties respond to their supporters. Chapter 6 takes up these models empirically, and again finds that the type of party drastically mediates the relationship between citizens' and parties' ideological preferences. Specifically, the general electorate model characterizes shifts of mainstream parties, while the partisan constituency model characterizes shifts of niche parties.

1.10 COMBINING CONCEPTS: INSTITUTIONS, TYPE OF PARTY, MODELS OF PARTY RESPONSIVENESS, AND ELECTION OUTCOMES

Figure 1.2 combines the concepts raised in Sections 1.6–1.9 to present an overview. Generally, electoral rules matter because they affect party system size, which

General relationships: Representation channels:

Democratic   →   Types of party   →   Models of representation and
institutions   electoral success

Specific relationships:

1) Disproportional   →   Mainstream party   →   General electorate model
   electoral rules[†]   competition   Party proximity model

2a) Proportional   →   Mainstream party   →   General electorate model
     electoral rules   competition   Party proximity model

                                AND

*2b)   Niche party   →   Partisan constituency model
                             competition   Party distinctiveness model

FIGURE 1.2 An overview of relationships: electoral rules, types of party, and political representation

Notes: † The dual ballot majority system employed in France is a special case. Although this system is comparatively
"disproportional," it does have significant levels of niche party competition (discussed in Chapter 4).
* Additional niche linkages between citizens and parties.

has implications for the types of parties (mainstream and niche) that compete in a
political system. The type of party mediates relationships between the citizens and
the parties in important ways: specifically, disproportional electoral systems (row
1) are associated with mainstream party competition, where the general electorate
and party proximity models apply. Proportional systems similarly display the
dynamics of mainstream party competition (row 2a), but they also offer niche
party competition (in row 2b) where the partisan constituency and party distinctiveness models characterize party responsiveness and electoral competition.

1.11 SIGNIFICANCE

There are several reasons why students of voting and elections should find this
study interesting. First, Chapter 2 tests out the plausibility of spatial models of
convergent and divergent party behavior in Western Europe. Second, the inquiry
introduces a macro-level empirical approach to the study of parties and voters in a
cross-national setting that provides the analyses with greater observational leverage. Third, the study clarifies expectations about how party support is generated,
incentives for party positioning, and how these factors interact with system-level

features. Finally, there are implications for our notions of democratic governance and representation.

The findings have direct implications for Downsian models of electoral competition insofar as one of the primary goals is to examine the relationship between citizens' ideological preferences and the Left–Right placements of competing parties or candidates.[14] Cross-sectional and temporal analyses have shown a connection between centrist policy positioning and electoral support for parties. Implicit in this outcome is the importance of policy positions – for voters and parties – in determining election outcomes. Had a different conclusion been reached, this would have suggested that party positioning along this abstract continuum is unrelated to electoral outcomes.

The study additionally takes advantage from its macro-level empirical approach as suggested by Erikson et al. (2002). Most studies tend to emphasize individual-level data on voting because it is easy to multiply the number of observations by increasing the number of survey respondents. Here data has been gathered from Eurobarometer surveys from 1976 to 2002, which permits the empirical analyses to be conducted cross-nationally. The scope of the data collection further enhances our ability to study how the *dynamics* of representation vary under different institutional contexts. Data have been scarce at aggregate levels of voting especially outside of the United States and, thus, there have been few studies focusing on proximity in several subnational or national elections over time.[15]

An additional reason why this study should be of interest is that it clarifies expectations about convergence in multiparty systems and shows how these expectations vary under different institutional arrangements. Using a Downsian framework in the United States creates clear predictions of convergence. However, in Europe, parties are capable of following several strategies, thus muddling predictions about their behavior. Parties that move toward the median voter to gain votes leave their traditional bases of support. Here, there are solid testable hypotheses – one says parties should gain votes by moving closer to more voters. The alternative hypothesis says these same parties will lose votes by deserting their core supporters. Additionally, the expectation is that proximity effects will be stronger in majoritarian systems than in proportional systems.

Finally, the study is of relevance to those with a general comparative interest in democratic representation. In what follows, the relationship between the voter–party correspondence and election outcomes is examined with particular

---

[14] Citizen Left–Right ideological placements are measured in the Eurobarometer 31A (1989).

[15] The primary set of analyses in Chapters 2–4 places candidates and parties on an ideological scale using the *perceptions of citizens*. Other scholars believe there are more accurate placements of candidates. These studies have used measures of candidates and/or parties based on: expert-placements (Powell 2000), roll-call voting behavior (Ansolabehere et al. 2001; Burden 2001), or the close scrutiny of party manifestos (Budge 1994). In each chapter, alternative analyses are conducted relying on these other measures of party placements so that the confidence in the findings is increased.

reference to how the dynamics of this relationship change under varying institutional settings. Thus, the work bears directly on "congruence" between policy makers and citizens (Huber and Powell 1994) and on the widely known comparative works that study the effects of constitutional design (Lijphart 1984, 1994, 1999; Powell 2000). The findings also relate to our normative ideals about how representation should work. Elections should function as a "link" between citizen policy preferences and elected representatives. From this standpoint, the analyses presented in the following chapters shed light on widely held conceptions of popular democratic governance.

1.12 PLAN OF THE BOOK

The book makes three basic arguments. First, electoral systems do not matter in the ways that are commonly accepted (Chapters 2 and 3). Electoral systems however do influence niche party competitiveness (Chapter 4). The role of niche parties in turn has dramatic implications for the way in which representation works (Chapters 5 and 6). Thus, electoral systems matter because they influence the level of niche party competition.

In particular, this study examines how system-level variables interact with election outcomes and party positioning incentives. The analyses address two questions that are of significant interest for students of voting and elections. The first area of inquiry asks: *do electoral systems affect whether it is electorally advantageous for parties to take centrist positions in elections?* Second, *do electoral systems affect the diversity of policy alternatives that parties offer citizens?* The following chapters will argue that important system-level factors, such as electoral institutions and the number of parties, do not systematically affect party policy positioning; nor do they systematically mediate the effects of party proximity (to the mean voter) on election outcomes.

Thus, Chapters 2 and 3 in Part II apply a macro-level cross-national approach and present evidence that *democracies are similar* in important ways that scholars have commonly overlooked. Across systems with different electoral rules there are similar patterns for election outcomes and party positioning. Chapter 2 presents theoretical arguments and empirical analyses that support the hypothesis that moderate parties tend to gain greater vote shares than their distinctly noncentrist counterparts, and that this relationship holds across *all* multiparty systems, regardless of electoral laws. The second half extends the argument by providing dynamic, over time, analyses that support the finding that parties gain votes when public opinion shifts in their direction between electoral contests.

In Chapter 3, I present evidence that party policy distinctiveness is roughly the same across proportional and plurality-based party systems, a finding that runs counter to the conventional wisdom that PR-based systems encourage radical party positioning. There is extensive theoretical research that explores the linkages between parties' policy positions, on the one hand, and the characteristics of the political system (i.e., voting rules and the number of parties) on the other, but empirical research on this topic is less developed. This chapter reports empirical analyses exploring the relationship between party policy extremism in eighteen party systems, and the proportionality of the electoral laws used to select representatives to the national legislature. Contrary to expectations, I find no evidence that average party policy extremism increases under PR. In addition, Chapter 3 explores several crucial measurement issues. Average party policy extremism, the dependent variable, requires three pieces of information per country: these are the ideological placements of parties, the ideological placements of voters, and the parties' vote shares. Scholars sharply disagree about how to aggregate these party position measures into a valid country-level estimate of party policy extremism. I explore the arguments relating to each approach. Then several constructions of the key variables are employed in the analyses of average party extremism in an effort to triangulate the central findings of this chapter.

While Chapters 2 and 3 highlight similarities across countries featuring different electoral rules, Chapters 4–6 emphasize how electoral rules can produce very important and meaningful differences in policy representation. The central effect of electoral rules is that they affect the influence of niche parties in the representative process (Chapter 4). This in turn has dramatic implications for party positioning (Chapter 5) and election outcomes (Chapter 6). Chapter 4 explores the relationship between voting rules – PR versus plurality voting – and the size and number of relevant niche parties. This chapter presents evidence for a strong association between PR voting rules and the existence of niche parties.

Chapters 5 and 6 argue that lowering the level of analysis, from the institutional level to the party-level, is crucial for understanding how democratic representation occurs. Chapter 5 revisits the two models of election outcomes (i.e., the party proximity model and the party distinctiveness model) and develops expectations about how these models fare in terms of explaining the election outcomes for niche and mainstream parties. Specifically, I argue that mainstream parties' vote shares will conform to expectations based on the party proximity model, while niche parties' vote shares are best explained by the party distinctiveness model. Next, I empirically evaluate these expectations.

Like Chapter 2, Chapter 5 analyzes how parties' policy positioning affects their vote shares. The additional step is to evaluate how the type of party mediates the relationship between party proximity to the center of the voter distribution, and election outcomes. The cross-sectional empirical results suggest that ideologically oriented niche parties presenting moderate policies fare poorly in elections. By contrast, the results suggest that if niche parties present distinctly noncentrist policy platforms, they fare well. In other words, while most parties benefit when they advocate moderate policies (relative to the Center of the voter distribution), the opposite is true of niche parties.

Chapter 6 examines whether political parties respond to the ideological shifts of their supporters or to those of the mean voter. Previous theoretical and empirical research stresses the primacy of the mean or median voter's policy preference as the starting point for democratic representation (Downs 1957; Powell 2000; Adams et al. 2004, 2006; McDonald and Budge 2005). An alternative and equally compelling vision of policy representation emphasizes the policy preference of the *mean party supporter* in explaining party–citizen linkages (Dalton 1985; Wessels 1999; see also Downs 1957: 120). My analyses show that these two theories in fact describe different styles of party behavior which complement each other. The *type of party* (i.e., "mainstream" versus "niche" parties) mediates linkages between parties' and citizens' policy preferences. Thus, I return to the two models of party responsiveness (i.e., the general electorate model and the partisan constituency model) and develop expectations about how these models would fare in terms of explaining the programmatic shifts of niche and mainstream parties. Specifically, I argue that mainstream parties' policy shifts are explained by the general electorate model, while niche parties' policy shifts are explained by the partisan constituency model. The empirical analyses examine political parties in fifteen Western European democracies from 1973 to 2003.

The results of my analyses support the following conclusions. First, mainstream parties tend to respond to shifts in the mean voter position as opposed to the policy shifts of their supporters. Second, the opposite pattern is true for niche parties. Specifically, niche parties are highly sensitive to shifts in the position of their mean supporter, and they do not respond systematically to the median voter in the general electorate. Thus, each model of representation is accurate at capturing parties' policy shifts, depending on the type of party being examined.

The findings are summarized in Chapter 7, and I identify paths for future study. In addition, striking normative implications of the study are highlighted. One implication is that systems that adopt PR should increase the number of *pathways* by which public preferences are translated into party programs. The evidence in the latter half of the study suggests that niche and mainstream parties offer radically different channels of political representation. Citizens in PR-based systems have access to niche party channels of political representation, and citizens in plurality-based systems do not. This suggests that citizens in PR systems are advantaged, because they have access to two pathways of representation rather than one.

On the other hand, in disproportional systems featuring some form of plurality voting, there is greater party responsiveness to the mean or median position, an important characteristic for democracy highlighted by McDonald and Budge (2005). However, it is less clear that partisans receive adequate representation in these systems (see Dalton 1985; Wessels 1999).

In spite of some of the trade-offs raised above, the book concludes with a positive evaluation of democratic representation for the countries under review. Though pathways of representation vary considerably across party families (and thereby party systems), the empirical survey of eighteen democracies nonetheless identifies concrete patterns, or policy linkages, between citizens and parties.

Part II

Observing Citizen–Party Linkages and Election Outcomes Under Different Institutions

2

Are Moderate Parties Rewarded in Multiparty Systems?

> Our simplification concentrates on the central notion that the policy prefer-
> ences of voters and the policy promises of parties both matter for elections.
> Despite the importance of this proposition, it has not been subject to serious
> macro-level testing.
>
> (Erikson et al. 2002: 256)

2.1 INTRODUCTION

Casual observers of politics often cite examples of major parties benefiting from policy moderation.[1] In particular, there are many "third way" examples – or instances in which Leftist parties adopt centrist strategies in order to appeal to greater portions of the electorate – to which scholars often point when they argue that there are electoral benefits for policy centrism. The US Democratic Party accomplished a successful move to the Center in 1992, co-opting several initiatives not so distant from the platform of the Republican Party on welfare reform and taxation. These moves were associated with the election of Bill Clinton and a relabeling of the party as the "New" Democrats. Following the New Democrats in the early 1990s were the victories of Tony Blair (and New Labour) in Britain, Gerhard Schroeder in Germany, Costas Simitis in Greece, and the Olive Tree coalition in Italy – each election success attributed to a centrist move by parties that had previously identified more with the Left.

The Labour Party of Britain successfully reemerged as the New Labour Party in 1997, emphasizing a broad-based movement that attracted the support of the median voter. Meanwhile, the Italian Olive Tree Coalition formed in 1995, led by Romano Prodi, assumed power in 1996 by taking a pragmatic and centrist approach. Similarly, Gerhard Schroeder revitalized the German Social Democratic Party with a move to the middle, taking over as Chancellor in 1998. In Greece, the Panhellenic Socialist Party (PASOK) moved more to the Center under Costas Simitis. Touted as the "modernization period," PASOK made gains in the elections taking power in 1996.

---

[1] Parts of this chapter are drawn from Ezrow (2005).

The Dutch Labour Party (Partij van de Arbeid, PvdA) also moved significantly toward Center in the 1990s to counter the centrist Christian Democrats. The PvdA under Wim Kok formed the Purple Coalition in 1994 coalescing with the Democrats '66 (D'66) and the People's Party for Freedom and Democracy (Volkspartij voor Vrijheid en Democratie, VVD), the latter closely linked to market liberalization principles. By contrast, Sweden's Social Democrats only received 38% of the votes in the 1991 Riksdag elections, when they failed to grasp that the median voter in Sweden had moved slightly to the Right.

The examples above speak to the validity of the party proximity model and the party distinctiveness model, that is, whether it is advantageous for parties to adopt centrist or distinctive policy positions. Recall from Chapter 1 that the party proximity model suggests that parties are rewarded for adopting positions closer to the center of the voter distribution (party proximity), and the party distinctiveness model is upheld when parties are rewarded for adopting radical or extreme positions. The instances of Leftist Centrism and electoral success cited above clearly speak to the party proximity model. Nevertheless, anecdotes and examples are not statistical regularities. The goal of this chapter is to determine whether these examples accurately describe the wider political phenomenon of policy centrism and electoral success.[2]

Can parties in Western Europe gain votes by converging toward the mean (or median) voter's position? Traditional spatial theory clearly predicts that, ceteris paribus, parties contesting two-party elections gain votes by converging toward the Center (Downs 1957). However, prior studies of models of multiparty elections report conflicting conclusions. Theoretical models that assume deterministic policy voting suggest that noncentrist positioning may be optimal[3] (Cox 1990; see also Adams 2001), while models with probabilistic voting suggest that parties increase their expected votes by shifting in the direction of the mean voter position (De Palma et al. 1990; Lin et al. 1999). However, recent work by Norman Schofield (2003; Schofield and Sened 2005) and by Adams and Merrill (1999, 2000; see also Adams 2001; Merrill and Adams 2002) has challenged this conclusion, suggesting that when measured nonpolicy-related voting influences are introduced into the probabilistic voting model, then parties may enhance their vote by shifting *away* from the center of the voter distribution.[4]

---

[2] Chapter 1 emphasized that niche parties benefit from policy radicalism while mainstream parties benefit from policy centrism. Here, in Chapters 2 and 3, I concentrate on (the lack of) variation across electoral systems, and in Chapter 5, I explore variation across types of party.

[3] Additional models with deterministic voting make similar noncentrist predictions by assuming that parties are motivated by policy preferences, or by including *valence* characteristics in their models (Wittman 1973, 1983; Ansolabehere and Snyder 2000; Groseclose 2001).

[4] Schofield and his coauthors emphasize the importance of "valence" dimensions of evaluation (such as voters' judgments about the competing party leaders' degrees of competence, integrity, and charisma), arguing that parties that are disadvantaged on valence grounds have electoral incentives to differentiate their policies from the policies of valence-advantaged parties, and that

Finally, simulations based on individual-level survey data from real-world elections also reach conflicting conclusions, with some studies finding that centrist positioning would increase support for parties contesting multiparty elections (Schofield et al. 1998*a*, 1998*b*; Alvarez et al. 2000*a*, 2000*b*), while other simulation studies conclude that parties may maximize votes by presenting distinctly non-centrist positions (Adams and Merrill 1999, 2000). These differing conclusions based on election survey data arise in part from differences in the historical elections under review, but also in part from the analysts' differing assumptions about voters' decision rules, and the number of parties contesting the election (Adams and Merrill 2001; Schofield 2001). However, note that none of the studies cited above actually analyze the linkages between parties' vote shares in real-world elections and their proximities to the center of the policy space in these elections.

The goal of this chapter is to conduct such an analysis. Specifically, a *macro-level* analysis is conducted of party positioning and election outcomes across Western Europe from 1984 to 1998, in which the dependent variables are the parties' vote shares in real-world elections, and the crucial independent variables are the policy distances between the parties and the mean voter positions in the countries included in the study. For this purpose the Eurobarometer surveys from the relevant election years are employed, allowing for the measurement of the mean citizen policy preference in each country, as well as for the policy distances between the parties' positions, as perceived by the citizens, and the mean citizen preference.[5] This macro-level approach has been used extensively in empirical studies of the electoral effects of candidates' or parties' positioning in American elections (Erikson and Wright 1993, 1997; Ansolabehere et al. 2001; Burden 2001; Canes-Wrone et al. 2002; Erikson et al. 2002), as well as in studies on the electoral effects of economic conditions both inside and outside the United States (Lewis-Beck 1988; Paldam 1991; Powell and Whitten 1993; Powell 2000). However, this approach has not previously been used to estimate the electoral effects of party positioning outside the United States.[6]

The empirical findings I report here support the conclusions developed in many of the existing studies of multiparty competition: *proximity to the mean voter position matters*. More specifically, I conclude that parties receive a statistically

---

valence-disadvantaged parties thereby enhance their vote shares by shifting to extreme or noncentrist positions (see also Adams 1999; Ansolabehere and Snyder 2000; Hug 1995). Adams and Merrill (see also Adams et al. 2005) present arguments that parties have electoral incentives to diverge from the center of the voter distribution, by appealing on policy grounds to voters who are biased toward them for nonpolicy reasons, notably party identification. Because the partisans of different parties typically occupy different regions of the policy space, this strategic incentive is likely to motivate policy differentiation by the competing parties.

[5] As discussed below, alternative sets of analyses are conducted which employ country experts' placements as a measure of the parties' positions.

[6] The Nagel and Wlezien (forthcoming) study of British elections represents a partial exception to this generalization.

significant electoral benefit from locating near the mean voter position. This benefit, however, is relatively modest in size, so that parties that advocate non-centrist positions may nonetheless be electorally competitive. This conclusion corroborates the findings suggested by Schofield's simulation studies (2003; see also Schofield et al. 1998*a*, 1998*b*), as well as the conclusions reported by Alvarez, Nagler, and their coauthors (Alvarez et al. 2000*a*, 2000*b*). Given that these conclusions are derived from a methodology that is completely different from the Alvarez–Nagler–Schofield approach, these results, in toto, increase the confidence that the estimates of the electoral effects of party positioning are accurate. This is an important finding because, as will be discussed later, these earlier studies employ a simulation approach, which relies on several strong assumptions that are not necessarily satisfied in practice.

The finding, that parties are rewarded for being perceived as close to the mean voter, is important for several reasons. Paramount to the spatial modeling enterprise is the notion that parties' issue positions matter for elections. If the empirical evidence shows that the party and voter positioning is unrelated to electoral outcomes, then this may call into question a central assumption that underlies spatial modeling. Second, the results have important implications for political representation. The ideological "congruence between citizens and policy makers" is one of the central features of democracy (Huber and Powell 1994). Democratic theory emphasizes that elections are supposed to reveal the will of the people. The title of G. Bingham Powell's seminal work *Elections as Instruments of Democracy* (2000) aptly summarizes this concept of representation.

Methodologically speaking, a cross-national "snapshot" comparing party proximities and vote shares provides an important measure of the extent to which elections fulfill the function that Powell ascribes to them.[7] Related to this idea, there is also a perceptible empirical relationship between government policy outputs and those of the median party in governing coalitions (Budge and McDonald 2006). In addition, this chapter speaks to issues of *dynamic representation* (Stimson et al. 1995) in that the electoral impacts of shifts in public opinion over time are evaluated, in order to determine whether parties benefit at the ballot box when public preferences shift in their direction between elections. Finally, there are implications for party strategies (Budge 1994) and their ideological positioning in elections.

Section 2.2, surveys the existing approaches that are used to study the electoral effects of party positioning in multiparty systems, highlights some of the limitations of these studies, and proposes an alternative approach relying on

---

[7] Of course, because government formation in multiparty parliamentary democracies revolves around postelection coalition negotiations, government policy outputs depend on more than the parties' vote shares. Nevertheless, because parties' bargaining power in coalition negotiations depends on their seat shares – which are obviously related to their vote shares – the empirical question of whether policy centrism enhances parties' vote shares is important for democratic representation.

the national level of observation. Section 2.3 develops hypotheses regarding proximity, and employs a cross-national approach. Section 2.4 highlights the strengths and limitations of the macro-level approach, and identifies avenues for future research.

2.2 EXISTING THEORY AND EMPIRICAL APPROACHES

Several empirical studies exist which explore multiparty systems and party behavior using the spatial modeling framework. In a series of important papers, Schofield and his coauthors examine party competition within several democracies: Britain, France, Belgium, Denmark, Germany, Ireland, Israel, Italy, Luxembourg, and the Netherlands (Schofield 1997, 2003; Schofield et al. 1998*a*, 1998*b*; Schofield and Sened 2005). In addition, Adams and Merrill (1999, 2000; Adams et al. 2005) analyze party competition in Norway, France, and Britain. Dow (2001) explores elections in Canada, France, the Netherlands, and Israel, while Alvarez and Nagler (1995, 1998; Alvarez et al. 2000*a*, 2000*b*) analyze elections in Canada, Britain, and the Netherlands.[8]

All of these analyses employ national election survey data. More specifically, they rely on three important measurements: the individual self-placements of the survey respondents along one or more policy scales, the respondents' placements of the parties along these same policy scales, and the respondents' reported vote

---

[8] When using citizen preferences as a determinant of vote choice, several assumptions are made about citizens. If citizens vote based on policy considerations, this assumes an accurate transmission of information from politicians to voters about their preferred policy positions. Under the policy-voting scenario, voters are well informed about their candidates, and they know where they place themselves on particular issues. Finally, voters must choose the candidate closest to their policy views.

Brody and Page (1972) argue that the appearance of policy voting is possibly an illusion. Two other processes could plausibly be taking place besides the aforementioned policy voting. When there are information gaps, voters might decide which candidate they support due to other characteristics such as partisan identification, the charisma of the candidate, or any other nonpolicy related factors. If this is the case, voters naturally assume their favored candidates match up with them on policy positions as well. Hence, the arrow of causality is reversed – and it is the *intended vote choice* that is determining the citizens' perceptions of candidates. Brody and Page label this first process "projection," which leads to a high correlation between issue position and vote. The second process is that some voters mold their own positions to more closely resemble those of their preferred candidates. Here, *persuasion* by the candidates causes high policy–vote correlation.

Discrete choice modelers deal with projection by using the mean candidate placement rather than respondents' personal placements of candidates (Alvarez and Nagler 1995; Adams and Merrill 2000). The logic behind using the mean placements of candidates is that positive projections of candidates offset the negative ones. Thus far, the examples of projection have served to place candidates and their supporters closer together. However, negative projection also exists where voters oppose candidates and perceive the candidates' platforms as further away than they might actually be.

decisions.[9] Starting with these three measurements – and in some cases including additional variables such as sociodemographic characteristics, evaluations of the party leaders' personal qualities, party identification, and retrospective evaluations of the economy – the authors cited above estimate the parameters of individual-level voting models, which are functions of the policy distances between the respondents' preferred positions and the positions of the competing parties. Using the parameter estimates from these individual-level models, the authors aggregate the individual responses in order to estimate the parties' expected vote shares in the elections under review. The major payoff of these analyses is that the analysts can estimate the expected changes in vote shares if parties shift their policy positions. They can then use these estimates to compute both the parties' vote-maximizing positions, *and* the magnitude of the vote losses that parties can expect to suffer as they diverge from these policy optima.

For the most part, the authors cited above find that, ceterus paribus, parties can expect to gain votes by presenting centrist policies, relative to the mean voter position (but see Adams and Merrill 1999, 2000; Schofield 2003; Schofield and Sened 2005). Interestingly, however these authors conclude that parties do not actually take their vote-maximizing positions. Schofield et al. (1998*a*, 1998*b*) argue that parties take positions that put them in a good "space" for the postelection coalition formation, while Dow maintains that noncentrist parties cannot feasibly shift to the moderate positions that would maximize their support, because the votes gained by taking more centrist positions are offset by the credibility and reliability concerns created by the shifting policy stances of the party (cf. Downs 1957: 96–112).

While the studies cited above have been invaluable for advancing the understanding of the electoral effects of party positioning, the simulation approach that each set of authors employs features several strong assumptions. First, the authors' simulations necessarily rely upon the coefficients estimated for individual-level voting specifications, so that their conclusions are only reliable to the extent that these individual-level vote models are correctly specified. Unfortunately, because behavioral researchers disagree sharply amongst themselves about the proper specification for models of individual voting behavior, it is difficult to know what the proper voting specification is.[10] Second, the authors' simulation

---

[9] Note that Schofield's studies (1998*a*, 1998*b*; 2003) typically rely on the self-placements of party elites to calibrate the parties' policy positions.

[10] The disagreements among behavioral researchers include, but are not limited to, the following topics: The empirical status of the party identification variable (see Fleury and Lewis-Beck 1993; Converse and Pierce 1993); the extent to which respondents' preferred policy positions (and their perceptions of the parties' positions) are subject to assimilation or contrast effects (Merrill et al. 2001; whether voters evaluate parties in terms of the policy distances between the parties' announced positions and the voters' policy preferences, or whether, alternatively, voters account for the fact that the parties may not be able to fully implement their announced policy agendas due to countervailing pressures from coalition partners or from other branches of government (Lacy and Paolino 1998, 2001;

approaches typically employ the assumption that parties can relocate costlessly in the policy space, and that parties' policy shifts do not affect voters' criteria for evaluating the parties. Recent empirical work by Stokes (1999) and Alvarez and Nagler (2001) calls both of these assumptions into question.[11] Furthermore, the simulation studies rely on an extreme counterfactual scenario, that when making predictions about the effects of a particular party's policy shift, they also assume that their competitors will not respond to these policy shifts by changing positions themselves. Intuitively, this "ceteris paribus" assumption is questionable, because it is unrealistic to believe that these parties would not respond to such shifts (however, for an example of a dynamic analysis that does allow competitors to shift their policy positions, see Quinn and Martin 2002). Saving the methodological details for Section 2.3, my analyses sidestep the problems encountered in the simulation studies, by actually observing shifts in party proximity, and expanding the scope of study across twelve Western European democracies.

2.3 HYPOTHESES, DATA, AND METHODS

2.3.1 Central hypotheses

The following hypotheses regarding the relationship between party positions, voter positions, and election outcomes are tested:

> H1: Parties occupying positions close to the mean voter position receive a higher proportion of the vote in national elections than do parties positioned farther away from the mean voter.

> H2: Parties gain votes in national elections when the mean voter position shifts in their direction between elections.

2.3.2 Introducing the data and developing key measurements

To test Hypotheses 1 and 2, it is necessary to develop measures of popular support (i.e., vote share) and proximity. The process of developing a measure for party support is relatively straightforward. Using Mackie and Rose (1991, 1997), it is

---

Kedar 2002). Chapter 2 in Adams et al. (2005) reviews the problems that behavioral researchers' disagreements pose for spatial modelers seeking to understand parties' policy strategies in real-world elections.

[11] Specifically, both the Stokes and the Alvarez–Nagler studies report results suggesting that the importance that voters attach to the parties' policy positions – relative to alternative influences on the vote such as economic conditions and the personal images of party leaders – varies with the parties' positions, that is, that voters' decision rules are *endogenous*.

possible to collect the absolute percentage of votes for each party in each election.[12] Still, one transformation is necessary, as it should be expected that successful parties will receive fewer votes in systems where there are more competitive parties. For example, the parties in the sample that receive a relatively large proportion of popular support in Belgium – a system that features at least six competitive parties – receive a lower absolute percentage of votes than the major parties in Britain, which features just three competitive parties. Thus, a normalized measure of vote share is appropriate, which takes into account the number of competitive parties in the given election. The measure that is employed is as follows:

$$Normalized\ vote\ share\ (NV) = V_i * N_j, \qquad (2.1)$$

where V_i equals the absolute share of the vote for party i, and N_j is the number of parties in election j receiving over 5% of the vote.

Developing a measure of proximity is also straightforward. The *Eurobarometer* 31A (1989) asks approximately 1,000 respondents in each of twelve countries across what was then known as the European Community to place themselves, and each of their significant national parties, on a "Left–Right" scale ranging from 1 (extreme Left) to 10 (extreme Right).[13] The party placements, for countries and parties listed in Appendix A2.1, are held for the analyses five years before and five years after the Eurobarometer was administered. Although this is not the ideal solution, there are several arguments for holding the party placements, with the most straightforward logic being that parties' announced policy preferences remain relatively stable over time (Budge 1994). To see this, Figure 2.1 plots the expert placements of parties in the Castles–Mair (1984) study, against the expert party placements reported in the Huber–Inglehart (1995) study approximately ten years later. The scattergram demonstrates that there is a rough correspondence between each set of party placements between the 1980s and 1990s ($r = .92$; $p < .01$). In addition, for this time period, the Eurobarometer 31A is the only available data source that avoids the problems that occur when researchers rely on different sources or "metrics" for placing parties and citizens (Achen 1978).[14] Finally, holding party placements has been recognized as a valid strategy for

---

[12] The remaining election returns (through 1998) were gathered using the CD-ROM accompanying Budge et al. (2001).

[13] The questions in the 1989 Eurobarometer (31A) are as follows: "In political matters, people talk of "the left" and "the right". How would you place your views on this scale? And, where would you place the political parties (of your country)?"

[14] The Comparative Survey of Electoral Systems (CSES) is an excellent data set that also sidesteps these problems by asking respondents to place *both* themselves and political parties on a Left–Right scale. However, the CSES does not extend back to the mid-1970s as the survey was first administered in 1996.

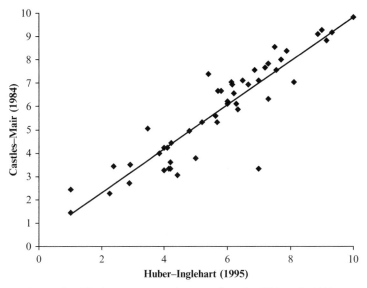

FIGURE 2.1 Plotting expert party placements from the 1980s to the 1990s

dealing with data limitations in similar studies that examine issues of representation (Powell 2000: 116).

The Eurobarometer respondent self-placements and party placements are then used to compute the mean voter's Left–Right position in each country, as well as the parties' mean perceived positions.[15] As an example, Figure 2.2 presents the voter distribution, and the parties' mean perceived Left–Right positions for France.

I emphasize the distributions of the respondents' self-placements across the countries included in the Eurobarometer survey were all similar to Figure 2.2 in that their shape approximates a bell curve, and their mode is in the middle of the scale, that is, 5 or 6 on the 1–10 scale. The exceptions are Greece and Denmark, where the distribution appears bimodal, and the mode is 8, respectively. Visual representations of these underlying voter distributions are found in Figure 2A.1. The unimodal distributions of citizen preferences across Western Europe are a significant detail for this analysis, because Downs (1957) discussed the possibility that multiparty systems were accompanied by multimodal voter distributions. If this were the case, he posited that convergent tendencies would not be as strong in multiparty systems. However, it appears in Appendix A2.1 that the multimodal assumption is hard to sustain empirically (see also Adams and Somer-Topcu 2009).

---

[15] Below, alternative sets of analyses are reported which employ country experts' party placements, in place of the mean positions ascribed to the parties by the Eurobarometer respondents.

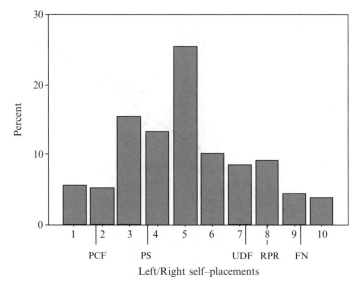

FIGURE 2.2 The ideological distribution of respondents and mean party placements in France

Notes: This sample is from the Eurobarometer (31A) survey in 1989. The locations of the parties are based on the respondents' placements from the same survey. The party labels are as follows: PCF – Communists, PS – Socialists, UDF – Union for French Democracy, RPR – Rally for the Republic (Gaullists), and FN – the National Front.

All of the measures presented in these analyses will derive from the difference between the mean citizen preference and the mean party placement. The party's proximity to the mean voter position is measured by squaring the difference between party position and the mean citizen placement:

$$Squared\ proximity = (A_i - X_i)^2, \tag{2.2}$$

where A_i is the position of the mean voter on a Left–Right continuum, and X_i is the (mean perceived) position of party X.

An alternative set of analyses was performed based on the parties' linear proximities to the mean voter position. These analyses supported substantive conclusions that were identical to the ones reported below, although the statistical fit of these models was not as strong as the fit for squared proximity, suggesting that this latter measure is the appropriate metric for evaluating the electoral effects of party positioning. This empirical finding suggests that the parties' vote shares are *concave* functions of their policy positions, that is that parties' vote shares drop off slowly at first as they diverge from their vote-maximizing positions, but then drop off more rapidly as the parties move further away. Adams and Merrill (2005) present theoretical arguments about why parties' vote shares can be expected to be concave functions of their positions. Interpreted, this means that parties are penalized more for each marginal unit further away they are from the mean voter position.

In addition to the squared proximity measure, a second and slightly more complicated measure of proximity is employed, which will help with the evaluation of the first hypothesis. This alternative proximity measure divides the squared proximity of a party by the average squared proximity of all the parties included in the analysis that are competing in the same election. The measure accounts for differing average proximities across countries, and is referred to as *relative squared proximity*. The variable is constructed as follows:

$$Relative\ squared\ proximity = \frac{Party\ squared\ proximity}{Average\ squared\ proximity} = \frac{(A_i - X_i)^2}{\Sigma_i(A_{ij} - X_{ij})^2/n} \quad (2.3)$$

The construction of the relative squared proximity variable controls for possible cross-national differences in respondents' interpretations of the Left–Right scale, and/or for differences in the dispersion of parties across different national settings.

2.3.3 The cross-sectional analysis (testing H1)

In Table 2.1, two specifications are estimated that relate the parties' vote shares to their proximities to the mean voter position for thirty-seven elections from 1984 to 1994: one using the squared proximity variable, and the other using the relative squared proximity variable. The first specification is

$$Normalized\ vote\ share = b_0 + b_1(A_i - X_i)^2 + e,$$
$$\text{H1.1: } b_1 < 0 \quad (2.4)$$

and the second specification is

$$Normalized\ vote\ share = b_0 + b_1(relative\ squared\ proximity) + e,$$
$$\text{H1.2: } b_1 < 0 \quad (2.5)$$

where e is a random disturbance term.[16]

---

[16] Note that these statistical analyses do not incorporate some of the panel data concerns raised by Katz and King (1999), who raise the issue that when estimating party vote shares, the observations are not completely independent, a standard assumption of ordinary least squares (OLS). The reason why party observations are partially dependent is that vote shares of *all* of the competitors necessarily add up to one in any given election.

Accordingly, the lack of independent observations in elections data results in another dilemma, that when predicting party vote shares, the error terms will be correlated. For example, in a three-party system, if two parties' predicted vote shares are above their observed values, then this necessarily means that the observed vote share for the third party will be lower than the expected value. The standard practice for correcting autocorrelation in panel data is to rely on panel-corrected standard errors that have been developed by Beck and Katz (1995). With this said, these issues are not as pronounced here because not every single party is included from each election in the empirical analyses. Consequently, the vote shares do not add up to one.

TABLE 2.1 *Coefficients for different measures of proximity when estimating normalized vote shares across the European Community*

| Coefficients | Eurobarometer placements (1984–94) | | Expert placements Huber–Inglehart (1988–98) | |
	Squared proximity (1)	Relative squared proximity (2)	Squared proximity (3)	Relative squared proximity (4)
Constant	69.31***	67.69***	80.77***	81.57***
	(4.84)	(5.04)	(5.51)	(5.63)
Proximity	**−2.18***	**−8.8***	**−2.46***	**−5.64***
	(.74)	(3.78)	(.79)	(1.77)
N	248	248	145	145
Adjusted R^2	.03	.02	.06	.06

Note: Parameters are ordinary least squares (OLS) coefficients. Estimated standard errors are in parentheses.

*p < .10, **p < .05, ***p < .01, two–tailed test

Reiterating some of the major points in Sections 2.2 and 2.3, the central hypothesis is that the coefficient estimates relating to the measures of proximity will be negative and statistically significant, that is, that parties lose votes as their policy distance to the mean voter position increases. The results reported in columns 1 and 2 of Table 2.2 support this hypothesis. For both measures of

TABLE 2.2 *Coefficients for the variables squared proximity gain $[(Prox_{t-1})^2 - (Prox_t)^2]$, and lagged changes in normalized vote shares $[NV_{t-1} - NV_{t-2}]$, when estimating changes in normalized vote shares $[NV_t - NV_{t-1}]$ across the European Community*

| Coefficients | Eurobarometer placements (1984–94) | | Expert placements Huber–Inglehart (1988–98) | |
	Basic (1)	Advanced (2)	Basic (3)	Advanced (4)
Constant	−1.88*	−2.52**	−1.97	−2.38
	(1.10)	(1.13)	(1.72)	(1.76)
Squared proximity gain	**3.27***	**2.72***	**3.34***	**3.16***
	(1.00)	(1.02)	(1.68)	(1.70)
Lagged ΔNV		−.14**		−.09
		(.06)		(.09)
N	228	211	134	133
Adjusted R^2	.04	.05	.02	.02

Note: Parameters are ordinary least squares (OLS) coefficients. Estimated standard errors are in parentheses.

*p < .10, **p < .05, ***p < .01, two-tailed test

proximity the coefficients are negative and statistically significant at the .05 level, which implies that the farther away a party is from the mean voter position in its national electorate, the fewer votes it receives.[17]

Columns 3 and 4 in Table 2.1 show the results for an alternative set of analyses in which the measure of the parties' positions was based on experts' placements, as reported in a survey of country experts conducted by Huber and Inglehart (1995). These analyses are important because, unlike the respondents' party placements, experts' placements are unlikely to be contaminated by assimilation and contrast effects, which have the potential to bias rank-and-file survey respondents' party placements.[18] The results for the analyses based on experts' party placements display the same pattern as the analyses based on the survey respondents' party placements, namely, for both the squared proximity measure and the relative squared proximity measure, the coefficients are negative and statistically significant at the .01 level.[19]

Note that although the proximity coefficients are significant, they are still quite small. Substantively, the coefficients for squared proximity represent marginal expected losses for parties closer to the citizen mean, and rapidly declining losses for those parties approaching the ideological extremes. For instance, consider the parameter estimate in column 1, which is -2.18. This implies that a party competing in a four-party system can expect to lose about six-tenths of 1% of the vote (0.55%) as it shifts from the mean voter's position to a position one unit away from the mean voter position, along the 1–10 Left–Right scale. By contrast, if this party shifts from one unit away from the mean voter to a position two units away, its expected vote loss approaches 2.2 percentage points; a further shift to a position three units from the mean is associated with an expected loss of about 4.9 percentage points, relative to positioning at the mean voter position.[20]

---

[17] Interestingly, if parties wish to maximize their chances of gaining office – as opposed to maximizing votes, these results still hold up. A probit model was estimated using a binary dependent variable indicating whether or not the party gained office in the election. There were no substantive changes in the results.

[18] Specifically, there is evidence that survey respondents tend to rationalize their vote choices by placing the parties they like unrealistically near to their own preferred ideological positions (an *assimilation effect*), while placing parties they dislike far from their own ideological positions (a *contrast effect*). See Merrill et al. (2001) for evidence on this point.

[19] Parallel analyses were conducted that rely on the estimates of parties' policy positions reported by the Comparative Manifesto Project (discussed in Chapter 6), and these analyses support identical substantive conclusions.

[20] The calculation of the expected vote loss for a party that is one unit from the mean voter position in a four-party system is $(-2.18 \times (1)^2)/4$ or only 0.55% of the vote. For two units, the vote loss is estimated to be $(-2.18 \times (2)^2)/4$ or 2.18%. The expected vote loss for three units is $(-2.18 \times (3)^2)/4$ or 4.91%.

Expected losses would be greater in a system with fewer than four parties, and less in a system with more than four parties.[21] The proximity coefficients reported in columns 2–4 support similar substantive conclusions.

2.3.4 The "proximity gain" specification (testing H2)

Although the cross-sectional analyses reported in Table 2.1 suggest that parties' vote shares increase modestly with proximity to the mean voter position, a limitation of these tests is that they have not controlled for nonpolicy-related sources of party strength, such as the charisma of party leaders, parties' campaign spending, economic conditions, and so on.[22] To the extent that parties' nonpolicy-related strength correlates with their policy positions, omission of these variables may bias the estimates of the electoral effects of party ideologies. Indeed, important work by Schofield (2003; see also Schofield and Sened 2005) suggests that parties that enjoy nonpolicy-related advantages have electoral incentives to present centrist positions, thereby providing theoretical support for such a correlation.

Here this problem is addressed by estimating the electoral effects of *changes* in the parties' proximities to the mean voter between elections.[23] Using the self-placement scores in the Eurobarometer, it is possible to determine the magnitude and direction of the ideological shift of the mean citizen between elections, and to use these shifts in the mean voter position to calculate changes in each party's proximity to the mean voter position. Specifically, squared proximity gain is measured by subtracting the current squared proximity from the squared proximity in the prior election. If a party is closer to the citizen mean in the current election

---

[21] For a three-party system (i.e., Britain), the expected vote losses due to proximity are expected to be greater than a system with six competitive parties (i.e., Denmark 1990). For example, if a party is positioned at two and a half units away from the mean voter position, then the expected loss in the British system is 4.5%, and in the Danish system, 2.3%.

[22] The omission of these variables stems from two considerations: (*a*) The fact that the Eurobarometer surveys do not contain information on most of the important nonpolicy-related variables that behavioral researchers have identified (i.e., they do not report respondents' assessments of party leaders, nor the parties' campaign spending). (*b*) There is extensive evidence that respondents' perceptions of many important nonpolicy variables – such as their perceptions of party leaders and their evaluations of economic conditions – are biased by their political loyalties, so that survey items tapping these variables may actually be surrogates for the respondents' policy preferences (see Alvarez and Nagler 2001).

Ideally, it would be possible to control for more factors in the specification. However, the Eurobarometers are commissioned by the European Union and, subsequently, these surveys are geared more toward attitudes about Europe than about domestic politics. Additionally, the surveys are not consistent over the time period included in the analyses. That is, the turnover is relatively high for the survey instruments that are included in the Eurobarometer.

[23] The Italian elections, post-1992, have been omitted due to the significant changes that were made to the electoral rules and the party system.

than in the prior election, the measure will be positive. To the extent that parties experiencing proximity gains also tend to increase their vote shares, there is additional evidence that proximity to the mean voter position enhances party support. Crucially, this test is not subject to the criticism that omitted nonpolicy-related sources of party strength bias the results. The reason is that even if parties that enjoy nonpolicy-related advantages do tend to locate nearer to (or further away from) the Center than do disadvantaged parties, to the extent that proximity matters it should still be expected that such parties will gain votes when the mean voter position shifts in the party's direction, and lose votes when the mean voter shifts away from the party's position.

The dependent variable in the analysis is the change in the party's normalized vote share (ΔNV) between elections. The expectation is that the coefficient for proximity gain should be positive and statistically significant. In other words, shifts toward the mean citizen should be rewarded with votes (H2). Thus, the basic proximity gain specification is

$$
\begin{array}{cc}
\Delta NV & (Squared)\,proximity\,gain \\
| & | \\
NV_t - NV_{t-1} = b_0 + b_1[(A_i - X_i)^2_{t-1} - (A_i - X_i)^2_{t}] + e
\end{array}
$$
$$
\text{H2.1: } b_1 > 0 \tag{2.6}
$$

An additional, advanced proximity gain specification controls for the lagged changes in normalized vote shares. This specification controls for prior shifts in the vote, because it is likely that, due to the regression to the mean, parties that gained votes in the previous election will lose support in the current election:

$$
\begin{array}{c}
Lagged\,\Delta NV \\
| \\
NV_t - NV_{t-1} = b_0 + b_1[(A_i - X_i)^2_{t-1} - (A_i - X_i)^2_{t}] + b_2[NV_{t-1} - NV_{t-2}] + e
\end{array}
$$
$$
\text{H2.2:} b_1 > 0
$$
$$
(\text{H3:} b_2 < 0) \tag{2.7}
$$

Table 2.2 supports the second hypothesis by showing that shifts in proximity are accompanied by shifts in vote shares. The squared proximity gain coefficients are positive and statistically significant in all of the specifications. In addition, note that the sizes of the proximity gain coefficients based on the Eurobarometer respondents' party placements (columns 1 and 2 in Table 2.2) are virtually identical to the coefficients based on the country experts' party placements (columns 3 and 4). These findings are extremely important because they substantiate the conclusions drawn by existing studies on the effects of proximity and party support across Western Europe, namely, proximity gains translate into only modest electoral benefits. The size of the coefficient in column 1 (3.27) indicates

TABLE 2.3 *Coefficients for different measures of proximity when estimating absolute vote shares across the European Community*

Coefficients	Eurobarometer placements (1984–94)		Expert placements Huber–Inglehart (1988–98)	
	Squared proximity (1)	Relative square proximity (2)	Squared proximity (3)	Relative square proximity (4)
Constant	25.86***	23.83***	31.60***	31.52***
	(2.75)	(2.57)	(3.14)	(3.16)
Proximity	**−.618***	**−2.51***	**−.72***	**−1.58***
	(.19)	(.97)	(.18)	(.41)
Effective number of parties	−2.02***	−1.67***	−2.70***	−2.63***
	(.512)	(.50)	(.61)	(.613)
N	245	245	138	138
Adjusted R^2	.07	.06	.18	.18

Note: Parameters are ordinary least squares (OLS) coefficients. Estimated standard errors are in parentheses.

*$p < .10$, **$p < .05$, ***$p < .01$, two-tailed test

that the gains in votes are relatively small for parties benefiting from proximity gains during inter-election periods.[24]

Additional statistical analyses are conducted, and reported in Tables 2.3 and 2.4, using parties' absolute vote shares as the dependent variable, and these analyses support the substantive conclusions based on normalized vote shares. In these analyses, the number of competitive parties is controlled for directly in the specifications, as opposed to accounting for this factor in the construction of the dependent variable.[25]

[24] Take, for example, a party moving from two units to one unit away from the mean voter position. Referring to Equation 2.6 in the text, the party's squared proximity gain value is $((2)^2 − (1)^2)$, or 3. Thus, $\Delta NV = −1.88 + 3.27(3)$ or 7.93. As the number of competitive parties in each system decreases or increases, 7.93 translates into more or less votes, respectively. For instance, for a four-party system, the expected gain is $7.93/4 \approx 2$ percentage points, while for a six-party system the expected vote gain is $7.93/6 \approx 1.5$ percentage points.

[25] Here, I rely on the *effective number of parties* as developed by Laakso and Taagepera (1979, see Chapter 3 for a detailed discussion of this measure) that is based on vote shares. This measure is calculated, $N = 1/\Sigma v_i^2$, where v_i is the proportion of votes of the ith party. It registers similar values as the one employed earlier in the chapter, which is based on the number of parties that receive over 5% of the popular vote ($r = .89$; the estimate is statistically significant at the .01 level).

TABLE 2.4 *Coefficients for the variables squared proximity gain* $[(Prox_{t-1})^2 - (Prox_t)^2]$, *and lagged changes in vote shares* $[V_{t-1} - V_{t-2}]$, *when estimating changes in vote shares* $[V_t - V_{t-1}]$ *across the European Community*

Coefficients	Eurobarometer placements (1984–94)		Expert placements Huber–Inglehart (1988–98)	
	Basic (1)	Advanced (2)	Basic (3)	Advanced (4)
Constant	−.36	−1.19	−.35	−2.38
	(.27)	(.77)	(.38)	(1.76)
Squared proximity gain	1.7*	1.2	.91**	.89**
	(1.03)	(1.04)	(.37)	(.38)
Lagged vote change		−.12**		−.04
		(.05)		(.09)
Effective number of parties		.15		−.02
		(.16)		(.24)
N	228	211	134	133
Adjusted R^2	.01	.02	.04	.02

Note: Parameters are ordinary least squares (OLS) coefficients. Estimated standard errors are in parentheses.

*$p < .10$, **$p < .05$, ***$p < .01$, two-tailed test

2.4 CONCLUSION – *PROXIMITY MATTERS*

These analyses supply the "serious macro-level testing" of the spatial model across the Western European party systems along the lines suggested by Erikson et al. (2002: 256, quoted at length at the beginning of the chapter). Based on citizen perceptions from the Eurobarometer surveys (1984–98), there is strong evidence to conclude that proximity is related to popular support (i.e., votes) across the multiparty systems in Western Europe. Specifically, parties occupying positions close to the mean voter position are likely to receive modest electoral benefits, compared to noncentrist parties. Using a macro-level approach, this finding confirms the claims arrived at by existing empirical studies that explore multiparty systems using the spatial modeling framework. An additional temporal component has also been added, and the finding here is that parties tend to gain votes when the mean voter position shifts in their direction between elections. Moreover, these results are strengthened by alternative specifications based on expert opinions of parties' positions from the Huber–Inglehart (1995) study.

This is simply a first look at an important and complicated question; a question that I will return to throughout the study. For instance, if proximity matters across multiparty systems, what are the implications of this finding for party positioning in these systems? How does this finding relate to dispersed or convergent positioning in these systems? I address these questions in detail in Chapter 3.

Even Anthony Downs was aware of the questionable applicability of his central convergence prediction to multiparty systems (Downs 1957: 126–7). Perhaps to the surprise of Downs, general connections between proximity and vote shares exist in such systems. There are other explanatory factors plausibly at work that have yet to be explored, such as the influence of electoral systems on positioning incentives. Additionally, positioning incentives may also vary by the type of party. It is not farfetched to expect the magnitude of the effects of proximity to vary under different contexts.

3

Parties' Policy Programs and the Dog that Did not Bark: No Evidence that Proportional Systems Promote Extreme Party Positioning

> "Is there any point to which you would wish to draw my attention?"
> "To the curious incident of the dog in the night-time."
> "But the dog did nothing in the night-time."
> "That was the curious incident," remarked Sherlock Holmes.
> (Dialogue between Sherlock Holmes and Inspector Gregory, from
> *Silver Blaze*, by Sir Arthur Conan Doyle)

3.1 INTRODUCTION

This chapter extends the analysis initiated in Chapter 2, which reported that parties' Left–Right policy positions are related to their popular support (i.e., votes) across the multiparty systems in Western Europe. The question that was addressed in that chapter is as follows: what are the electoral effects of parties' positions? This chapter takes a step back to analyze the *causes* of party positions; in particular, it examines the relationship between electoral systems and parties' Left–Right policy positions.[1]

On first glance, it seems obvious that plurality systems encourage policy centrism. In systems like Britain and the United States, candidates gravitate toward the Center of political competition in an attempt to win elections. They lose if they do otherwise. Casual observation of these systems suggests this proposed relationship is slightly more complex. While there are periods of convergence in these systems, there are also periods of polarization. British party competition in the mid-1990s, with the arrival of Tony Blair and "New Labour," was noticeably centrist. By contrast, however, Margaret Thatcher initiated a decade of polarized politics in the 1980s. The gap between Democrats and

---

[1] Sections of this chapter are based on Ezrow (2008*b*).

Republicans in the United States has been growing steadily since the mid-1970s (McCarty et al. 2006). Putting recent levels of polarization into context (in the wake of the Bush Administration), McCarty, Poole, and Rosenthal observe that "partisan differences in congressional voting behavior have grown dramatically to levels not seen since the early twentieth century" (McCarty et al. 2009: 666).

These examples point to difficulties that arise when generalizing about the effects of electoral systems on party positioning. This chapter highlights plausible factors that would explain why parties adopt more extreme positions in plurality systems (e.g., activists and valence), and centrist positions in PR systems (e.g., coalition seeking motivations). These factors perhaps counterbalance conventional expectations, which suggest that plurality and PR systems promote centrist and differentiated party positioning, respectively.

While there is extensive theoretical research that explores the linkages between parties' policy positions on the one hand, and the characteristics of the political system (i.e., voting rules and the number of parties) on the other, empirical research on this topic is less developed. Building on earlier work by Jay Dow, I report empirical analyses that explore the connections between the average party policy extremism in fifteen-party systems (defined as the average party policy distance from the party system Center), and two important system-level variables: the proportionality of the electoral laws used to select representatives to the national legislature and the number of political parties. Contrary to expectations – but consistent with recent theoretical work by Norman Schofield and his coauthors – I find no evidence that average party policy extremism increases under proportional representation (PR), nor that policy extremism increases in countries that feature large numbers of parties.

There is an emerging body of work that seeks to understand the factors that affect the degree of policy distinctiveness offered by parties and candidates across political systems, that is the extent to which competing parties or candidates offer divergent sets of platforms that provide voters with diverse sets of policy options (Budge and McDonald 2006; see also McDonald and Budge 2005). The spatial modeling literature has identified several features of voting behavior that plausibly influence vote-seeking parties' position-taking incentives, and through this, the degree to which parties or candidates take divergent policy positions. These factors include (but are not limited to) the following: the electoral salience of policies relative to unmeasured sources of voters' party evaluations, the importance of "valence" dimensions of voters' party evaluations relative to policy dimensions of evaluation, the spatial distribution of voters' partisan affiliations, and the strategic effects of voter abstention (see, e.g., Lin et al. 1999; Schofield 2003; Schofield and Sened 2006; Adams and Merrill 1999; Hinich and Ordeshook 1970).

While the theoretical literature on the topic of party polarization is extensive, there has been little empirical work that evaluates the predictions derived from formal theory. Indeed, Jay Dow has written the only comparative empirical study that explores the factors that influence the degree of policy differentiation among political parties or candidates that are observed in real-world party systems. In this chapter, the enquiry initiated by Dow is extended to encompass the party systems in fifteen postwar democracies. Specifically, with respect to these fifteen-party systems, I address the following question: How extreme are parties, on average, with respect to the center of the voter distribution within a political system? This query is further subdivided by considering two, related, questions: Is there a *direct* relationship between electoral laws and party policy extremism? and Do electoral laws exert an *indirect* effect on party policy extremism via their influence on the number of political parties? The latter question is motivated by Duverger's well-known law and hypotheses (Duverger 1954), which posit that the number of political parties is influenced by the electoral system (see also Rae 1967; Riker 1982; Taagepera and Shugart 1989; Cox 1997).

Contrary to expectation, the empirical analyses suggest that the answer to each of the above questions is *no*. Specifically, there is little evidence to suggest that electoral laws (specifically the proportionality of the electoral system) exert an effect – either directly or indirectly – on parties' tendencies to propose extreme as opposed to moderate policy positions. Furthermore, to the extent that linkages are uncovered between electoral systems and party policy extremism, the relationships that are found are in the *opposite* direction than expected: namely, the analyses suggest that more proportional electoral systems may actually motivate greater policy moderation by political parties. This finding runs contrary to the conventional wisdom that proportional electoral systems motivate parties to present more extreme policies; as stated in an early analysis of voting systems *Democracy or Anarchy?*, where F. A. Hermens (1941: 19) posits that PR made "it natural that there be a party to represent every shade of political opinion. This means that political differences are not only more clearly expressed, but multiplied and intensified."

However, although some evidence is uncovered to suggest that more proportional voting systems actually motivate party policy moderation, the weight of the evidence is most consistent with the finding of *no effect*, that is, that electoral system proportionality does not systematically influence extreme party positioning. This suggests that the role of the country's electoral system in explaining party policy extremism is analogous to the role of the "dog in the night-time" in the Sherlock Holmes story *Silver Blaze*, namely, that contrary to the expectations of political scientists, electoral system proportionality does *not* systematically increase or depress the distinctiveness of political parties' policy offerings. Thus, I conclude that when exploring the factors that affect divergent party positioning, electoral systems are the dog that did not bark.

However, these conclusions come with four caveats. First, due to measurement issues (discussed below), the empirical analyses are limited to fifteen-party systems in Western democracies. While the scope of the study thereby covers a significant portion of the population that I wish to describe (i.e., reasonably stable and well-developed democracies), I am nevertheless cautious about extrapolating these conclusions to political systems outside of the study. Second, the fluidity of the more elegant two-dimensional spatial mapping in a smaller number of countries has been consciously exchanged for unidimensional measurements of ideology in order to widen the geographical scope of this study.[2] Nevertheless, an analysis of Left–Right policy extremism can still be illuminating. With respect to this point, Ian Budge and Michael McDonald comment that "while the issues involved in Left–Right divisions do not cover the whole spectrum of democratic politics, few would deny they are at the centre of them" (Budge and McDonald 2006: 453). There is convincing empirical research that complements these authors' remarks, and suggests that the Left–Right dimension captures an important and meaningful component of political competition across the national settings and time period that are under review here (see, e.g., Powell 2000; Huber and Powell 1994; Powell and Vanberg 2000; Huber 1989; McDonald and Budge 2005).

Third, I emphasize that the conclusion, that electoral system proportionality does not systematically affect the incentives for parties to take noncentrist positions, does *not* imply that electoral laws exert no influence on party elites' policy strategies; indeed, given the extensive theoretical and empirical literature suggesting that politicians do indeed account for electoral laws, such a conclusion would be remarkable. What the findings *do* suggest is that, in the fifteen democracies in the study, electoral system proportionality does not exert a significant *net* effect on party policy extremism. Thus, to the extent that proportionality presents parties with incentives to moderate their policies in some circumstances, the results imply that there may be other circumstances where proportionality motivates parties to shift toward more radical policies.

The fourth caveat relates to the first two caveats discussed above, namely that in exploring the research question significant theoretical and practical difficulties are confronted in measuring the dependent variable, average party policy extremism. These issues are explored extensively in Section 3.3, where several alternative measures of average party policy extremism are developed. The fact that the central substantive conclusions hold regardless of which measure is used increases the confidence in the results.

The above limitations notwithstanding, these results have important implications for institutional design, for democratic representation, and for spatial models of elections. With respect to institutional design and democratic representation, these findings suggest that scholars need to rethink the proposition that proportional election systems promote more extreme party positioning, an assumption that underlies the long-standing debate over the relative virtues of proportional

---

[2] For examples of spatial mappings on more than one dimension, see Schofield (1997; see also Dow 2001).

versus plurality voting systems. This posited policy divergence is seen as an advantage by some scholars, who argue that it enhances mass-elite policy linkages (Dalton 1996), but as a potential disadvantage by other scholars who point out that too much party policy divergence may also be destabilizing (Carter 2004). These findings suggest that, regardless of the virtues and drawbacks of greater average party policy extremism, both sides in this debate should be cautious of their underlying assumption that electoral proportionality actually promotes extreme position-taking by the competing parties within a political system. With respect to spatial models of elections, the findings suggest an important puzzle on parties' policy programs, that may prove susceptible to the spatial modeling approach, namely: What are possible rational choice explanations for the finding that parties do *not* tend to present more radical policy programs in proportional systems? I will offer some possible answers to this question, following the presentation of the initial results.

In Section 3.2, I develop hypotheses that link institutional variables (i.e., electoral rules and the number of parties) to average party policy extremism. Section 3.3 develops measures of party policy extremism based on previous work by Alvarez and Nagler (2004), and presents data from fifteen long-standing democracies that are used to evaluate the hypotheses. Sections 3.4 and 3.5 specify the statistical models that are used to test the hypotheses, and discuss the empirical findings. Section 3.6 outlines possible reasons for why the hypotheses developed in Section 3.2 are not supported by the data. The final section summarizes comments on the findings.

3.2 HYPOTHESES ON VOTING SYSTEMS, THE NUMBER OF PARTIES, AND AVERAGE PARTY POLICY EXTREMISM

Following Gary Cox (1990), *centripetal incentives* refer to factors that reward parties that converge to the Center of the voter distribution, while *centrifugal incentives* refer to the factors that cause parties to take distinctly noncentrist positions. The conventional understanding developed in the influential spatial modeling study by Cox is that proportional electoral rules exert centrifugal incentives that motivate parties to present noncentrist policy programs. Assuming deterministic policy voting along a unidimensional continuum, Cox establishes the independent effects of electoral rules (specifically, the electoral formulae, district magnitude, and ballot structure) and the number of competitors (discussed in more detail later in the section) on the positioning incentives for parties. Cox concludes that proportional electoral formulae create incentives for parties to present noncentrist policies.

Jay Dow (2001) advances the debate by presenting intuitive arguments and empirical analyses suggesting that proportionality does indeed exert centrifugal policy incentives on political parties. Dow's argument is that parties have weaker incentives to maximize votes in proportional systems than they do in disproportional or plurality systems, and given the expectation that centrist policy positioning tends to enhance parties' vote shares (an expectation that was supported in the empirical analyses I reported in Chapter 2), this implies that disproportional electoral systems motivate centrist party positioning compared with proportional systems.[3] Dow bases this argument about vote-seeking incentives on the logic that, because disproportional electoral laws tend to punish small parties by awarding them seat shares in parliament that are less than their national vote shares – while correspondingly awarding seat shares to large parties that exceed their vote shares – disproportional electoral laws give office-seeking parties added motivations to maximize their electoral support.

In addition, votes are less directly tied to office in proportional systems – that is, parties with smaller vote shares can still participate in governing coalitions in PR systems. By contrast disproportional, plurality-based voting systems frequently manufacture single-party parliamentary majorities, as is the case in Britain, as well as in New Zealand prior to its switch to PR for the 1996 election.[4] In these cases, "losing" parties have no chance of becoming part of the government. Alternatively, proportional systems give small parties the opportunity to coalesce with larger parties and take part in the governing coalition. An example of small parties gaining office is the Free Democratic Party (FDP), which took part in governing coalitions throughout much of the postwar period in Germany.

Thus, in disproportional systems fewer parties are capable of "winning" parliamentary seats, and maximizing votes entails staking out popular positions. This suggests that there are strict limits to the viable *policy space* for competition in disproportional systems, that is, the expectation is to see in plurality systems a "clustering" of a small number of competitive parties close to the mean or median voter position.

By contrast, given that electoral thresholds in proportional systems permit more parties to win seats in the legislature, the competing parties in proportional systems can afford to be less concerned about whether they are occupying moderate, vote-maximizing positions. Thus, parties competing in PR systems

---

[3] There is both a theoretical and empirically based literature suggesting that parties in multiparty elections (i.e., elections involving at least three parties) maximize votes by presenting centrist positions. Theoretically, when voting is probabilistic and voters do not attach too much salience to policy distance compared with unmeasured, nonpolicy motivations, then a unique vote-maximizing equilibrium exists in which all parties in a multiparty election locate at the mean voter position (Lin et al. 1999). Empirically, scholars report computations on survey data from real-world elections which suggest that the noncentrist parties that contested these elections could have increased their support in elections held in Britain, France, the Netherlands, Germany, and Canada (see Alvarez et al. 2000*b*, 2000*a*; Adams and Merrill 2000; Adams, Merrill and Grofman 2005; for static analyses, see Ezrow 2005). I revisit this point about policy moderation and vote shares at the end of the chapter.

[4] For a review of evidence on this issue, see McDonald et al. (2004).

are plausibly free to advocate their sincere policy beliefs, even if these preferred policies are distinctly noncentrist. It is in this fashion that in systems with proportional electoral rules, the viable policy space for politics should be larger than is the viable policy space in disproportional systems. This provides the basis for the first hypothesis – the Proportionality Hypothesis – that seeks to explain variation in average party policy extremism across systems:

> H_1 (The Proportionality Hypothesis): Proportionality increases average party policy extremism along the Left–Right dimension (i.e., an effect that is independent of the number of parties).

The second hypothesis is also motivated by the work of Gary Cox (1990). In addition to voting rules, Cox considers the effects of the *number of competitors* on the incentives for party positioning in a spatial model with deterministic policy voting. Cox concludes that the greater the number of competitors in a political system, the stronger the expectation that at least some of these parties will present noncentrist positions (see also Eaton and Lipsey 1975). This conclusion is also supported by Merrill and Adams' theoretical results (2002) on multiparty elections with probabilistic voting, which conclude that vote-seeking politicians' centrifugal incentives grow stronger as the number of parties increases. Roughly speaking, the logic that underlies both the Cox and the Merrill–Adams conclusions is that the greater the number of parties contesting an election, the greater the danger that centrist parties will be "squeezed" by less centrist competitors, thereby depressing the centrist parties' vote shares and making noncentrist positioning more attractive.

The conclusions of Cox, Merrill and Adams, and others on the relationship between the number of parties and centrifugal policy incentives are independent of the proportionality of the electoral system. However, these conclusions are nevertheless related to electoral systems research, since there is extensive empirical evidence that electoral laws exert effects on the number of viable parties in a political system. Specifically, dating back at least to Duverger's formulation of his famous law (1954) – namely, that single-ballot plurality systems favor two-party political systems[5] – scholars have argued that the number of parties increases with electoral system proportionality (Taagepera and Shugart 1989; Lijphart 1999). This suggests in turn that electoral systems may exert an *indirect* effect upon average party policy extremism, via their influence on the number of parties. This provides the basis for the second hypothesis – the Party System Size Hypothesis – that seeks to explain variation in average party policy extremism across systems:

> H_2 (The Party System Size Hypothesis): Proportionality increases average party policy extremism along the Left–Right dimension, indirectly, via its influence on the effective number of parliamentary parties.

---

[5] Related to this is Duverger's Hypothesis, that proportional voting systems are associated with multipartyism (Duverger 1954).

3.3 DATA AND MEASUREMENT

3.3.1 Measuring the independent variables: electoral system proportionality and the number of parties

The two independent variables that are central to the Proportionality and the Party System Size Hypotheses are the proportionality of the electoral system and the number of parties in the political system. The measures of these institutional characteristics are reported by Arend Lijphart (1999) for thirty-six democracies over the period 1945–96. Lijphart's measure of electoral system disproportionality, which is based on the index developed by Gallagher (1991), varies with the squared differences between parties' vote shares and their subsequent seat shares in parliament. The equation for the Gallagher Index of Disproportionality is $\sqrt{\frac{1}{2}\Sigma\left(v_i - s_i\right)^2}$, where v_i and s_i are the vote shares and subsequent seat shares for party *i*. According to this measure larger differences between votes and seats indicate greater disproportionality. Column 3 of Table A3.1 reports measures of these variables for the fifteen countries included in the study.[6] These measures indicate that countries such as Denmark, Germany, Sweden, and Norway feature quite proportional voting systems, while Britain, the United States, France, and Canada – the four countries in the study that employ some form of plurality – are comparatively disproportional. These measures conform to common sense.

In addition to Gallagher's Index, the specifications were estimated in Equations 3.3–3.5 using alternative measures developed to assess the level of disproportionality based on a dichotomous variable that indicates whether a country has single member districts (SMD) or some form of PR, the "effective district magnitude" measure developed by Taagepera and Shugart (1989),[7] and Lijphart's "effective threshold" (Lijphart 1999: 27). The substantive conclusions that are reported in the subsequent empirical analyses persist when disproportionality is measured based on each of these measures.[8]

The *effective number of parliamentary parties* (ENPP) developed by Laakso and Taagepera (1979) and applied by Lijphart (1999) is used to estimate the number of competitors in the party system. The equation for ENPP is $N = 1/\Sigma s_i^2$, where s_i is the proportion of seats of the *i*th party. The Laakso-Taagepera (L–T) measure is constructed so that large parliamentary parties are counted more heavily than small parties. Thus, if four parties are competing and each receives 25% of the seats in

---

[6] The criteria are discussed below that are used to select these fifteen countries.

[7] See table 12.1 in Taagepera and Shugart (1989: 136–7).

[8] These additional analyses, using an alternative measure of proportionality, also directly address endogeneity concerns for the specifications identified in Equations 3.3 and 4.4, that is, the concern that vote share is a component of the Gallagher Index as well as the weighted version of average party policy extremism (the dependent variable). The results from these analyses are presented in Tables A3.3–A3.8.

parliament, the L-T measure of the effective number of parties is four, while if two large parties each control 40% of the seats in parliament and two smaller parties each control 10% of the seats, the effective number of parties is about three.[9] Column 4 of Table A3.1 reports the L–T estimates of the ENPP for the fifteen countries included in the analysis.

3.3.2 Measuring the dependent variable: average party policy extremism

While the measurements for the two key independent variables are straightforward – in the sense that widely accepted measures of these variables have already been developed – measurement of the dependent variable, *average party policy extremism*, is more complicated. Although the measure of average party policy extremism requires only three pieces of information per country (these are the ideological placements of parties, the ideological placements of voters, and the parties' vote shares), scholars sharply disagree both over how best to measure the parties' policy positions and also about how to aggregate these party position measures into a valid country-level estimate of party policy extremism.

With respect to the measurement of parties' policy positions, for instance, some scholars argue for *expert placements* of party positions (Castles and Mair 1984; Huber and Inglehart 1995), others rely on *citizen placements* of parties as recorded in national election surveys (Adams and Merrill 1999, 2000; Alvarez et al. 2000), and still other scholars emphasize the virtues of locating parties based upon content analyses of their *election manifestos* (Budge et al. 2001; Klingemann et al. 2006).[10] With respect to aggregating the party position measures into a measure of average party policy extremism, scholars disagree about whether or not the parties' positions should be weighted by their size (Kollman et al. 1998; Alvarez and Nagler 2004).

The argument for weighting average party policy extremism by party size is that such weighting accounts for the fact that the small parties in some countries (e.g., the American Green Party, the British Socialist Party, and so on) have virtually no political influence, so that their policy proposals do not enlarge the menu of policy choices available to voters in any meaningful sense. The arguments for relying on

---

[9] The authors' alternative measure, the effective number of elective parties (ENEP) is based on votes (i.e., $N = 1/\Sigma v_i^2$, where v_i is the proportion of votes of the ith party). The measure based on seats (ENPP) is employed in the empirical analyses reported below. However, I also ran these analyses using the Laakso–Taagepera measure based on vote share weightings (ENEP), as well as a third measure which is based on the number of parties receiving over a minimum threshold of votes (5%) in the election. In all cases, the substantive conclusions were unchanged. The results from these analyses are presented in Tables A3.9–A3.12.

[10] In addition, scholars have employed the technique of multidimensional scaling, which involves estimating the parties' positions relative to voters' positions via analyses of voters' policy preferences in combination with their party evaluations (see Dow 2001; Schofield and Sened 2006).

an unweighted measure of party policy extremism (UPE) are, first, that any weighting system is unavoidably arbitrary given that parties' policy influence does not necessarily correlate with vote (or seat) share, and, second, that small parties provide a vehicle through which voters can express their policy preferences, regardless of whether or not such parties significantly influence government policy outputs.

In order to ensure that the substantive conclusions are not artifacts of the measurement approach, Hypotheses 1 and 2 are evaluated using both weighted and unweighted measures of average party policy extremism. Furthermore, while there are disagreements over how to most accurately place parties along a Left–Right policy dimension, these debates are sidestepped by evaluating each of the hypotheses using the three alternative approaches discussed above, namely, those that rely on citizen placements, expert placements, and party manifesto codings.[11]

To measure average party policy extremism, it is necessary to measure the mean voter position so that it is possible to determine how far parties' policies deviate from the center of the voter distribution. I rely on the Eurobarometer surveys from each election year of the countries in the empirical analyses to estimate the mean voter position. Specifically, these surveys ask approximately 1,000 respondents per country to place themselves on a 1–10 Left–Right ideological scale, and the mean respondent self-placement score constitutes the measure of the Center of the party system.[12] Furthermore, in order to make the coefficients in the subsequent empirical analyses reasonably comparable, the ideological scales based on experts (ranging from 0 to 10) and manifestos (ranging from −100 to 100) have been recalibrated so that these placements are also on the traditional 1–10 scale that is used in the Eurobarometer surveys. Note that to the extent that "different metrics" issues arise due to the use of multiple data sources and scales (see Achen 1977, 1978), the analyses based on the

[11] A comprehensive set of studies are presented in Marks (2007), which analyze the trade-offs that accompany each approach used to estimate parties' policy positions.

[12] I rely on the Eurobarometer surveys from 1980 (13), 1981 (15), 1982 (17), and 1983 (19) for the analyses based on experts and manifestos, and the Eurobarometer surveys from 1987 (27), 1988 (29), 1989 (31A), and 1990 (33) for the analyses that are based on the citizen placements of parties' Left–Right policy positions. The questions in the Eurobarometer are phrased: "In political matters, people talk of 'the left' and 'the right'. How would you place your views on this scale? [The following question is included *only* in the Eurobarometer 31A (1989)] And, where would you place the political parties (of your country)?"

For analyses of political systems outside of the European Community, I rely on table 7.1 in Powell (2000: 168) for Left–Right self-placements of voters. The benefit of using the information from this table is that it allows for the addition of Australia, Canada, Finland, Norway, Sweden, and the United States to the analysis of Western European countries in the early 1980s. Also, note that the Castles–Mair survey does not ask experts to place parties in Greece, Luxembourg, and Portugal.

Eurobarometer surveys address these concerns directly because the *source* and *scale* of party and voter ideological measurements is the same (i.e., voters).

The average party policy extremism measure also requires data about the dispersion of voter ideologies in each country, as well as data on parties' vote shares.[13] Citizen policy dispersion is defined as the standard deviation of respondents' Left–Right self-placements in the country, calculated for all respondents who were willing to place themselves on the Left–Right scale.

Thus, the countries were selected based on the availability of underlying voter distributions, and of reliable Left–Right party placements. The specific national elections were chosen based on the proximity to the time at which experts (1982) and citizens (1989) were asked to place parties along a Left–Right policy dimension. In sum, it was possible to gather fifteen country-level observations for the elections between 1980 and 1983, and twelve additional observations from 1987 to 1990. Table A3.2 presents the list of countries and elections that are included in the empirical analyses (for more information about the data, see also Footnote 11).

Here is an illustration of why it is important to measure the party policy extremism relative to the dispersion of the voter distribution. Suppose that two countries A and B have parties that present, on average, platforms that are equally noncentrist – but that country A has a more dispersed voter distribution than country B. If we look only at the party platforms the countries' party policy extremism scores will be the same. However, when we account for the differing voter distributions, we conclude that the party system in country B is more extreme because the parties in this system are more widely distributed *relative to the voter distribution*. The decision to normalize the measure of average party policy extremism based upon the voter dispersion in the country is consistent with the arguments advanced by Alvarez and Nagler (2004) and Kollman et al. (1998), both of whom develop voter-normalized party dispersion measures. Note, however, that all of the analyses reported below have been replicated using measures of average party policy extremism that are not normalized for the dispersion of the voter distribution, and that these analyses support identical substantive conclusions.

With these considerations in mind, I employ a measure of average party policy extremism that is analogous to the *Party System Compactness* measure developed by Alvarez and Nagler (2004). *Party System Compactness* is expressed as voter dispersion divided by net party policy differentiation. In the following empirical analyses, however, the numerator and the denominator are reversed so that higher scores indicate increased party policy extremism. An additional variation is that the Center of the party system is defined as the ideological Center of the voter distribution (i.e., public opinion) as opposed to the weighted mean of the parties'

---

[13] The Manifesto Research Group provides vote shares in a CD-ROM in its 2001 and 2006 publications.

ideological positions.[14] The *weighted* measure of average *party* policy *extremism (WPE)* is defined as follows:

$$WPE_k = \frac{\Sigma_{j=1} VS_j |(P_{jk} - \bar{V}_k)|}{\sigma_{vk}},$$ (3.1)

where

$\bar{V}_k$ is the mean voter Left–Right ideological self-placement in country k,
P_{jk} is the ideological position of party j in country k,
VS_j is the vote share for party j, and
σ_{vk} is the standard deviation of voter self-placements in country k.

The alternative to weighing parties' positions by their vote shares is to weight all parties equally. This measure is the *unweighted* measure of the average *party* policy *extremism (UPE)*, and it is constructed as follows:

$$UPE_k = \frac{[\Sigma_{j=1} |(P_{jk} - \bar{V}_k)|]/n}{\sigma_{vk}},$$ (3.2)

where

n = the absolute number of parties included in the analysis for country k.

To visualize the mechanics of the UPE and WPE, refer to Figures 3.1a and b. Each figure depicts the 1983 elections in Great Britain, and measures party policy extremism based on UPE and WPE. WPE measures the average party extremism at .96, while UPE registers .76.[15] The explanation for the difference is straightforward – in 1983, the two largest parties, the Conservatives and Labour, were relatively noncentrist, while the two smaller parties, the Liberals and Social Democrats, were centrist. Thus, the UPE score of the British political system

---

[14] The Alvarez and Nagler formula is $\sigma_{vk}/[\Sigma_{j=1} VS_j |(P_{jk} - P_k)|]$, which is identical to Equation 3.1 with the noted exceptions that the party system Center is identified as the mean voter's ideological position, and that the numerator and dominator have been switched. However, empirical analyses have been conducted that substitute the weighted mean party position, $\bar{P}_k$, as the measure for the party system Center. Furthermore, the parameters have been estimated for each of the specifications featured in Equations 3.3–3.5, employing a version of the dependent variable that squares the party policy deviations from the party system Center (i.e., based on *variances*), and the results for each of these analyses support the substantive conclusions reported in this study. The results from this set of analyses are in Tables A3.13 and A3.14.

[15] Specifically, WPE is calculated (.289 * | 3.07–5.87| + .144 * |5.14–5.87| + .122 * |5.50–5.87| + .444 * |8.02–5.87|) / 2 = .96, where the parties' deviations from the Center of the voter distribution are weighted by their relative shares of the vote, and the denominator (which equals 2) represents the standard deviation of the British respondents' Left–Right self-placements on the 1983 Eurobarometer survey. Alternatively, UPE is calculated (.25 * |3.07 – 5.87| + .25 * |5.14 –5.87| + .25 * |5.50 – 5.87| + .25 * |8.02 – 5.87|) / 2 = .76, where each of the four parties' deviations from the mean party placement on a Left–Right scale is counted equally, so that consequently each is weighted at .25.

(a)

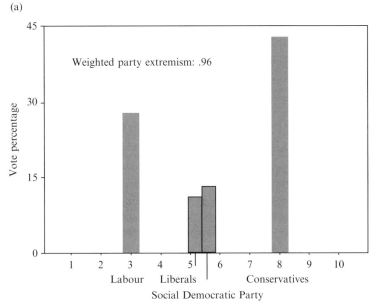

Experts' Left–Right party placements

(b)

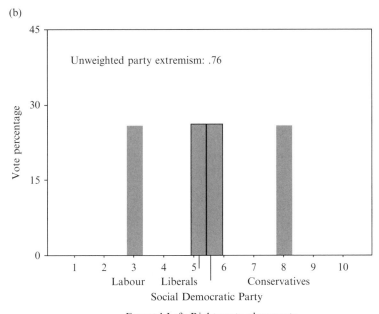

Experts' Left–Right party placements

FIGURE 3.1a and b Demonstrating the weighted (WPE) and unweighted (UPE) measures of average party policy extremism: the 1983 British National Elections

Notes: Although the Social Democratic Party and the Liberals were allied for the 1983 Elections, the two parties are each coded separately in the Castles and Mair (1984) study, as well as by the Comparative Manifesto Project (CMP). Their Left–Right scores are 5.14 and 5.50, respectively, on a 1–10 scale. After the "Alliance" performed poorly in the 1987 Elections, the parties formally merged in 1989 to become the Liberal Democrats, and are thus coded as a single party by the CMP from this time onwards.

decreases when the Liberals and Social Democrats are treated on equal footing with the Conservatives and Labour.

3.4 TESTING THE PROPORTIONALITY AND THE PARTY SYSTEM SIZE HYPOTHESES

Recall that the Proportionality Hypothesis predicts a positive relationship between the degree of proportionality and the average party policy extremism, that is, that as the electoral system becomes more proportional, party policy extremism increases. The Party System Size Hypothesis posits that there is a positive relationship between the effective number of parties and the average party extremism variable. The parameters of an ordinary least squares (OLS) regression model are estimated in order to evaluate these hypotheses. The full specification is given as follows:

$$Average\ party\ policy\ extremism = B_0 + B_1[Degree\ of\ proportionality] +$$
$$B_2[Effective\ number\ of\ parliamentary\ parties]$$
$$H_1: B_1 > 0,$$
$$H_2: B_2 > 0. \tag{3.3}$$

However, the independent variables relating to proportionality and the effective number of parties are correlated, which raises concerns about collinearity and its effects on the efficiency of the parameter estimates.[16] Consequently, bivariate regression equations are also estimated to test Hypotheses 1 and 2. The bivariate *proportionality* specification is

$$Average\ party\ policy\ extremism = B_0 + B_1[Degree\ of\ proportionality],$$
$$H_2: B_1 > 0. \tag{3.4}$$

The bivariate *number of parties* specification is

$$Average\ party\ policy\ extremism = B_0 + B_1[Effective\ number\ of$$
$$parliamentary\ parties],$$
$$H_2: B_1 > 0. \tag{3.5}$$

Results for the WPE: Table 3.1 reports parameter estimates for the full specification, the bivariate proportionality specification, and the bivariate number of parties

---

[16] Based on the countries included in the analyses, the correlation coefficient between proportionality and the effective number of parties is .58, which is statistically significant at the .05 level.

TABLE 3.1 *Estimating weighted average party policy extremism (WPE)*

L–R party placements based on the following	Experts (1980–3)		Citizens (1987–90)			Manifestos (1980–3)		
Specification: variable	Full	Bivariate	Full	Bivariate	Bivariate	Full	Bivariate	Bivariate
Degree of proportionality	**–.009**	**–.004**	**–.02****	**–.02****		**–.001**	**.001**	
	(.01)	(.01)	(.007)	(.006)		(.01)	(.008)	
Effective number of parliamentary parties (ENPP)	.03	.01	.01		–.03	.02		.02
	(.06)	(.05)	(.03)		(.04)	(.05)		(.04)
Constant	.78***	.85***	1.09***	1.12***	.96***	.39**	.43***	.38**
	(.20)	(.15)	(.12)	(.09)	(.15)	(.15)	(.11)	(.14)
N	15	15	12	12	12	15	15	15
Adjusted R^2	–.12	–.06	.38	.44	–.03	–.15	–.07	–.06

Notes: Parameters are ordinary least squares (OLS) coefficients. Estimated standard errors are in parentheses. The dependent variable is the average party's policy distance from the Left–Right position of the mean voter weighted by its relative share of the vote, divided by the standard deviation of voter Left–Right self-placements (refer to Equation 3.1 in the text). The definitions of the independent variables are given in the text. The ideological scales based on experts and manifestos have been recalibrated so that these placements are also on the 1–10 scale that is used in the Eurobarometer surveys. Each country is observed only once for each set of analyses. The specific countries included in each set of analyses are presented in Table A3.2.

$*p = .10$, $**p = .05$, $***p = .01$, two-tailed test

specification, with each specification estimated using the weighted version of the average party policy extremism variable. Each specification was estimated in turn for each of the three different versions of the party policy extremism variable – one based on expert placements, another on voter placements, and another on codings of party manifestos – so that there are nine regressions in all.[17]

The most striking feature of the results reported in Table 3.1 is the consistent lack of support for the Proportionality and the Party System Size Hypotheses. None of the estimated coefficients for the degree of proportionality and for the number of parties is positive and statistically significant. Indeed, half of the twelve parameter estimates for these independent variables are negative, that is, these coefficients suggest that the average party policy extremism actually *declines* as the electoral system proportionality and the number of parties increases. While most of these parameter estimates do not attain statistical significance, the estimates are significant (and negative!) for the full and the bivariate proportionality specifications, when citizen placements are used to locate the parties (see Table 3.1, columns 4 and 5).

Results for the UPE: Table 3.2 reports analyses that are identical to those reported in Table 3.1, *except* that the results in Table 3.2 are based on the unweighted version of the party policy extremism variable. Once again, there is no support for the Proportionality Hypothesis and the Party System Size Hypothesis. That is, none of the estimated coefficients estimating the effects of the degree of proportionality and for the number of parties are positive and statistically significant and, in fact, once again half of the parameter estimates for these independent variables are negative.

Overall, I find no evidence to support the Proportionality or the Party System Size Hypotheses, and that average party policy extremism increases with the electoral system proportionality and with the number of parties. This conclusion persists despite the fact that these hypotheses have been evaluated using alternative measures of party policy extremism (weighted and unweighted) and of party positions (expert placements, citizen placements, and party manifestos). I conclude that in the fifteen postwar democracies included in the study, increased electoral proportionality and larger numbers of parties were not systematically linked to the average party policy extremism in the party system.

---

[17] The parameters for each of these specifications were also estimated using the Left–Right estimates of party positions presented in Huber and Inglehart (1995) for the early 1990s. These estimates are presented in Table A3.15. The substantive conclusions based on these results are identical to the ones reported below.

TABLE 3.2 *Estimating unweighted average party policy extremism (UPE)*

L–R party placements based on the following	Experts (1980–3)			Citizens (1987–90)			Manifestos (1980–3)		
Specification: variable	Full	Bivariate	Bivariate	Full	Bivariate	Bivariate	Full	Bivariate	Bivariate
Degree of proportionality	**-.01**	**-.003**		**-.02**	**-.02***		**.00004**	**.0007**	
	(.01)	(.01)		(.01)	(.01)		(.01)	(.009)	
Effective number of parliamentary parties (ENPP)	.02		.002	-.05		-.08	.006		.006
	(.06)		(.04)	(.05)		(.05)	(.05)		(.04)
Constant	.82***	.86***	.80***	1.33***	1.21***	1.24***	.44**	.45***	.44**
	(.18)	(.13)	(.17)	(.18)	(.14)	(.18)	(.17)	(.13)	(.16)
N	15	15	15	12	12	12	15	15	15
Adjusted R^2	-.14	-.07	-.08	.25	.24	.17	-.17	-.08	.08

Notes: Parameters are ordinary least squares (OLS) coefficients. Estimated standard errors are in parentheses. The dependent variable is the average party's policy distance from the Left–Right position of the mean voter, divided by the standard deviation of voter Left–Right self-placements (refer to Equation 3.2). The definitions of the independent variables are given in the text. The ideological scales based on experts and manifestos have been recalibrated so that these placements are also on the 1–10 scale that is used in the Eurobarometer surveys. Each country is observed only once for each set of analyses. The specific countries included in each set of analyses are presented in Table A3.2.

*p = .10, ** p = .05, *** p = .01, and two-tailed test

3.5 EXPLAINING THE RESULTS (I): MEASURING THE MEDIATING EFFECTS OF ELECTORAL SYSTEMS

Given that the previous scholarly research discussed in Section 3.2 tends to support the Proportionality and the Party System Size Hypotheses, the empirical findings reported above are surprising. What accounts for the finding that average party policy extremism does not systematically increase with electoral system proportionality and with the number of parties? Here I rely on the empirical framework from Chapter 3 and discuss recent theoretical research – much of it by Schofield and his coauthors – to illuminate the findings.

I begin by summarizing the previous arguments in the chapter concerning vote-seeking and policy convergence. Keeping Duverger's mechanical effect (1954) in mind, these arguments posited that disproportional systems motivate parties to maximize votes. The most efficient strategy for enhancing votes, ceteris paribus, is to adopt policy positions near the Center of the voter distribution – thereby minimizing the policy distance between the party or the candidate and as many voters as possible. This expectation is indeed borne out empirically in Chapter 2. Then if the evidence suggests that the party proximity model holds across developed democracies, we would expect these party proximity effects to be greater in disproportional electoral systems.

Using the framework developed in Chapter 2, we can actually investigate whether this is the case, and whether party proximity effects are enhanced in disproportional systems. For the twelve Western European democracies from 1976 to 1998 in Chapter 2, we have already developed a measure of *party policy distance*, which is the distance between the party's Left–Right policy position and the mean voter preference, and we can further rely on Gallagher's measure of *disproportionality* introduced earlier in this chapter. Thus, the degree to which centrifugal and centripetal incentives exist across countries featuring different electoral systems by estimating the following regression model specification:

$$Normalized\ vote\ share = B_1 + B_2[Party\ policy\ distance]$$
$$+ B_3[Party\ policy\ distance \times Disproportionality]$$
$$+ B_4[Disproportionality] + e. \qquad (3.6)$$

Recall we found in Chapter 2 that a *negative* relationship exists between party policy distance and party support, that is that parties' vote shares decrease with the distance between the party's Left–Right position and the mean voter position. By contrast, if there are sharp differences in electoral incentives across systems that feature different levels of (dis)proportionality, then we would expect the coefficient, B_3, on the interaction term [*party policy distance* × *disproportionality*] to be statistically significant. In particular, if party policy proximity matters more in disproportional systems, leading to the expectation of clustering of parties at the Center of the voter distribution, then this coefficient is expected to be negative and statistically significant, because parties in disproportional systems would experience additional punishment at the polls for adopting policies further from the mean voter position.

Column 1 of Table 3.3 presents the results from estimating the parameters of the model specification in Equation 3.6. The coefficient on the [*party policy distance*] variable is negative (-3.27) and statistically significant, which is consistent with the findings reported in Chapter 2 that parties further from the Center of the voter distribution tend to gain fewer votes than parties closer to the middle of the electorate. With respect to the key expectation formulated in this section that electoral systems mediate the effects of proximity, there is no statistically significant evidence that moderate parties gain more votes in disproportional systems than in proportional systems. If the coefficient on the interaction term was negative and statistically significant, this would suggest that electoral systems mediate party proximity effects. However, the estimates on the interaction term in column 1 are neither positive nor statistically significant. Furthermore, the estimates in columns 2–4 continue to support the finding that electoral systems do not mediate the effects of party proximity on electoral success. Table 3.4 reports the parameter estimates of the model specification, controlling for vote share on the right-hand side of the regression equation. The estimates in columns 1–4 on the interaction term support the finding that electoral systems do not mediate the effects of party proximity in the expected direction.

Furthermore, we can simply stratify the sample into disproportional systems and proportional systems, and directly compare the coefficients on the [*party policy distance*] variables. The disadvantage accompanied by stratification is that we lose degrees of freedom in the estimation process. On the other hand, stratifying the sample leads to a more direct interpretation of the results. The disproportional systems include France, Britain, Greece, and Spain – all countries that score above 8 on the Gallagher Index for the time period under investigation – and the proportional systems include Belgium, Denmark, Germany, Ireland, Italy, Luxembourg, the Netherlands, and Portugal.[18]

Tables 3.5 and 3.6 estimate the parameters of a bivariate OLS model estimating parties' normalized vote share for countries featuring disproportional and proportional electoral systems, respectively. All of the estimates on the [*party policy distance*] variables are negative, as expected, but insignificant. In Table 3.6, which

---

[18] The countries are divided into "disproportional" and "proportional" categories based on the disproportionality scores reported in appendix A in Lijphart (1999) where a (relatively sizeable) four-point gap divides the two groupings.

TABLE 3.3 *Coefficients for different measures of proximity, and their interaction with electoral system disproportionality when estimating normalized vote shares*

Coefficients	Eurobarometer placements (1984–94)		Expert placements Huber–Inglehart (1988–98)	
	Squared proximity (1)	Relative squared proximity (2)	Squared proximity (3)	Relative squared proximity (4)
Constant	64.23***	59.34***	81.63***	78.18***
	(7.49)	(8.00)	(7.71)	(10.21)
Proximity	**−3.27***	**−8.47**†	**−4.28***	**−19.39***
	(1.16)	(6.32)	(1.12)	(9.94)
Proximity × disproportionality	.11	−.07	.17†	.19
	(.15)	(1.12)	(.10)	(1.27)
Disproportionality	1.53	1.73	.41	.85
	(1.28)	(1.35)	(1.02)	(1.45)
N	248	248	145	145
Adjusted R^2	.06	.03	.09	.03

Note: Parameters are ordinary least squares (OLS) coefficients. Estimated standard errors are in parentheses. Coefficient for proximity in column 2 is statistically significant at the .10 level, one-tailed test.

*p < .10, **p < .05, ***p < .01, and two-tailed test; $^†p$ < .10, one-tailed test

TABLE 3.4 *Coefficients for different measures of proximity and their interaction with electoral system disproportionality when estimating absolute vote shares*

Coefficients	Eurobarometer placements (1984–94)		Expert placements Huber–Inglehart (1988–98)	
	Squared proximity (1)	Relative squared proximity (2)	Squared proximity (3)	Relative squared proximity (4)
Constant	23.34***	21.00***	32.59***	33.00***
	(3.42)	(3.21)	(3.64)	(4.19)
Proximity	**−.79***	**−2.63***	**−1.09***	**−6.03****
	(.29)	(1.52)	(.28)	(2.35)
Proximity × disproportionality	.02	.07	.037†	.17
	(.04)	(.28)	(.024)	(.30)
Disproportionality	.43	.35	.04	−.02
	(.33)	(.34)	(.25)	(.34)
Effective number of parties	−1.86***	−1.49***	−2.66***	−2.78***
	(.51)	(.50)	(.61)	(.64)
N	248	248	145	145
Adjusted R^2	.10	.08	.20	.15

Note: Parameters are ordinary least squares (OLS) coefficients. Estimated standard errors are in parentheses.

*p < .10, **p < .05, ***p < .01, two-tailed test; $^†p$ < .10, one-tailed test

TABLE 3.5 *Coefficients for different measures of proximity under electoral systems characterized as disproportional, estimating normalized vote shares*

Coefficients	Eurobarometer placements (1984–94)		Expert placements Huber–Inglehart (1988–98)	
	Squared proximity (1)	Relative squared proximity (2)	Squared proximity (3)	Relative squared proximity (4)
Constant	73.04***	73.53***	73.57***	78.15***
	(10.85)	(10.82)	(9.90)	(13.68)
Proximity	**−.62**	**−4.37**	**−.74**	**−9.71**
	(1.34)	(8.30)	(1.09)	(12.41)
N	57	57	40	40
R^2	.004	.005	.01	.02

Note: Parameters are ordinary least squares (OLS) coefficients. Estimated standard errors are in parentheses.

*p < .10, **p < .05, ***p < .01, two-tailed test

TABLE 3.6 *Coefficients for different measures of proximity in electoral systems characterized as proportional, when estimating normalized vote shares*

Coefficients	Eurobarometer placements (1984–94)		Expert placements Huber–Inglehart (1988–98)	
	Squared proximity (1)	Relative squared proximity (2)	Squared proximity (3)	Relative squared proximity (4)
Constant	70.36***	65.79***	85.95***	86.84***
	(5.37)	(5.68)	(6.65)	(8.93)
Proximity	**−3.33***	**−9.96**	**−4.07***	**−20.59**
	(.89)	(4.24)	(1.10)	(8.80)
N	191	191	105	105
R^2	.07	.03	.12	.05

Note: Parameters are ordinary least squares (OLS) coefficients. Estimated standard errors are in parentheses.

*p < .10, **p < .05, ***p < .01, two-tailed test

estimates the parameters of the same model for proportional systems, the estimates in columns 1–4 are much larger than for disproportional systems (columns 1–4 in Table 3.5). Indeed, these two tables suggest that, if anything, party proximity matters more in the more proportional systems (although the standard error estimates are too large on the interaction terms in Tables 3.3 and 3.4 to convincingly support this claim).

3.6 EXPLAINING THE RESULTS (II): RESEARCH ON PARTY STRATEGIES

Thus far, this chapter has reported empirical results that parties are not more dispersed under PR, and that the effects of party policy distance do not vary across electoral systems. The latter empirical finding plausibly explains the former, but what theories of party competition can illuminate these results? The answer is that scholars often confuse, or conflate vote- and office-seeking incentives. That is, it seems perfectly reasonable to assume that parties wishing to gain office would naturally seek votes to this end.

Robertson (1976) theorizes that when systems that feature plurality voting like Britain hold competitive elections this will induce parties to converge on the median. Parties abandon their preferred parties and move toward the Center in a Downsian fashion when the outcome of the election "hangs in the balance." On the other hand, the situation looks very different for these same plurality systems in circumstances where the outcome can be easily predicted ahead of time. If the election outcome as described in this situation is uncompetitive, then the winning party will want to claim a mandate and implement its preferred policies. Meanwhile, under the uncompetitive scenario, the losing party would much rather "go down fighting" and stick to its principles than lose the election while pandering to the Center. The latter situation puts losing party leaders in a precarious position for any postmortem analysis (Andrews and Jackman 2008).

There is evidence to suggest that plurality systems have less competitive elections than PR systems (Franklin 2004; see also Blais 2002). A vote in PR systems is more likely to change representative outcomes than in a plurality system. Under the first scenario, the probability that a citizen casts a vote that adds one more seat to her party's total in the legislative chamber is far greater than the probability of casting the winning vote in "first past the post" elections. The arguments based on Robertson (1976) above suggest that the lack of competitiveness could foster policy divergence quite regularly in plurality voting systems.[19]

Research on valence, party activists, and coalitions also explain the findings reported in this chapter. In the past few years, Norman Schofield has identified two factors that can motivate vote-seeking parties to shift *away* from the Center of the voter distribution, thereby increasing the policy divergence of the party system. The first is the strategic implications of "valence" dimensions of party evaluation, that is dimensions related to voters' impressions of party elites' competence, honesty, or charisma (see Stokes 1963). Schofield and his coauthors argue that "valence-disadvantaged" parties have electoral incentives to

---

[19] The crucial assumption of these arguments is that parties can diagnose the competitiveness of elections ahead of time.

differentiate themselves on policy grounds, because if they present centrist policies that are similar to those advocated by valence-advantaged parties, then voters will choose based on the valence dimension – that is, they will choose parties that have superior valence images (Adams 1999; Schofield and Sened 2005, 2006; see also Macdonald and Rabinowitz 1998). To the extent that Schofield's argument captures real-world parties' electoral strategies, we should not expect all vote-seeking parties to converge toward the center of the policy space. In this case, then even if plurality systems motivate parties to attach greater weight to vote-seeking, this will not in turn imply that plurality elections motivate policy convergence.[20]

Miller and Schofield (2003), building on Aldrich (1983*a*, 1983*b*, 1995), develop a second motivation for vote-seeking parties to diverge from the center of the policy space, which revolves around strategic incentives related to *party activists*. The Miller-Schofield argument is that parties can enhance their vote shares by appealing to party activists who provide scarce campaign resources (i.e., time and money) – and that these activists typically hold extreme views. Specifically, the authors argue that parties can use the added campaign resources they acquire via their policy appeals to activists to enhance their images along valence dimensions such as competence and integrity – and that this in turn will increase the parties' electoral support among rank-and-file voters.

A final interpretation is that while maximizing votes is obviously important, maximizing the likelihood of being included in the governing coalition is more important. If this is the case then centrist positioning in proportional systems should not be surprising. Schofield et al. (1998*a*) examine Dutch and German elections and determine that parties (intentionally or unintentionally) forgo their vote-maximizing positions, and try to put themselves in good positions for the post-coalition negotiations. This entails presenting policies that are acceptable to potential coalition partners, which may provide incentives for policy moderation. If proportional systems motivate parties to present policies that are acceptable to coalition partners, then these parties may well present centrist positions. This finding is also in line with that of the other prominent coalition scholars who present theoretical and empirical results that support the claim that in proportional systems, gaining membership in the governing coalition is closely linked with centrist positioning (Axelrod 1970; Huber and Powell 1994; Laver and Shepsle 1996; Powell 2000).

Thus, factors like election competitiveness, valence, party activists, and post-election coalition negotiations potentially blur what might otherwise be a straightforward relationship between electoral systems, parties' policy positions, and election outcomes.

---

[20] Adams and Merrill (1999, 2000) present an alternative argument that voters' partisan loyalties can motivate vote-seeking parties to diverge from the Center, in the direction of the policies favored by the members of their partisan constituencies (see also Adams et al. 2005).

3.7 CONCLUSION

Political scientists and casual political observers have long been in agreement that proportional electoral rules enhance the distinctiveness of parties' policy programs. Conversely, plurality and plurality-runoff systems are thought to produce Downsian "Tweedledum and Tweedledee" political competition where the number of competitors is low and policy moderation is the dominant party strategy. The empirical analyses reported in this chapter – which are based on several alternative measures of average party policy extremism – do not support these claims. In this analysis of fifteen democratic party systems, I find no evidence that average party policy extremism systematically increases with electoral system proportionality. Nor do I find evidence for an "indirect effect" of proportionality on party extremism, via the influence of electoral systems on the number of political parties.

The limitations for this chapter, stated in Section 3.1, are also avenues for future research on the relationship between institutional settings and party behavior. Future studies would benefit by having more than fifteen countries and/or by analyzing parties' positions along multiple policy dimensions. However, preliminary evidence suggests that by excluding analyses of a second dimension the average party policy extremism along the Left–Right dimension is *not* being artificially reduced. Indeed, an appraisal of the spatial mappings of Schofield and Sened (2006) for the Netherlands and Italy (two proportional systems) and for the United Kingdom and the United States (systems that feature plurality voting) suggests that there is at least as much variation in party positions along the second dimension in the plurality-based party systems as there is in the PR-based systems (see Figures A3.1a–d).

To summarize, the relationship has been evaluated between proportionality and average party policy extremism over a much larger set of countries than has been explored in previous empirical work, and the results are robust across several alternative measures of parties' positions. Proportional electoral systems do not systematically encourage party extremism.

Part III

Effects of Electoral Institutions

Part II

4

Electoral Rules, the Number of Parties, and Niche Party Success

> Although we are only part way along in this history, it still seems to me that the law is much more defensible than when the Ashworths uttered it eighty years ago. Many – perhaps most – political scientists who specialize in the study of political parties now accept the law.
>
> (William Riker (1986: 41) on Duverger's Law)

4.1 INTRODUCTION

The modest goal of this chapter is to demonstrate an association between the electoral rules that have been adopted in a political system and the subsequent competitiveness of niche parties in electoral competition. The competitiveness of niche parties refers to the number of viable niche competitors in a particular country and/or their combined vote share.

Why does niche party influence matter? While Chapters 5 and 6 address this question, the short answer for now is that political systems that allow for nontrivial niche party competition provide their citizens with access to two fundamentally different channels of political representation. By contrast, political systems with relatively nonexistent niche party influence offer their citizens access to only one channel of political representation. *Policy responsiveness* is quite different for mainstream and niche parties – across institutional settings – in that the former responds to the mean voter position and the latter to their core supporters (detailed in Chapter 6). Furthermore, when analyzing election outcomes, niche parties are rewarded for their *policy distinctiveness*, while mainstream parties generally gain more votes when they adopt moderate positions (Chapter 5). Thus, Chapters 5 and 6 expand on the idea that niche and mainstream parties function very differently in terms of political representation. This chapter steps back to approach the question about what leads to the relative influence of niche and mainstream parties in the first place.

While Chapters 2 and 3 report surprising empirical similarities across countries in spite of differences in their institutional design, this chapter departs by focusing on differential *effects of electoral systems*. The central finding of Chapter 2 is that moderate party position-taking has a common effect across democracies. That is, moderate parties gain relatively higher vote shares in comparison to their more extreme counterparts. Furthermore, the relationship between party policy distance from the mean voter position and vote share is not mediated by the electoral system in which parties compete. Disproportional political systems like Great Britain should reward moderate parties with more votes than proportional electoral systems, but the findings from Chapter 2 do not support that this finding holds comparatively.[1]

Chapter 3 reports no evidence supporting conventional wisdom that proportional systems promote more dispersed party positioning, that is electoral systems are the "dog that didn't bark." Taken together, the empirical analyses reported in Chapters 2 and 3 suggest a far more modest role for electoral systems in influencing party positions and election outcomes than scholars had previously thought.

This chapter moves away from Chapters 2 and 3 by demonstrating that – while voting rules are not accompanied by the direct effects on the causes and consequences of party positioning – voting rules do affect the level of influence that niche parties are likely to wield in a political system.

4.2 RELATIONSHIPS BETWEEN ELECTORAL SYSTEMS, THE NUMBER OF PARTIES, AND THE NUMBER OF NICHE PARTIES

The literature on electoral systems and the number of parties is well developed (Benoit 2006). Maurice Duverger (1954) is credited with two important well-known propositions on the relationship between voting rules and party system size. Duverger posited a "law" for which he is famous, and then a related hypothesis. Duverger's Law states that, "the simple-majority, single-ballot system favors the two-party system" (Duverger 1954: 217). And the "weaker" hypothesis posits that "the simple-majority system with second ballot and proportional representation favour multipartism" (p. 239). While there has been some controversy in the past about who should be credited with these propositions, and, in particular the "law," Duverger's legacy is credited to a few factors.[2] Benoit (2006) identifies three of these in particular. The first is that Duverger was the first to

---

[1] Furthermore, the experience of the centrist Liberals, Social Democrats, and the allied Liberal Democrats suggests that policy proximity to the mean voter position in Britain is not the sole determinant of vote share. These parties have competed in the 'middle' of Labour and the Conservative parties, and they have never exceeded the vote of either party.

[2] For a history of this controversy, see Riker (1982; see also Riker 1986).

explicitly make these assertions. Second, Duverger brought a wealth of historical evidence into the fold to systematically argue for the law and hypothesis. Third, Duverger introduced the mechanical and psychological effects, that is, the causal mechanisms, through which electoral systems are linked to party system size (see also Riker 1986: 26).

Since Duverger, there have been many important studies on electoral systems and party system size (e.g., Taagepera and Shugart 1989; Lijphart 1994, 1999; Cox 1997). Electoral systems research is an area of political science research where data collection has been relatively strong. One reason why data has been quick to accumulate is that concrete measures are in relative abundance. For example, it is easier to measure a country's voting laws than it is to measure its political culture.

In this vein, Lijphart (1999, chapter 8) evaluates thirty-six democracies in the postwar period and finds a fairly strong association between the proportionality of voting systems and greater numbers of political parties. Here, the relationship between the electoral system and the niche party existence is raised in a fashion similar to Lijphart (1999). There are several studies that target the effects of electoral rules on the electoral success of particular types of niche parties. The rise of the extreme Right received considerable attention in this regard (see e.g. Jackman and Volpert 1996; Givens 2004; Golder 2003*a*, 2003*b*; Carter 2004; Kitschelt with McGann 1995). Additionally, several studies focus on Green party electoral fortunes (Kitschelt 1988; Taggart 1996). By singling out party families in a few political systems, the number of observations that can be leveraged in any of these analyses is, naturally, limited. This often leads to difficulties in making generalizations about what explains the electoral success of one party family. With respect to the extreme Right parties, Kai Arzeimer (2009) employs a sophisticated multilevel setup to analyze the impact of democratic institutions (centralization and electoral laws) on these parties' vote support. Arzeimer reports that neither the decentralization nor proportionality of the political system directly affects individual likelihoods of supporting extreme Right parties. Golder's studies (2003*a*, 2003*b*) also highlight the difficulties with tying electoral systems to the extreme Right party support. First, Golder (2003*a*) concludes, "that it would be much harder to contain the electoral growth of extreme Right parties through policy intervention than Jackman and Volpert believe. This is because there is no convincing evidence that changing electoral rules would influence their electoral success in one way or another." Then he reports findings that suggest electoral systems play a slightly greater role in explaining far Right support, but that their effects are conditional on levels of immigration (Golder 2003*b*).

Indeed, a review of the literature above is what makes Bonnie Meguid's studies (2005, 2008) so unique, because she is able to identify conditions of individual niche party success and failure. The two circumstances she identifies are when a mainstream party engages niche parties on their primary issue dimension (e.g., the environment for Green parties), and when a mainstream party adopts an "adversarial" position on the issue dimension of the niche party. Thus, in Meguid's model, *issue salience* and *differentiation* contribute to the electoral success of niche parties.

The present analysis looks at all niche parties, rather than focusing on one particular party family. I analyze niche parties along the lines of Lijphart (1999), plotting in scattergrams institutional arrangements and the existence of niche parties, thereby illustrating relationships between the voting rules, party system size, and niche party competition. The discussion above motivates Hypotheses 1a and 1b:

> H1a: *proportional electoral systems are associated with greater numbers of niche parties.*
>
> H1b: *proportional electoral systems are associated with greater combined niche vote share.*

These propositions are logical extensions of Duverger (1954) and Lijphart (1999). Through their influence on party system size, electoral systems should also affect the level of competitiveness of niche parties. Several studies examine the relationship between electoral rules and the electoral success of single issue parties, and these scholars suggest that smaller parties benefit under proportional representation (PR) (Lijphart 1994; Ordeshook and Shvetsova 1994; Cox 1997; see also Norris 2005).

Thus far, the expectation is that the proportionality of the electoral system adopted is conducive to allowing a greater number of smaller parties to compete. Niche parties tend to be smaller than mainstream parties, and so proportional electoral systems should be conducive to a greater niche party presence in the political system. However, to the extent that any disagreement exists over the connection between the electoral rules and party system size (i.e., the number of parties), it is also possible via Table 4.1 to evaluate another simple proposition, which is that systems that have greater numbers of parties should also have an increased role for niche parties in general. By extension, we would also expect that the greater number of competitors would also facilitate greater numbers of niche parties that are able to compete in a political system. Furthermore, the greater the number of niche parties, the more likely that the aggregated niche party share of the vote will also increase in a political system. Hypotheses 2a and 2b posit relationships between party system size and niche party competitiveness:

> H2a: *party system size is directly related to the number of significant niche parties that compete within that system.*
>
> H2b: *party system size is directly related to combined niche vote share.*

Figure 4.1 summarizes the relationships discussed above, and depicts the four hypotheses (1a, 1b, 2a, 2b).

TABLE 4.1 *The average number of niche party competitors and their combined vote shares, stratified by country*

Country	Number of niche parties	Combined niche vote percentage	Disproportionality score[a]	Effective number of parliamentary parties[b] (ENPP)	Effective number of elective parties[c] (ENEP)	Number of elections
Australia	0	0	10.37	3.07	2.44	10
Austria	0.875	4.82	1.66	3.11	2.95	8
Belgium	1.44	5.88	3.41	8.54	7.37	9
Britain	0.29	0.15	15.5	3.27	2.21	7
Canada	0	0	13.69	3.37	2.39	7
Czech Republic	1.6	16.21	7.42	5.13	3.71	5
Denmark	2.4	13.45	1.55	5.19	4.92	10
Finland	1.71	17.37	3.33	5.82	5.07	7
France	2.29	21.05	15.22	5.28	3.22	7
Germany	1.25	6.68	2.23	3.52	3.22	8
Greece	1.22	9.84	7.24	2.81	2.28	9
Hungary	0.25	1.39	12.25	5.23	3.08	4
Iceland	1	14.98	2.47	4.27	3.99	8
Ireland	1.22	3.41	4.15	3.33	2.86	9
Italy	4.38	42.77	4.75	5.54	4.94	8
Japan	1	9.65	7.33	3.91	3.07	10
Luxembourg	1.6	8.96	4.22	4.36	3.74	5
The Netherlands	1.22	7.41	1.2	4.7	4.44	9
New Zealand	0.22	1.35	11.19	3.3	2.54	9
Norway	1	7.3	4.27	4.57	3.89	7
Poland	1	3.38	9.6	8.18	5.32	4
Portugal	2.8	14.61	4.44	3.33	2.83	10
Slovakia	2.4	34.26	6.1	6.24	4.69	5
Spain	1	7.85	7.96	3.66	2.68	8
Sweden	1.56	9.03	1.69	3.92	3.7	9
Switzerland	3.14	7.98	3.01	6.26	5.52	7
United States	0	0	5.2	2.11	1.95	8

Notes: Scores in the columns are averages for 1976–2003. Country election year observations are in the Table A4.1.

[a] *Source*: "Index of Disproportionality" developed by Michael Gallagher (1991). Gallagher and Mitchell (2008) report election year estimates in their appendix B.

[b] *Source*: Laakso and Taagepera (1979) measure of the effective number of parliamentary parties (ENPP).

[c] *Source*: Laakso and Taagepera (1979) measure of the effective number of elective parties (ENEP).

(a)   (b)   (c)

Electoral system → Number of parties → Influence of niche parties (number of, and
                                              combined vote share)

Specifically:

Proportional   → More parties   → Greater

Disproportional   → Fewer parties   → Smaller

FIGURE 4.1 Posited relationships between electoral systems, the number of parties, and
the role of niche parties

Hypothesis 1 is depicted by the relationship between (a) and (c). And Hypothesis 2 is depicted by the
relationship between (b) and (c).

4.3 MEASURES AND MODEL SPECIFICATION

4.3.1 *The dependent variables: the number of niche parties and combined vote percentage of niche parties*

To measure the number and combined size of niche parties (i.e., the role or presence of niche parties), I rely on the CD-ROM that comes packaged with the Comparative Manifesto Project (CMP). The CMP is well known for systematically analyzing parties' policy programs, and using codings of manifestos to measure party policy positions over time. In this chapter, I focus on the sampling frame of the CMP investigators rather than estimates of the parties' policy positions.

Namely, how do the coders decide which parties to code? On the one hand, they do not want to miss any important parties. And, on the other, there are limited resources for the project, and so the investigators would prefer to avoid innumerable hours involved in coding platforms for irrelevant parties. The guidelines are set clearly by Ian Budge (Budge et al. 1987: 31), where he relies on Sartori (1976) to judge which parties are "significant." The parties whose policy programs are coded by the CMP are those that are judged to have blackmail and/or coalition potential. That is, parties are significant if they are able to disrupt the legislative schedule in the lower house of parliament, or if there is any possibility that they may join the governing coalition. An additional, more concrete indicator of significance that is employed by the authors is if the party receives over 5% of the vote in any postwar election contest.

I measure the number of niche parties by counting the number of niche parties that the CMP investigators deemed significant enough to code for a country election year. The combined niche vote percentage is similarly measured as the total percentage of votes that niche parties received in a country election year. Table A4.1 includes the number and combined size of niche parties competing in

Organization for Economic Cooperation and Development (OECD) country election years dating from 1976 to 2003, and Table 4.1 presents the averages, by country, of the number of niche parties and combined niche party support.

4.3.2 Measuring electoral system proportionality and the number of parties

The two independent variables that are central to the hypotheses explaining the role of niche parties are the proportionality of the electoral system and the number of parties in the political system. While these measures were outlined in previous chapters, I briefly describe them here. For disproportionality, I rely on the index developed by Gallagher (1991), which varies with the squared differences between parties' vote shares and their subsequent seat shares in parliament. The

equation for the Gallagher Index of Disproportionality is $\sqrt{\frac{1}{2}\Sigma(v_i - s_i)^2}$, where v_i and s_i are the vote shares and subsequent seat shares for party i. According to this measure larger differences between votes and seats indicate greater disproportionality.[3]

To measure the number of parties, I use the *effective number of parliamentary parties* (ENPP) measure developed by Laakso and Taagepera (1979). The ENPP is calculated using the following equation: $N = 1/\Sigma s_i^2$, where s_i is the proportion of seats of the ith party. I also employ the authors' alternative measure, the *effective number of elective parties* (ENEP) which is instead based on votes (i.e., $N = 1/\Sigma v_i^2$, where v_i is the proportion of votes of the ith party).[4]

Columns 6 and 7 of the Table A4.1 reports the L–T estimates of the ENPP and the ENEP for twenty-seven OECD countries in their election years.[5] Table 4.1 condenses Table A4.1, reporting the average estimates of the number of niche parties, the combined niche vote percentage, the disproportionality index, the ENEP, and the ENPP for the twenty-seven OECD countries from 1976 until 2003.[6]

---

[3] These measures indicate that countries such as Denmark, Germany, Sweden, and Norway feature quite proportional voting systems, while Britain, the United States, France, and Canada – the four countries in our study that employ some form of plurality – are comparatively disproportional.

[4] The Laakso–Taagepera (L–T) measure is constructed so that large parliamentary parties are counted more heavily than small parties. Thus, if three parties are competing and each receives a third of the seats in parliament, the L–T measure of the effective number of parties is three, while if one large party controls 60% of the seats in parliament and the other smaller parties each controls 20% of the seats, the effective number of parties is about 2.27.

[5] Turkey is not included in the analysis, because Gallagher and Mitchell (2008) do not report the disproportionality estimates.

[6] I note that when we constrain the number of observations to only countries included in the empirical analyses in Chapters 2 and 3, the results remain the same. These results are reporter below.

4.4 MODEL SPECIFICATION

I specify bivariate regression models in order to test the disproportionality hypotheses (1a and 1b), and the effective number of parties hypotheses (2a and 2b)[7]:

$$Number\ of\ niche\ parties = B_0 + B_1[Disproportionality] \qquad (4.1)$$

$$Combined\ of\ niche\ party\ vote\ percentage = B_0 + B_1[Disproportionality] \quad (4.2)$$

$$Number\ of\ niche\ parties = B_0 + B_1[Effective\ number\ of\ parties] \qquad (4.3)$$

$$Combined\ niche\ party\ vote\ percentage = B_0 + B_1[Effective\ number\ of\ parties] \qquad (4.4)$$

The disproportionality hypotheses (1a and 1b) posit that non-proportional electoral systems produce lower levels of niche party competitiveness (the number of niche parties and combined niche party vote percentage). Hypotheses 2a and 2b (the Party System Size Hypotheses) posit that as the party system size increases, niche party competitiveness will also increase. Thus, for all of the model specifications above we expect the coefficients on [*Disproportionality*] to be negative and statistically significant, and the coefficients on [*Effective number of parties*] to be positive and statistically significant.

4.5 ESTIMATING THE PARAMETERS OF THE MODEL SPECIFICATIONS

The next step is to estimate the parameters of the model specifications given by Equations 4.1–4.4. The results are fairly straightforward and easy to interpret. The coefficients on [*Disproportionality*] are negative when the parameters are estimated for the model specifications in columns 1 and 2 estimating the number of niche parties and their combined vote percentage.

Since we are positing that electoral systems matter for niche party competition through their effect on party system size, it makes sense to treat France and its two-round system as a special case in a similar fashion to Duverger who grouped France with PR systems in the "hypothesis" (discussed earlier in the chapter). The dual ballot majority system encourages French citizens to cast their ballots for several parties in the first election, and then to cast their ballots for more established parties in the runoff election. This leads to high scores on the effective

---

[7] The independent variables relating to proportionality and the number of parties are correlated, which raises concerns about collinearity and its effects on the efficiency of the parameter estimates.

number of parties based on first round voting, and high levels of disproportionality resulting from the outcomes of the second round. Accordingly, when we estimate the parameters for the "number of niche parties" and "combined niche vote share" model specifications without France, it should strengthen evidence that supports the relationship between (dis)proportionality and niche party competitiveness. The coefficient on the [*Disproportionality*] variable in the number of niche parties model specification when France is omitted, decreases from $-.09$ in column 1 to $-.13$ in column 3. For the combined niche vote share model, the coefficient decreases from $-.49$ to $-.84$ ($p < .10$). Thus, modest electoral system effects are reported for models that include France (column 1), and much stronger effects are reported for when France is omitted (columns 3 and 4).

Interpreting the coefficients in the bivariate models is quite straightforward. The intercept is 2.13, which means that a system registering perfect proportionality (i.e., disproportionality equals zero) will on average feature 2.13 niche parties. For each unit of disproportionality this point estimate decreases by .13. Thus, a system like Britain that is highly disproportional (15.5) is predicted to have on average .11 niche parties; not too far from the observed average of .29 niche parties competing

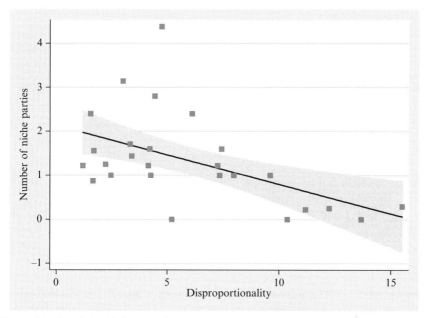

FIGURE 4.2 The relationship between disproportionality and the number of niche parties that compete in an election across Organization for Economic Cooperation and Development (OECD) countries

Notes: Shaded area indicates 90% confidence interval for the predicted estimate. The French observation is omitted. Disproportionality scores are based on the least squared index developed by Michael Gallagher (1991). The number of niche parties is the number of niche parties that are reported in a country election year by the authors of the CMP dataset (Budge et al. 2001; Klingemann et al. 2006).

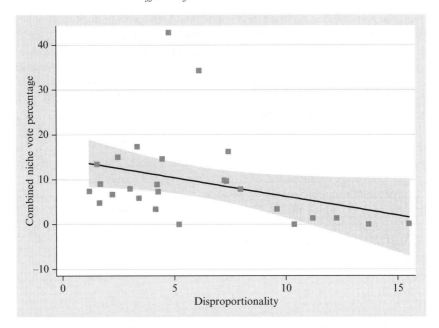

FIGURE 4.3 The relationship between disproportionality and the number of niche parties that compete
in an election across Organization for Economic Cooperation and Development (OECD) countries

Notes: Shaded area indicates 90% confidence interval for the predicted estimate. The French observation is omitted.
Disproportionality scores are based on the least squared index developed by Michael Gallagher (1991). Combined
niche vote percentage is the combined vote percentage for niche parties reported for a country election year by the
authors of the CMP dataset (Budge et al. 2001; Klingemann et al. 2006).

in its elections. To see the relationship between disproportionality and the average
number of niche parties more closely, Figure 4.2 plots the two variables, and the
slope estimate with 90% confidence interval.

Figures 4.2 and 4.3 illustrate the relationship between disproportional outcomes of electoral systems, and the role niche parties play in a political system.
Figure 4.2 plots the relationship between the average disproportionality and the
average number of niche parties that compete in elections, and the "best-fit" line is
based on the parameter estimates in column 3 of Table 4.2. The line slopes steadily
downward ($\beta = -.13$), from an average of two significant niche parties in the most
proportional systems (i.e., disproportionality equal to 1) to an average of close to
zero niche parties in the most disproportional systems where the disproportionality
score is equal to 15.

The cutoff in Figure 4.2 for having a niche party or not is about 10 on the
disproportionality scale. Countries above 10 have had very few niche parties

TABLE 4.2 *Explaining the number and combined size of niche parties*

	Number of niche parties (1)	Combined niche vote share (2)	Number of niche parties omitting France (3)	Combined niche vote omitting France (4)
Disproportionality	−.09**	−.49	−.13***	−.84*
	(.04)	(.46)	(.05)	(.48)
Intercept	1.95***	13.07***	2.13***	14.61***
	(.34)	(3.50)	(.33)	(3.46)
N	27	27	26	26
Adjusted R^2	.12	.01	.24	.07

Notes: Standard errors are in parentheses. The dependent variable in columns 1 and 3 is the average number of niche parties that compete from election to election in a country since 1976. The dependent variable in columns 2 and 4 is the average combined niche party vote share in a country since 1976. The definitions of the independent variables are given in the text.

$*p < .10, **p < .05, ***p < .01$, two-tailed tests

competing in elections over the past thirty years. Note that countries for which the CMP counts close to zero niche parties are the United States, Canada, and Australia. New Zealand registers one niche party for the election after they switched to a more proportional system in 1996 (the Green Party of Aotearoa).

Figure 4.3 similarly depicts the relationship estimated in column 4 of Table 4.2. The difference between Figures 4.3 and 4.2 is that rather than estimating the number of niche parties, the *y*-axis is instead combined niche vote percentage. I examine votes, because it is another indicator of how significant a role niche parties play in a political system. The slope line again trends downward ($\beta = -.84$) with the predicted combined vote percentage losing almost a full percentage point per unit of disproportionality. Thus, in the most proportional systems the predicted percentage is about 15, and in the least proportional systems (disproportionality > 15) approximately 2%. Note that there are four countries that score between 7 and 8 on the disproportionality scale. These are the Czech Republic (7.42), Greece (7.24), Japan (7.33), and Spain (7.96). These countries range from an average of 8% combined niche vote to 16%. Then note the steep drop-off at approximately 8 on the disproportionality scale: the rest of the countries with disproportionality scores of above 8 are associated with at most approximately 3% niche vote. Poland is the next country to the right with disproportionality of 9.6 and it registers 3.38% combined niche vote. Australia, Canada, New Zealand, the United States, and Great Britain register below 1% niche vote.

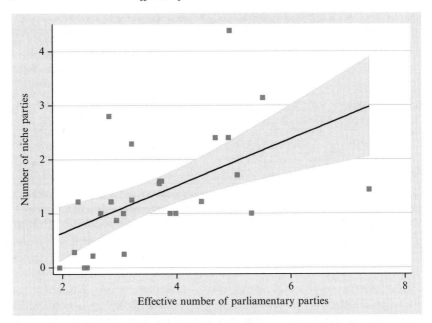

F<small>IGURE</small> 4.4 The relationship between the effective number of parliamentary parties (ENPP) and the number of niche parties that compete in an election across Organization for Economic Cooperation and Development (OECD) countries

Notes: Shaded area indicates 90% confidence interval for the predicted estimate. The effective number of elective parties (ENEP) is based on the measure developed by Laakso and Taagepera (1979). The number of niche parties is the number of niche parties that are reported in a country election year by the authors of the CMP dataset (Budge et al. 2001; Klingemann et al. 2006).

Figures 4.4–4.7 portray a similar story. These scattergrams plot the relationships in Table 4.3, where the effects of party system size are examined. The difference between Figures 4.2 and 4.3 and Figures 4.4–4.7 is that in the latter grouping different measures of party system size (i.e., ENPP and ENEP) are plotted on the *x*-axis instead of disproportionality scores. All of the coefficients in Table 4.3 on the party system size variables are positive and statistically significant, which provides evidence for the number of parties hypotheses (2a and 2b) that the number and combined size of niche parties increases with party system size.

Figure 4.4 depicts the relationship based on the parameter estimates in column 1 of Table 4.3. Here again, it is clear that party system size is associated with greater numbers of niche parties. Thus, while there may be some disagreement over the relationship between electoral institutions and party system size, we should be

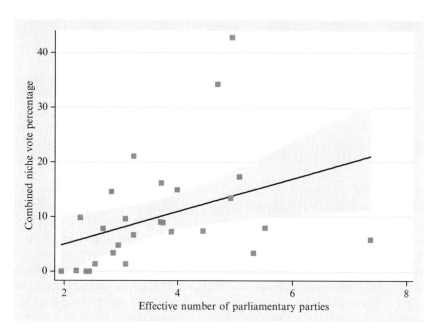

FIGURE 4.5 The relationship between effective number of parliamentary parties (ENPP) and combined niche vote percentages across Organization for Economic Cooperation and Development (OECD) countries

Notes: Shaded area indicates 90% confidence interval for the predicted estimate. ENPP is based on the measure developed by Laakso and Taagepera (1979). Combined niche vote percentage is the combined vote percentage for niche parties reported for a country election year by the authors of the CMP dataset (Budge et al. 2001; Klingemann et al. 2006).

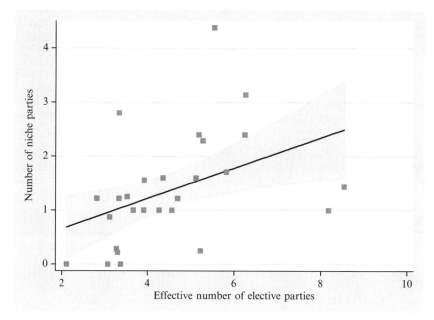

FIGURE 4.6 The relationship between the effective number of elective parties (ENEP) and the number of niche parties that compete in elections across Organization for Economic Cooperation and Development (OECD) countries

Notes: Shaded area indicates 90% confidence interval for the predicted estimate. The effective number of elective parties (ENEP) is based on the measure developed by Laakso and Taagepera (1979). The number of niche parties is the number of niche parties that are reported in a country election year by the authors of the CMP dataset (Budge et al. 2001; Klingemann et al. 2006).

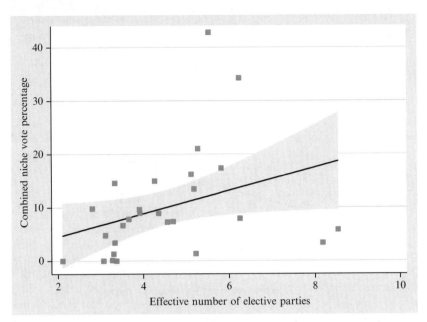

FIGURE 4.7 The relationship between effective number of elective parties (ENEP) and combined niche vote percentages across Organization for Economic Cooperation and Development (OECD) countries

Notes: Shaded area indicates 90% confidence interval for the predicted estimate. The ENEP is based on the measure developed by Laakso and Taagepera (1979). Combined niche vote percentage is the combined vote percentage for niche parties reported for a country election year by the authors of the CMP dataset (Budge et al. 2001; Klingemann et al. 2006).

TABLE 4.3 *Explaining the number and combined size of niche parties*

	Number of niche parties	Combined niche vote	Number of niche parties	Combined niche vote
	(1)	(2)	(3)	(4)
Effective number of parliamentary parties (ENPP)	.43***	2.99*		
	(.14)	(1.47)		
Effective number of elective parties (ENEP)			.28**	2.17*
			(.12)	(1.22)
Intercept	.23	−.97	.10	.20
	(.53)	(5.69)	(.58)	(5.84)
N	27	27	27	27
Adjusted R^2	.26	.11	.14	.08

Notes: Standard errors are in parentheses. The dependent variable in columns 1 and 3 is the average number of niche parties that compete from election to election in a country since 1976. The dependent variable in columns 2 and 4 is the average combined niche party vote share in a country since 1976. The definitions of the independent variables are given in the text.

$*p < .10, **p < .05, ***p < .01$, two-tailed tests

able to agree that whatever factors contribute to party system size will ultimately present niche parties with greater opportunities.[8]

4.6 CONCLUSION

This chapter studies the implications of electoral systems and party system size for the number and size of niche parties. I find that proportional electoral systems promote greater numbers of niche parties and their combined vote share via their impact on party system size. This finding highlights the permissive role that electoral rules play in fostering niche party success. It perhaps sheds light on why it is difficult to generalize about the electoral fortunes of any particular niche party family. Simply, the number of observations is few. However, the necessary or permissive role of electoral systems in fostering greater niche party competitiveness is recognized when we analyze niche parties together.

There are of course several routes of further inquiry to explore from here. In a cross-national analysis, Abedi (2002) examines antiestablishment parties and links mainstream party policy convergence to these parties' success. The logic is fairly straightforward that when the large parties focus on the median voter there is opportunity for smaller parties on the periphery. If we use Abedi's framework in a longitudinal setting, one would expect that niche opportunities would increase under circumstances where mainstream parties represent the median position at the expense of the extremes *over time*, that is, when party systems converge, niche party competition will be enhanced.[9]

I have presented results that suggest that electoral rules that foster greater number of parties will tend to produce a greater role for niche parties in these systems. This may not be an entirely new insight into the effects of electoral rules. Nevertheless, Chapters 5 and 6 highlight the importance of this observation, because the existence and size of niche parties have nontrivial implications for the manner in which political representation occurs.

---

[8] Wagner (2010) corroborates this finding in a study that clarifies the definition and measure of niche parties.

[9] It would actually be possible to test this proposition by employing the average party extremism measure introduced in Chapter 3. If average party extremism decreases between elections, we would expect indicators of niche party competition to increase.

5

Proximity and Votes for Mainstream and Niche Parties

> If we have to stress anything it is precisely our "Eurocommunism" ... Because so far social democracy has been equivalent to capitalism, to the loyal administration of capitalist interests, and will continue to be so until the social democrats undergo a transformation and converge with the aims of the "Eurocommunists."
>
> (Santiago Carrillo 1977).[1]

5.1 INTRODUCTION

With respect to the quotation above, one question that could be posed is what if Santiago Carrillo had, instead, advised the Central Committee of the Spanish Communist Party (Partido Comunista de España, PCE) to moderate its policies to fall in line with the policies of the social democratic Spanish Socialist Workers' Party (Partido Socialista Obrero Español, PSOE)? Would the Spanish Communist Party (Partido Comunista de España, PCE) have increased its vote share in subsequent national elections? More generally, do niche parties (like the PCE) occupying Left–Right policy positions that are farther from the center of the voter distribution gain more popular support than those moderately positioned along the Left–Right continuum?

In this chapter, cross-sectional analyses, based on observations from twelve Western European countries from 1984 to 1998, are presented that suggest the answer is *yes* – niche parties perform better in elections by adopting radical positions.[2] By contrast, these analyses strongly suggest that, for mainstream parties, policy radicalism depresses popular support. The implication of these findings is that, for niche parties, it is the distinctiveness of their Left–Right positions that enhances their competitiveness in democratic elections. While this

---

[1] Santiago Carrillo, General Secretary, Spanish Communist Party. "Genuine Democratisation of Society and its Institutions." (Transcript from a speech to the Central Committee of the Spanish Communist Party, June 25–26, 1977, printed in *Marxism Today* (October 1977: 309)).

[2] This chapter draws material from Ezrow (2008a).

finding runs counter to the intuition of standard spatial theory (see Downs 1957), it is consistent with recent dynamic accounts of niche party responsiveness to shifts in public opinion, and electoral support for niche parties (Meguid 2005; Adams et al. 2006). These findings have implications for party strategies, spatial theories, and our understanding of political representation.

Traditional spatial theory predicts that, ceteris paribus, candidates and political parties gain electoral benefits when they moderate their policy positions (Downs 1957; Enelow and Hinich 1984). Recent studies, however, suggest that the logic of spatial theory applies differently to different *types* of parties (Meguid 2005; Adams et al. 2006). Specifically, these studies suggest that *niche parties* – namely, parties that occupy the extreme Left (i.e., Communists), the extreme Right (i.e., radical nationalist parties), or a distinctly noncentrist niche (i.e., the Greens) – do not necessarily enhance their electoral appeal by presenting moderate policy programs. Here, I extend this line of research by presenting two new insights about the relationship between parties' policy programs and their electoral success.

The first contribution extends on a central conclusion in an article by Adams and his coauthors (2006) where the authors conclude that niche parties are penalized for moderating their Left–Right positions, because this alienates their ideological clienteles who perceive that these parties are "pandering" or "selling out." While this finding – the *costly policy moderation result* – is an important one, it does not directly address the question of whether niche parties would gain popular support if they *entered* a political system as more moderate in the first place. The cross-sectional empirical results reported below suggest that even if these ideologically oriented niche parties entered the party system while presenting moderate policies, they would do poorly in elections. By contrast, the results suggest that if niche parties entered the system adopting distinctly noncentrist policy platforms they would increase their electoral success. In other words, while most parties benefit when they advocate moderate policies (relative to the center of the voter distribution), the opposite is true of niche parties.

The second contribution relates to the *American Political Science Review* (APSR) article by Bonnie Meguid (2005) which argues that popular support for Green and radical Right parties is largely determined by the actions of mainstream parties in the political system.[3] Meguid concludes that the electoral competitiveness of Green and radical Right parties is greatest when two conditions are met: first, that a mainstream party must engage such parties on their primary issue dimension (e.g., immigration policy for radical Right parties, and the environment for Green parties), thereby enhancing the salience of this dimension; second, that the mainstream party adopts an "adversarial" position along the issue dimension of the niche party. The highly plausible implication of Meguid's argument is that

---

[3] Unlike Adams et al. (2006), Meguid does not directly explore the electoral fortunes of communist parties.

issue salience and *differentiation*, taken together, contribute to the electoral success of niche parties.

While Meguid rightly emphasizes additional issue dimensions of party competition, the results reported here suggest that her logic of policy differentiation extends to the central axis of party competition, the Left–Right dimension, across twelve democratic political systems. Specifically, niche parties do better in elections when their Left–Right positions are perceived as radical rather than centrist.

Cross-sectional analyses of parties' vote shares in twelve Western European democracies are presented, which produce two central findings.[4] The first is that parties, in general, gain more vote shares when they are positioned closer to the center of public opinion in the political systems under observation. This finding is labeled the *Mainstream Party Centrism Result*, and is consistent with previous macro-level empirical research on the effects of Left–Right policy positioning in multiparty systems (Ezrow 2005). The second and central finding of the chapter is the *Niche Party Radicalism Result*. This result states that radical niche parties receive more popular support than niche parties positioned nearer to the center of the Left–Right dimension.

In Section 5.2, I explain the logic behind expectations about the relationship between party policy distance (defined as the party's Left–Right policy distance from the Center of the voter distribution) and vote share. Section 5.3 describes the data and constructs the variables that are necessary to test these expectations. Section 5.4 analyzes the results, and Section 5.5 comments on niche party success (or failure).

5.2 HYPOTHESES ON MAINSTREAM AND NICHE PARTY SUPPORT

The first hypothesis posits that political parties are rewarded for presenting policies that are centrist relative to the voter distribution. Though the first expectation is not the central concern of this analysis, it is nevertheless important because it is necessary to first identify the nature of the relationship between party positioning and popular support for all of the parties in a political system (and then compare this relationship to that for niche parties). Previous macro-level research on the linkages between parties' vote shares in *real-world* elections and their proximities to the Center of the policy space in multiparty elections

---

[4] This chapter relies on party-level observations from Belgium, Great Britain, France, Germany, Spain, the Netherlands, Italy, Portugal, Ireland, Luxembourg, Denmark, and Greece.

conclude that parties typically gain votes when they are positioned closer to the Center of the voter distribution (Ezrow 2005). This expectation motivates the first hypothesis:

> H_1 (*The Mainstream Party Centrism Hypothesis*): Parties occupying Left–Right positions close to the mean voter position receive a higher proportion of the vote in national elections than do parties positioned farther away from the mean voter.

While the mainstream party centrism hypothesis posits that the traditional spatial model possesses explanatory power for understanding party support across political systems, one might expect that the assumptions of the model do not hold for niche parties. In their analyses of the electoral consequences of changes in parties' ideological positions, Adams et al. (2006) conclude that niche parties – defined as Communist, Green, and radical Right parties – tend to lose vote shares when they moderate their positions. The implications of Meguid's argument (2005) similarly suggest that niche parties are unable to increase their vote shares through unilateral strategic positioning decisions, and, instead, that niche parties' popular support largely depends on the behavior of the mainstream parties in the system, and whether these parties engage niche parties on the additional dimensions that they are attempting to introduce to party competition. Meguid adds that it is in cases when mainstream parties take "adversarial" positions to niche parties on immigration or the environment that the niche parties are expected to have the highest likelihood of electoral success. Here, Meguid's logic of niche party differentiation is simply transferred to the Left–Right dimension.

Taken together these analyses produce the counterintuitive expectation that, contrary to the Mainstream Party Centrism Hypothesis, niche parties will in fact gain *fewer* votes when they are perceived as "centrist" in the party system. Thus, the work of Adams et al. (2006) and Meguid (2005) motivates the second hypothesis:

> H_2 (*The Niche Party Radicalism Hypothesis*): Niche parties occupying positions close to the mean voter position will receive a lower proportion of the vote in national elections than will niche parties positioned farther away from the mean voter.

5.3 DATA AND METHOD

To test Hypotheses 1 and 2, it is necessary to develop measures of popular support and party proximity to the mean Left–Right voter position. Mackie and Rose (1991, 1997) report the absolute percentage of votes for each party in each election.[5] The measure of popular support, vote share, is reconstructed because it is expected that successful parties will receive fewer votes in systems where there are more competitive parties. The normalized measure takes into account the number of competitive parties in the given election. The measure employed is as follows:

$$Normalized\ vote\ share\ (NV) = V_i * N_j, \eqno(5.1)$$

where V_i equals the absolute share of the vote for party i and N_j is the number of parties in election j receiving over 5% of the vote.[6]

The measure of party policy distance relies on the Eurobarometer 31A (1989). The survey asks approximately 1,000 respondents in each of the twelve members in the European Community to place themselves, and each of their significant national parties, on a Left–Right scale, ranging from 1 (extreme Left) to 10 (extreme Right).[7] These placements are used to compute the mean voter's Left–Right position in each country, as well as the parties' mean perceived positions in each country's election year from 1984 through 1998.[8]

All of the measures of party policy distance presented in these analyses are defined as the difference between the mean citizen Left–Right self-placement – that is, the center of public opinion – and the party placements based on citizen perceptions, as well as placements by a survey of experts (discussed later).[9] The measure party policy distance is based on the squared difference between the party position and the mean citizen placement[10]:

---

[5] The remaining election returns (through 1998) were gathered using the CD-ROM accompanying Budge et al. (2001).

[6] Note that additional statistical analyses are conducted employing as the dependent variable, instead, the parties' absolute vote shares (reported in Tables 5.1 and 5.2) and the natural logs of the parties' vote shares, and that these analyses support the substantive conclusions based on normalized vote shares that are reported below.

[7] The questions in the 1989 Eurobarometer (31A) are worded: "In political matters, people talk of 'the left' and 'the right'. How would you place your views on this scale? And, where would you place the political parties (of your country)?"

[8] Alternative sets of analyses are reported later, which employ country experts' party placements in place of the mean positions ascribed to the parties by the Eurobarometer respondents. Also, note that in addition to the Eurobarometer 31A (1989), Eurobarometers 21 (1984), 23 (1985), 25 (1986), 27 (1987), 29 (1988), 33 (1990), 35 (1991), 37 (1992), 39 (1993), 41 (1994), 43 (1995), 45 (1996), 47 (1997), and 49 (1998) were relied upon to calculate the mean voter's Left–Right position for each country during its election year.

[9] Note that party policy distance and party proximity are, to some extent, interchangeable, insofar as each refers to the *ideological distance* between a party and the Center of the voter distribution. The measures are inversely related, that is, as the policy distance for a party increases, proximity to the mean voter position necessarily decreases (in a one-to-one fashion). In a few instances, I refer to *proximity* because it is more familiar of the two terms, and in the rest I refer to *party policy distance* to facilitate the substantive interpretation of the results.

[10] An alternative set of analyses was performed based on the parties' linear proximities to the mean voter position. These analyses supported substantive conclusions that were identical to the ones reported below, although the statistical fit of these models was not as strong as the fit for squared

$$Party\ policy\ distance = (A_i - X_i)^2, \tag{5.2}$$

where A_i is the position of the mean voter on a Left–Right continuum and X_i is the (mean perceived) Left–Right position of party X.

I further rely on the surveys of panels of country experts conducted by Huber and Inglehart (1995) that ask experts for their opinions of parties' ideological placements on a Left–Right continuum.[11] In so doing, it is possible to develop additional measures of party policy distance for the empirical analyses. An interesting by-product of these analyses is that the following substantive conclusions remain robust, regardless of the measure of party policy distance that is employed.

5.4 TESTING HYPOTHESES 1 AND 2

Recall that the Mainstream Party Centrism Hypothesis (H_1) posits a *negative* relationship between party policy distance and party support, that is, that parties' vote shares decrease with the distance between the party's Left–Right position and the mean voter position. By contrast, the Niche Party Radicalism Hypothesis (H_2) suggests that this expected relationship will be *positive* for niche parties. The most straightforward method to evaluate these hypotheses is to stratify the sample of parties into niche and mainstream (i.e., non-niche) groups.[12] For each set of parties, the parameters of an ordinary least squares (OLS) regression model are estimated in order to evaluate these hypotheses. The specification is given as

$$Normalized\ vote\ share = B_1 + B_2\ [Party\ policy\ distance] + e, \tag{5.3}$$

where

Party policy distance is the squared Left–Right distance between the party's position and the mean voter position.

In order to ensure that our substantive conclusions are not artifacts of our measurement approach for the dependent variable, additional regression models

---

proximity, suggesting that this latter measure is the appropriate metric for evaluating the electoral effects of party positioning. This empirical finding suggests that the parties' vote shares are *concave* functions of their policy positions, that is, that parties' vote shares drop off slowly at first as they diverge from their vote-maximizing positions, but then drop off more rapidly as the parties move further away. Adams and Merrill (2005) present theoretical arguments about why parties' vote shares can be expected to be concave functions of their positions. Interpreted, this means that parties are penalized more for each marginal unit of distance between their Left–Right position and the mean voter position.

[11] Note that all of the party scores have been recalibrated to the traditional Eurobarometer 1–10 scale so that all of the analyses fit the data on public opinion.

[12] A list of the niche parties that are included is presented in the Table A5.1.

TABLE 5.1 Regression coefficients for party policy distance when estimating vote shares for mainstream parties

	Eurobarometer placements (1984–94)		Expert placements Huber–Inglehart (1988–98)	
	Normalized vote shares (1)	Absolute vote shares (2)	Normalized vote shares (3)	Absolute vote shares (4)
Party policy distance	−**1.93***	−**.50***	−**3.98****	−**1.03****
	(1.11)	(.28)	(1.13)	(.26)
Effective number of elective parties[a]		−2.55***		−3.18***
		(.60)		(.69)
Constant	75.91***	29.51***	89.50***	35.51***
	(5.78)	(3.26)	(6.30)	(3.51)
N	189	189	120	120
Adjusted R^2	.01	.08	.09	.21

Notes: Estimated standard errors are in parentheses. The dependent variable that is estimated in columns 1 and 3 is normalized vote share, which is calculated as the party's vote share multiplied by the number of competitive parties in the election (see Equation 5.1). The mainstream political parties included in the statistical analyses are those that do not belong to the Green, Communist, or Nationalist party families. The Comparative Manifesto Project (CMP) designates to which "party family" a party belongs in their published CD-ROM.

[a] *Source*: Laakso and Taagepera (1979).

*$p < .10$, **$p < .05$, ***$p < .01$, two-tailed test

are estimated as checks on robustness. Specifically, the parameters are estimated for an alternative specification for which the dependent variable is the party's *absolute vote share*. For these analyses it is necessary to also control for the number of competitors in the political system, and here I employ the *effective number of elective parties* (ENEP) measure that is developed by Laakso and Taagepera (1979).[13] The specification is given as

$$Absolute\ vote\ share = B_1 + B_2\ [Party\ policy\ distance]$$
$$+ B_3\ [Effective\ number\ of\ elective\ parties] + e$$
$$H_1: B_2 < 0,\ for\ mainstream\ parties;$$
$$H_2: B_2 > 0,\ for\ niche\ parties. \qquad (5.4)$$

Table 5.1 reports the parameter estimates for Equations 5.3 and 5.4, which estimate popular support for the mainstream parties that are included in the

---

[13] The effective number of elective parties (ENEP) is calculated using the following equation developed by Laakso and Taagepera (1979): $N = 1/\Sigma v_i^2$, where v_i is the proportion of votes of the *i*th party that is represented in parliament. The authors' alternative measure, the effective number of parliamentary parties (ENPP) is based on seats (i.e., $N = 1/\Sigma s_i^2$, where s_i is the proportion of seats of the *i*th party in the legislature). In the following empirical analyses, the results that are reported are based on votes (ENEP), though analyses have also been conducted using the measure based on seat share weightings (ENPP). In each case, the substantive results remained unchanged.

empirical analysis. Each specification was estimated in turn for each of the two measures of proximity – one based on citizen party placements, and another based on expert placements reported in the Huber–Inglehart survey.

The parameter estimates in the first table support the mainstream party centrism hypothesis, and this finding is plainly labeled the *mainstream party centrism result*. The four coefficients that estimate the relationship between *party policy distance* and (normalized and absolute) *vote share* are negative, and each of these coefficients reach statistical significance. Interpreted, the parameter estimates indicate that as party policy distance increases, vote share decreases for the mainstream parties included in the analyses – a finding that is consistent with the standard spatial model. Thus, moderate party positioning and popular support appear to be linked across the multiparty Western European democracies.

The results presented in Table 5.2, which reports parameter estimates based on the set of niche parties included in the dataset, support the Niche Party Radicalism Hypothesis, and this finding is labeled the *niche party radicalism result*. Each of the parameter estimates for *party policy distance* is positive and reaches statistical significance. These estimates indicate that as niche parties are perceived as farther away from the Center of the voter distribution, they tend to receive larger vote shares. The central implication of the niche party radicalism result is that it is the ideological distinctiveness along the Left–Right dimension that contributes to niche party electoral success.

TABLE 5.2 *Regression coefficients for party policy distance when estimating vote shares for niche parties*

	Eurobarometer placements (1984–94)		Expert placements Huber–Inglehart (1988–98)	
	Normalized vote shares (1)	Absolute vote shares (2)	Normalized vote shares (3)	Absolute vote shares (4)
Party policy distance	**1.21***	**.40*****	**1.37*****	**.21****
	(.62)	(.13)	(.45)	(.08)
Effective number of elective parties[a]		.20		−.59
		(.41)		(.35)
Constant	17.76***	1.81	30.49***	9.48
	(5.97)	(2.53)	(5.29)	(2.01)
N	59	59	25	25
Adjusted R^2	.05	.11	.25	.28

Notes: Estimated standard errors are in parentheses. Niche parties belong to the Green, Communist, or Nationalist party families.

[a] *Source*: Laakso and Taagepera (1979).

*$p < .10$, **$p < .05$, ***$p < .01$, two-tailed test

(a)

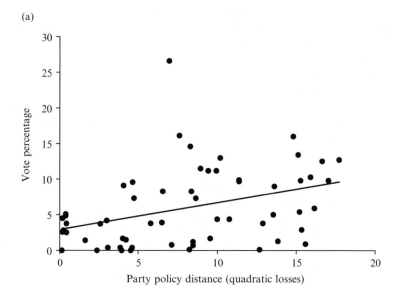

(b)

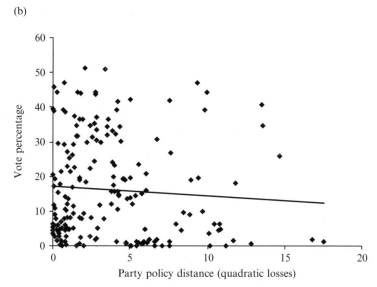

FIGURE 5.1 Party policy distance and vote percentage for (a) niche parties and (b) mainstream
parties, based on respondents' Left–Right policy perceptions of parties from the
Eurobarometer 31A (1989)

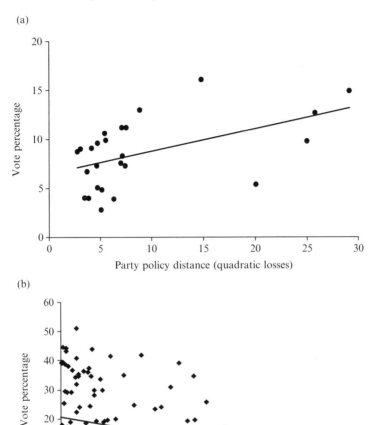

FIGURE 5.2 Party policy distance and vote percentage for (a) niche parties and (b) mainstream parties, based on the estimates of parties' Left–Right policy positions reported in the Huber-Inglehart (1995) survey of country experts

Figures 5.1a and 5.1b, as well as 5.2a and 5.2b illustrate the central conclusion, that niche parties tend to gain fewer votes, and mainstream parties more votes, when they are perceived by their citizens as centrist parties. These figures plot the policy distances of niche parties (Figures 5.1a and 5.2a) and mainstream parties (Figures 5.1b and 5.2b) along the *x*-axes, and their absolute vote percentages along the *y*-axes – based on each approach for estimating parties' Left–Right ideological positions.

The slope estimates of the "best-fit" lines for the niche party scattergrams are distinctly positive, indicating that niche parties tend to receive greater vote shares as their policy distance (or distinctiveness) from the center of the voter distribution increases. Alternatively, the negative slope-lines for mainstream (i.e., non-niche) parties suggest that the conventional spatial theory generally applies to the rest of the parties that are included in the analyses.

While the niche party radicalism result is relevant to the studies by Adams et al. (2006) and Meguid (2005) that were cited in the introduction, there are several related authors whose empirical results also fit neatly with the central conclusion of this chapter. Instead of dividing parties into the "niche" and "mainstream" camps, Andrews and Money (2005) separate parties into "champions" and "challengers," that is, parties that have been a part of a governing coalition at one time, and those that have not. The central finding from the Andrews–Money study is that challengers gain votes by adopting a strategy of policy extremism while champions enhance their electoral support via a strategy of policy moderation. The result also relates to Schofield and Sened's remarkable book (2006) on party competition. One of the authors' central findings relates to parties' valence qualities in elections,[14] specifically that parties possessing low valence scores tend to do better in elections when they differentiate themselves from higher-valence parties. To the extent that niche parties tend to be the "challengers" or valence-disadvantaged parties, and that mainstream parties are generally the "champions" or valence-advantaged parties, the niche party radicalism result is consistent with the arguments put forward in the Schofield–Sened and the Andrews–Money studies.[15]

5.5 CONCLUSION

Policy centrism influences mainstream and niche party success in elections though, remarkably, in the opposite direction for each type of party. Policy centrism is generally rewarded with votes in multiparty systems. However, when a line is drawn between niche parties and the rest of the parties in a political system, an interesting relationship emerges: namely, niche parties that present moderate policy positions receive fewer votes than their more radical counterparts.

[14] The term "valence" was introduced in an article by Stokes (1963), where valence characteristics refer to nonpolicy-related traits of parties that influence election outcomes (e.g., leadership ability, competence, integrity, and unity).

[15] It is also worth noting that the niche party radicalism result is relevant to the studies on party decision rules (Budge 1994; Laver 2005). The empirical results reported in this section imply that different types of parties may employ different decision rules when they are choosing their policy strategies.

These results are robust across several model specifications, and remain valid for alternative measures of the theoretically relevant variables (i.e., party policy distance and party support).[16] Moreover, these conclusions corroborate and expand upon the contributions of several recent studies (Meguid 2005; Adams et al., 2006).

In addition, the cross-sectional feature of the empirical analyses in this chapter implies that the *costly policy moderation result*, raised by Adams et al., applies to niche party *entry* into party competition. Based on the findings reported here, budding niche parties would be well advised to start off by adopting radical Left–Right policy positions. Moreover, the logic of niche party policy differentiation, raised by Bonnie Meguid, appears to hold along the traditional Left–Right dimension of party competition. Together these studies have introduced significant modifications to the conventional spatial model by considering the *type of party* competing in elections. The next chapter continues to explore how the type of party matters for political representation.

---

[16] A promising direction for future research in this area is to examine how well specific niche parties differentiate themselves from their 'closest' mainstream party competitors. The comparative analysis by Spoon (2010) estimates Green parties' support based on how distinctive their policies are from their Social Democratic competitors. Spoon reports a curvilinear relationship, i.e., Green parties enhance their support when they differentiate their policies from Social Democratic parties. However, their support fades when these policy differences exceed certain thresholds.

Mean Voter Representation Versus Partisan Constituency Representation: Do Parties Respond to the Mean Voter Position or to Their Supporters?

Representation is a complex phenomenon. It has been addressed from a variety of angles and dimensions and through different normative lenses. The smallest common denominator in normative terms, though, is that in a democracy there should be some match between the interests of the people and what representatives promote.

(Wessels 1999: 137)

6.1 INTRODUCTION

Chapter 5 identifies a stark contrast in explanations for niche party and mainstream party electoral success. This chapter extends this argument that this distinction matters for understanding political representation in Western Europe over the past thirty years. Instead of addressing the electoral consequences of citizen–party linkages (as in Chapter 5), I turn to *responsiveness*, and whether political parties *respond* to the ideological shifts of their supporters or to those of the mean voter (or to neither).[1]

Previous theoretical and empirical research stresses the primacy of the mean or the median voter's policy preference as the starting point for democratic representation (Downs 1957; Huber and Powell 1994; Stimson et al. 1995; Powell 2000; Erikson et al. 2002; Adams et al. 2004, 2006; McDonald and Budge 2005). However, an alternative and perhaps equally compelling vision of policy representation emphasizes the policy preference of the *mean party supporter* in explaining party–citizen linkages (Weissberg 1978; Dalton 1985; Wessels 1999).

---

[1] This chapter is based on a manuscript that is coauthored with Catherine De Vries, Erica Edwards, and Marco Steenbergen (Ezrow, De Vries, Steenbergen, and Edwards forthcoming.

The first model of political representation is referred to as the *general electorate model*, and the second is referred to as the *partisan constituency model*.

With respect to the general electorate model and the partisan constituency model, this chapter will address the following questions: First, are shifts in the preference of the mean voter position in the general electorate accompanied by roughly corresponding policy shifts of the parties in a given party system? Alternatively, are shifts in the preferences of the party's supporters accompanied by roughly similar shifts in the party's position? Finally, are these citizen–party linkages mediated by the *type of party* – niche or mainstream – under examination?

The empirical analyses examine political parties in fifteen Western European democracies from 1973 to 2003.[2] The results reported later support the following conclusions. First, mainstream parties (i.e., parties belonging to the Social Democratic, Conservative, Christian Democratic, or Liberal party families) tend to respond to shifts in the mean voter position as opposed to the policy shifts of their supporters. Second, the opposite pattern is true for niche parties (i.e., parties belonging to the Communist, Nationalist, and Green party families). Specifically, niche parties are highly sensitive to shifts in the position of their mean supporter, and they do not respond systematically to the median voter in the general electorate. *Thus, each model of representation is accurate at capturing parties' policy shifts, depending on the type of party being examined.*

I should note that these conclusions come with one caveat. While parties are assumed to *respond* to public preferences, an equally plausible alternative exists that parties shape or "cue" the preferences of the electorate (see Steenbergen et al. 2007). The measurement instruments do not allow me to completely parse out the direction of causality in the empirical analyses. However, I employ similar methods of Steenbergen et al. (2007) to address endogeneity (discussed later), and the results from these analyses suggest that the assumption that parties respond to shifts in public preferences is a reasonable one. Under either causal scenario, to the extent that reciprocal influences are uncovered on party and citizen policy preferences, these findings contribute to our understanding of party competition in Western European democracies.

This limitation notwithstanding, these results have important implications for political representation, party strategies, and for spatial models of elections. With respect to political representation, Huber and Powell (1994) argue that the ideological "congruence between citizens and policy makers" is one of the central features of democracy. Following from this perspective, G. Bingham Powell presents two visions of democracy that are based on constitutional design: the nature of party–citizen linkages varies depending on whether the political system is characterized as "majoritarian" or "proportional" (Powell 2000; see also

---

[2] The following fifteen countries are included: Austria, Belgium, Denmark, Finland, France, Germany, Great Britain, Greece, Ireland, Italy, Luxembourg, the Netherlands, Portugal, Spain, and Sweden.

Lijphart 1999). Complementing Powell, the typology emphasized here requires lowering the level of analysis from the country to the party level. Specifically, when parties are classified along the lines of James Adams and his colleagues (2006) and Bonnie Meguid (2005, 2008) into niche and mainstream parties, an equally powerful narrative emerges that explains how parties represent the viewpoints of citizens,[3] namely, that the general electorate model is accurate in explaining the policy shifts of mainstream parties and that the partisan constituency model is accurate in explaining the policy shifts of niche parties.

The findings reported in this chapter also relate to the dynamic representation model of elections developed by Stimson et al. (1995; see also Erikson et al. 2002), which identifies party responsiveness to shifts in public opinion as a key component to political representation.[4] Similarly, the empirical validity is assessed of a partisan constituency model that is based on several influential studies addressing party–constituency agreement (see Dalton 1985; Weissberg 1978; Wessels 1999). Furthermore, the results corroborate and expand upon the conclusions of recent studies by Adams et al. (2006) and Meguid (2005, 2008) who present theoretical and empirical arguments suggesting that spatial theories of electoral competition (Downs 1957; Enelow and Hinich 1984) should account for the party families competing in elections. That is to say that not all parties are the same.

Finally, the overall finding that different parties respond to different constituencies highlights the importance of developing more contextualized spatial models, particularly among the growing group of scholars who explore parties' policy strategies in real-world elections (Erikson and Romero 1990; Schofield et al. 1998*a*, 1998*b*; Adams and Merrill 1999, 2000; Lin et al. 1999; Merrill and Grofman 1999; Alvarez et al. 2000*a*, 2000*b*; Dow 2001; Quinn and Martin 2002; Adams et al. 2005; Glasgow and Alvarez 2005; Kedar 2005; Schofield and Sened 2005, 2006; Andrews and Money forthcoming).

6.2 HYPOTHESES

Two hypotheses are developed in this chapter; one is based on the general electorate model, and the other on the partisan constituency model. The first

---

[3] This framework is not wholly different from that of Powell (2000). Chapter 4 reports that some types of political systems (i.e., systems featuring proportional electoral rules) encourage niche party competition more than others.

[4] Mean voter representation and dynamic representation do differ conceptually. While the former concerns the party–citizen linkage and "giving voice" to electors, the latter refers to responsiveness of governing institutions in terms of policy outputs.

hypothesis concerns the linkage that is relevant to mean voter representation, namely the connection between the shifts in the mean policy preference of the electorate as a whole, and shifts in parties' policy programs:

> H_1: *Mean Voter Hypothesis*: Changes in the mean voter position in the general electorate cause corresponding shifts in mainstream parties' policy positions.

Based on whether one assumes that parties are motivated by vote-seeking, office-seeking, or policy-seeking objectives (see Müller and Strøm 1999), there are persuasive arguments suggesting that shifts in the mean voter position will influence mainstream parties' policy shifts, perhaps at the expense of being responsive to shifts in their supporters' positions. Many scholars analyzing party strategies in Western Europe have reported that these parties do indeed tend to be vote-maximizing and center-oriented. These studies characterize mainstream parties as steadily pitching larger ideological tents in an attempt to "catch" more voters, and this requires that these parties shed their "ideological baggage" (Kirchheimer 1966; see also Kitschelt 1997; Van Kersbergen 1999). The result is that major parties have become ideologically unhinged from particular voting subconstituencies and instead are sensitized to policy shift signals from the center of political systems.

Maximizing votes, as suggested by the Mean Voter Hypothesis, may not be an end goal in itself: vote-maximization is an efficient strategy for office- and policy-seeking parties. In the former case, to the extent that a party in a multiparty system gains votes, *ceteris paribus*, this will enhance its position for postelection coalition negotiations. In the latter case, it is plausible to assume that as a policy-seeking party's electoral strength increases, the party will gain more leverage to pull the governing coalition's policy in its preferred direction. Adams and Merrill's theoretical study (2009) on policy-seeking parties' strategies in multiparty systems concludes that parties are motivated to adjust their policy strategies in response to their beliefs about the median voter's position, rather than in response to the diversity of voter ideologies in the electorate. In sum, there are persuasive theoretical arguments to suggest that parties – whether they are vote-, office-, or policy-seeking – will be responsive to changes in the median voter position in the general electorate.

> H_2: *Partisan Constituency Hypothesis*: Changes in the mean party supporter positions cause corresponding shifts in niche parties' policy positions.

While the general electorate model discussed above is proposed to explain the party policy shifts of mainstream parties, should we believe that it holds true for all types of parties? The growing number of studies on niche parties indicates that this is unlikely to be the case, as there are strong arguments to suggest that the type of party would mediate party–citizen linkages. A central implication of studies on elites and activists in the Green and Communist parties (see Kitschelt 1994; D'Alimonte 1999; Tarrow 1989) is that the partisan constituency model would be more useful for examining the policy shifts of niche parties. Specifically, I expect niche parties to be more sensitive to shifts in their supporters' policy preferences, and less concerned with voter shifts at the center of the political system.

The studies of Kitschelt (1994) and D'Alimonte (1999) suggest that niche party elites will be more responsive to their supporters than to the mean voter. Niche party elites who are willing to shift their policy orientations toward the mean voter position run the risk of being perceived as pandering or "selling out." This notion that niche parties are "fundamentally different" is in line with the conclusions of Adams et al. (2006) who report a statistical tendency for niche parties to lose votes when they moderate their policy positions.

A second, related argument introduces electoral time horizons and assumes that niche parties are concerned primarily with *preserving* their electoral support in the long term, while mainstream party elites are more oriented to the short term (Przeworski and Sprague 1986). To the extent that niche parties' elites and activists have longer electoral time horizons than do mainstream party elites, we should expect niche parties to be less responsive to short-term trends in public opinion and more responsive to maintaining the loyalty of their supporters by appealing to them on policy grounds (Adams et al. 2005).

A third line of reasoning emphasizes the structure of niche party organizations. These organizations are smaller and more "horizontal" in contrast to larger and more hierarchical mainstream *party organizations*. To these qualities, Kitschelt (1988) highlights several additional party features that would lead to partisan constituency representation, such as a more active and *participatory membership*; *weak political executives* (with higher turnover); and informal or personal linkages between these two groups. These considerations suggest that the "distance" is much smaller for niche parties between their rank-and-file supporters and party executives, and that policy responsiveness to core constituencies is far more likely given their organizational setting.

To summarize, Figures 6.1 and 6.2 depict the predictions based on the two central hypotheses. Figure 6.1 demonstrates the Mean Voter Hypothesis, where a party's focal point in a political system is the center of public opinion. Under this scenario, the expectation is that the hypothetical parties *a, b, c,* and *d* will respond to shifts in the mean voter position. Figure 6.2 clarifies expectations about party position shifts based on the Partisan Constituency Hypothesis. The major difference between the first and second figures is the conceptualization of voter preferences. While in the former, the overall distribution of voters is central to understanding the parties' policy shifts, the latter emphasizes each party's constituency (i.e., set of supporters) by distinguishing between the voter distributions A, B, C, and D. The prediction based on the Partisan Constituency Hypothesis

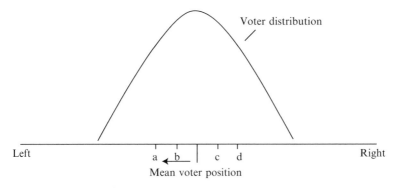

FIGURE 6.1 Demonstrating the Mean Voter Hypothesis

Notes: *a, b, c,* and *d* are hypothetical parties. Similarly, the arrow denotes a hypothetical Left–Right shift in the mean voter position.

Voter distributions A, B, C, and D

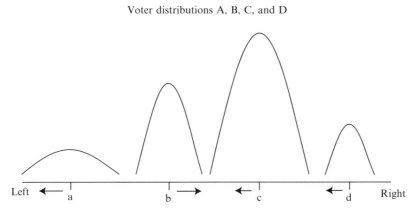

FIGURE 6.2 Demonstrating the Partisan Constituency Hypothesis

Notes: *a, b, c,* and *d* are hypothetical parties. The arrows denote shifts in the Left–Right positions of the mean party supporter for each party.

represented in Figure 6.2 is that parties *a, b, c,* and *d* will respond to Left–Right shifts of their particular constituencies (more so than to shifts in the mean voter position). In total, these hypotheses suggest that mainstream parties will respond to public opinion in a manner consistent with Figure 6.1 and that niche parties will respond to citizens as suggested in Figure 6.2.

6.3 DATA AND MEASUREMENT

6.3.1 Measuring parties' policy positions and public policy preferences

Each hypothesis posits that the changes in the voters' ideological preferences are somehow linked to parties' policy positions. Thus, to test these propositions, longitudinal, cross-national measures of parties' policy programs need to be developed, as well as measures of voters' policy preferences.

To measure party policy positions over time, the estimates from the Comparative Manifesto Project (CMP) are employed. These data are comprised of party manifestos from the main political parties in twenty-five democracies in the postwar period and provide the only longitudinal and cross-national estimates of party policies. The analytical payoff of the CMP data is that it allows us to map party positions over the entire time period and in all of the countries under investigation.[5] Moreover, as the content of party programs is often the result of intense intra-party debate, the CMP estimates should be reliable and accurate statements about parties' positions at the time of elections. Indeed, these measures are generally consistent with those from other party positioning studies, such as those based upon expert placements, citizen perceptions of parties' positions, and parliamentary voting analyses. This provides additional confidence in the longitudinal and cross-national reliability of these estimates (see Hearl 2001; McDonald and Mendes 2001; Laver et al. 2003).

While the methods used by the CMP to map party policy positions based on election programs are described at length elsewhere, I briefly review them here.[6] Under the CMP framework, policy preferences are characterized by systematic examination of party stances on policies, based on content analysis of election programs (Budge et al. 2001). Individual coders isolate "quasi-sentences" in a party's policy program and pair them with policy categories (e.g., education, defense, law and order, morality, etc.) using a preestablished, common classification scheme. The classification scheme is made up of fifty-six categories and the percentages of each category provide the basis for estimating the policy priorities of a party. The Left–Right ideological scores for parties' policy programs range from −100 (extreme Left) to +100 (extreme Right).

The measure of public opinion is based on Eurobarometer surveys dating from 1973 (the first year that the Left–Right self-placement item appears on the Eurobarometer survey)[7] until 2002 (the last year for which the "vote intention" item

[5] In *Mapping Policy Preferences II*, the CMP updates their estimates of parties' policy positions through 2003 and expands the number of countries for which they place parties (Klingemann et al. 2006).

[6] For a more thorough description of the coding process, see appendix 2 in Budge et al. (2001).

[7] The *Mannheim Eurobarometer Trend File, 1970–2002* (Schmitt and Scholz 2005) is relied on for the public opinion data. The Trend File has compiled the Eurobarometers for the time period under investigation.

discussed below appears on the survey). In these surveys, approximately 2,000 respondents in each country in each year are asked to place themselves on a 1–10 Left–Right ideological scale.[8]

Finally, to estimate the policy position of the mean party supporter, I rely on the "vote intention" question in the Eurobarometer surveys in combination with the Left–Right self-placement data described above. Specifically, the question asks respondents the following: "If there were a 'general election' tomorrow, which party would you support?" The mean party supporter is calculated as the mean Left–Right self-placement for all respondents that indicated that they would support the party in the upcoming parliamentary elections.[9] Table A6.1 presents the countries, parties, inter-election periods, party family designations, and the mean Left–Right party supporter positions, and Table A6.2 lists the mean general voter positions (stratified by year and by country) that are used in the empirical analyses.[10]

6.4 TESTING THE MEAN VOTER REPRESENTATION AND THE PARTISAN CONSTITUENCY HYPOTHESES

6.4.1 Model specification for the hypotheses

In order to test the Mean Voter Hypothesis (H_1) and the Partisan Constituency Hypothesis (H_2), I specify the following multivariate regression model (referred to as the core model specification):

$$
\begin{aligned}
\textit{Change in party position } (t) \\
= B_1 + B_2 \left[\textit{Mean shift} - \textit{All voters } (t) \right] \\
+ B_3 \left[\textit{Mean shift} - \textit{Party supporters } (t) \right] \\
+ B_4 \left[\textit{Niche} \times \textit{Mean shift} - \textit{All voters } (t) \right] \\
+ B_5 \left[\textit{Niche} \times \textit{Mean shift} - \textit{Party supporters } (t) \right] \\
+ B_6 \left[\textit{Niche} \right] \\
+ B_7 \left[\textit{Change in party position } (t-1) \right] \quad (6.1)
\end{aligned}
$$

---

[8] Specifically, the Eurobarometer surveys ask, "In political matters, people talk of 'the left' and 'the right.' How would you place your views on this scale?".

[9] The mean party supporter estimates are based on at least fifty responses to the Left–Right self-placement item in each country in each year. There were a relatively large number of respondents per country year (approximately 2,000) so that only a few parties did not reach this criterion for inclusion. In addition, only parties that were observed in at least three successive elections are included in the empirical analyses.

[10] Addressing this research question requires aggregating individual-level observations up to party and country levels of analysis. Thus, while the statistical analyses that are reported are based on over 309 party-level observations, it should be clarified that these aggregated observations are based on slightly over 800,000 individual responses for the time period and countries under consideration.

where,

Change in party position (*t*) is the change in a party's Left–Right policy position in the current election compared to its position in the previous election (election *t* − 1), based on the CMP data.

Change in party position (*t* − 1) is the difference in the CMP Left–Right estimates of a party's policy position between election *t* − 1 and election *t* − 2.

Mean shift − *All voters* (*t*) is the change in the mean Left–Right self-placement score of *all* respondents in a country between the year of the current election and the year of the previous election (election *t* − 1), based on the Eurobarometer data.

Mean shift − *Party supporters* (*t*) is the change in the mean Left–Right self-placements for all of the respondents who indicated that they would vote for the party in the upcoming national election, between the year of the current election and the year of the previous election.

Niche is 1, if the party is classified by the CMP as a niche party, and 0 otherwise.

The dependent variable [*Change in party position* (*t*)] represents the inter-election shift in parties' Left–Right policies. The variable is constructed so that positive scores indicate that the parties' policies are moving "rightward" between elections and negative scores denote "leftward" party shifts. The key independent variables [*Mean shift* − *All voters*] and [*Mean shift* − *Party supporters*] are similarly constructed.

Recall that the Partisan Constituency Hypothesis (H_2) states that party–citizen linkages are mediated by the type of party. To test this proposition, I include two interaction variables in the core model specification, [*Niche* × *Mean shift* − *All voters*] and [*Niche* × *Mean shift* − *Party supporters*], which interact public opinion shifts and mean party supporter shifts with the dummy variable [*Niche*]. The [*Niche*] variable equals 1 if Klingemann et al. (2006) classify the party as a niche party (i.e., Communist, Green, or Nationalist), and zero otherwise.[11] The interaction terms allow us to estimate differences in the degree to which public opinion or party supporters influence niche parties' policy positions as compared to the mainstream parties.

The interpretation of models containing interaction terms can be challenging, making a more detailed explanation of the results worthwhile (see Brambor et al. 2006). Fortunately, the interaction terms are each comprised of the dichotomous variable [*Niche*], which simplifies the interpretation of the model. Let us first consider the effects of the variables [*Mean shift* − *All voters*] or [*Mean shift* − *Party supporters*] on the policy shifts of mainstream parties. For mainstream parties, the dummy variable [*Niche*] equals zero, and the coefficients B_2 and B_3

---

[11] Table A6.1 presents these party family designations, in addition to a list of the specific countries, parties, and elections that are included in the empirical analyses.

on the variables [*Mean shift − All voters*] and [*Mean shift − Party supporters*] estimate the effects of public opinion shifts and party supporter shifts on mainstream parties' policy shifts. If mainstream parties are generally responsive to shifts in public opinion and to their supporters, coefficients B_2 and B_3 will be positive and statistically significant. Specifically, the *Mean Voter Hypothesis* (H_1) is supported if the coefficient on the [*Mean shift − All voters*] variable (B_2) is positive and statistically significant.

Second, the effect of public opinion shifts and party supporter shifts on the policy shifts of niche parties is considered. In this instance, the dummy variable for niche parties equals 1. The effects of changes in public opinion on niche parties' policy programs will be captured by the sum of the coefficients B_2 and B_4 on the variables [*Mean shift − All voters*] and [*Niche × Mean shift − All voters*] in Equation 6.1. Similarly, the sum of the coefficients B_3 and B_5 on variables [*Mean shift − Party supporters*] and [*Niche × Mean shift − Party supporters*] will estimate the influence of changes in the mean Left–Right position of niche party supporters on the policy shifts of niche parties. The second hypothesis, the *Partisan Constituency Hypothesis* (H_2), is supported if $B_3 + B_5 > 0$ and is statistically significant.

Two additional variables in the core model specification are included. First, a lagged version of the dependent variable [*Change in party position* $(t − 1)$] is included, which measures the party's policy shift between election $t − 2$ and election $t − 1$. The lagged dependent variable addresses autocorrelation (discussed further below). Additionally, the [*Change in party position* $(t−1)$] variable addresses policy alternation, a possibility raised by Budge (1994) and Adams (2001), that party elites may have electoral incentives to move their party's position in the opposite direction from their shift in the previous election. Policy alternation, according to Budge, is a rational response by party leaders to placate different wings within the party (see also Budge et al. forthcoming). Adams emphasizes the existence of nonpolicy related factors such as the party identification of voters that would explain similar zigzag patterns of party movement.[12] Under either scenario, the direction of parties' policy shifts in the previous election might influence party leaders' Left–Right strategies in the current election. The [*Niche*] variable is also included on its own in the model specification to ensure

---

[12] There are two additional considerations that would also explain party policy alternation. Burt (1997) proposes a random ideologies model that explains policy alternations by assuming a random selection of three successive party ideologies from a random probability distribution. Measurement error in the CMP estimates of parties' Left–Right positions is a fourth factor that would explain policy alternation. To the extent that parties' "true" positions do not vary over time, and to the extent that the CMP estimates contain measurement error, the estimates will shift in the pattern predicted by Burt's random ideologies model.

that the effects of the interaction terms are measured accurately (Brambor et al. 2006; see also Braumoeller 2004).[13]

6.4.2 Evaluating the Mean Voter and Partisan Constituency Hypotheses

The mean voter and partisan constituency hypotheses are evaluated using time series cross-sectional data from fifteen Western European democracies over the period 1973–2002. One possible concern is the existence of unobserved differences between countries or parties: estimating a simple regression on the pooled data containing these unobserved differences could lead to erroneous inferences (Green et al. 2001; Hsiao 2003). In Table 6.1 (columns 1 and 2), estimates are reported for the core model specification that controls for country- and party-specific effects.[14] The results indicate that unobserved differences between countries or parties are not driving the major findings.

The parameter estimates for the core model specification are presented in column 1 of Table 6.1. The coefficient estimate on the [*Change in party position* $(t-1)$] variable is negative and statistically significant, which is consistent with the theoretical arguments of Budge (1994; see also Budge et al. forthcoming) and Adams (2001) that parties tend to shift their positions in the opposite direction from their shifts in the previous inter-election period. With respect to the key hypotheses, the parameter estimates suggest that mainstream parties respond to shifts in the mean voter position: specifically, the parameter estimate on the [*Mean shift – All voters* (t)] variable is positive and statistically significant (+8.47). Furthermore, the magnitude of this estimate suggests that the effect is *substantively* significant: the coefficient indicates that when the mean Left–Right self-placement of respondents in a country shifts by a unit along the 1–10 Eurobarometer Left–Right scale during an inter-election period, then mainstream parties' Left–Right positions tend to shift 8.47 units in the same direction along the 200-point CMP Left–Right scale. If we recalibrate the party shifts so that the 200-point CMP Left–Right scale is on the same 1–10 Left–Right Eurobarometer scale, a one unit

---

[13] One of the central implications of the study by Braumoeller (2004) is that properly estimating the effects of interaction terms involves including the constitutive (i.e., lower-order) terms in the model specification.

[14] The [*Niche*] variable does not vary within parties (i.e. party family designations do not change over time), which makes running a fixed-effects model for the original specification problematic, as this term naturally drops out of the model specification. Thus, column 2 reports the results from a random-effects model specification where unobserved differences between parties are controlled for. Note that when party-specific intercepts are estimated (and the [*Niche*] variable drops out of the model), the results from these analyses also support the substantive conclusions reported below.

TABLE 6.1 Explaining parties' policy shifts

	Country-specific effects (1)	Party-specific effects (2)	Past election results (3)	Party moderation (4)	Fully specified model (5)	Public opinion model (6)	Party supporter model (7)
Mean shift – All voters (t)	8.47**	7.26*	8.38**	8.47**	8.38**	7.52*	
	(4.01)	(3.77)	(4.00)	(4.02)	(4.01)	(3.95)	
Mean shift – Party supporters (t)	−1.63	−1.33	−1.28	−1.60	−1.26		−.89
	(1.78)	(1.80)	(1.77)	(1.79)	(1.78)		(1.75)
Niche × Mean shift – All voters (t)	−5.94	−7.46	−6.20	−6.02	−6.24	−5.07	
	(7.84)	(7.83)	(7.78)	(7.86)	(7.80)	(7.84)	
Niche × Mean shift – Party supporters (t)	8.47**	6.51*	8.25**	8.42**	8.23**		7.54**
	(3.84)	(3.85)	(3.81)	(3.86)	(3.82)		(3.83)
Niche	−1.02	−.75	−1.22	−.87	−1.14	−.82	−1.01
	(1.73)	(1.63)	(1.72)	(1.86)	(1.84)	(1.74)	(1.74)
Change in party position (t−1)	−.43***	−.42***	−.44***	−.44***	−.44***	−.44***	−.44***
	(.05)	(.05)	(.05)	(.05)	(.05)	(.05)	(.05)
Change in party position (t−1) × Vote change (t−1)			.025**		.025**		
			(.012)		(.012)		
Vote change (t−1)			−.23*		−.22*		
			(.14)		(.14)		
Party ideology				.19	.09		
				(.81)	(.80)		
Intercept	1.88**	1.78**	1.79**	1.88**	1.80**	1.92***	1.55**
	(.73)	(.74)	(.73)	(.73)	(.73)	(.74)	(.72)
N	309	309	309	309	309	309	309
R^2	.19	.19	.20	.19	.20	.18	.18

Notes: Standard errors are in parentheses. The dependent variable is the change in a party's Left-Right policy position, based on the codings of parties' policy programs that are reported in the CD-ROM in Budge et al. (2001) and Klingemann et al. (2006). The definitions of the independent variables are given in the text. Column 2 estimates the parameters of a random effects model specification (see Footnote 14). The country-specific intercepts for columns 1, 3, 4, 5, 6, and 7 are not shown.

$*p < .10$, $**p < .05$, $***p < .01$, two-tailed tests

mean voter shift translates into a party shift of 0.38.[15] Accordingly, the evidence supports the *Mean Voter Hypothesis* (H$_1$) indicating that shifts in mainstream parties' Left–Right policy positions systematically respond to shifts in the mean voter position. This finding is labeled the *General Electorate Result*.

Table 6.1 also reports the coefficient estimates for the [*Niche* × *Mean shift – Party supporters*] variable, which are positive and reach statistical significance, lending support to a finding that niche parties are systematically more responsive to their supporters than are mainstream parties. Furthermore, the conditional coefficient and conditional standard error were computed to determine if niche parties are responsive to their supporters in absolute terms (and not just more responsive to their supporters than mainstream parties). The conditional coefficient on niche party responsiveness to their supporters is positive and statistically significant ($B_3 + B_5 = 6.84$; SE $= 3.41$; $p = .046$).[16] The magnitude of the conditional coefficient on niche party responsiveness to their supporters is also *substantively* significant: these estimates suggest that on a recalibrated 200-point CMP scale (to fit on the 1–10 Eurobarometer scale), a one unit party supporter shift produces, on average, a 0.31 unit niche party shift.[17] Consequently, the conditional parameter estimates support the Partisan Constituency Hypothesis (H$_2$). This second finding is labeled the *Partisan Constituency Result*.[18]

In addition to reporting these central results (i.e., the general electorate result and the partisan constituency result), it is important to consider consequential

---

[15] Furthermore, although the theoretical range of the CMP scale is 200 points, it has been noted that in practice the range of the CMP scale is from −50 to 50 (Mikhaylov et al. 2008; see also Budge and McDonald 2006). If the CMP scale is treated as a 100-point scale rather than a 200-point scale as these authors suggest (and adjusted to the 1–10 Left–Right Eurobarometer scale), a mean voter shift of one unit is expected to induce mainstream parties to shift their positions approximately three-quarters of a unit (.76) on this scale in the same direction. Under either scenario, mainstream political parties appear highly responsive to the shift in the mean voter position.

[16] The conditional coefficients are calculated based on the following (see Equation 6.1 for notation): $\frac{\partial \Delta P(t)}{\partial \Delta S(t)} = B_3 + B_5 \times [Niche]$, while the conditional standard errors are given by s.e. $\left(\frac{\partial \Delta P(t)}{\partial \Delta S(t)}\right) = \sqrt{var(B_3) + [Niche]^2 \times var(B_5) + 2[Niche] \times cov(B_3, B_5)}$ (see Brambor et al. 2006), where $P(t)$ and $S(t)$ stand for the variables [*Change in party position (t)*] and [*Mean shift – Party supporters (t)*]. The coefficient and standard error for mainstream parties (when [*Niche*] $= 0$) are simply B_3 and s.e.(B_3) (the coefficient and standard error estimating the effects of the [*Mean shift – Party supporters*] variable). For niche parties (when the [*Niche*] variable $= 1$), the coefficient is ($B_3 + B_5$), and the conditional standard error is calculated using the equation above.

[17] If the range of the CMP data is treated as being on a 100-point scale (as discussed in Footnote 15), then a one unit party supporter shift is expected to induce niche parties to shift their policy positions in the inter-election period by almost two-thirds of a unit (.62).

[18] The partisan constituency result suggests an answer to the puzzle raised in Adams et al. (2006) where the authors find that niche parties do not respond to shifts in the mean voter position. The lingering question then is to whom do niche parties respond? This second finding suggests that niche parties respond to shifts in their supporters' positions in contrast to responding to shifts in the general electorate's mean position.

"null" results. Relying on the equations presented in Footnote 16, the conditional parameter estimates for niche party responsiveness to the [*Mean shift − All voters*] variable ($B_2 + B_4 = 2.53$; SE $= 7.07$, $p = .72$) indicates that public opinion does not appear to systematically influence the policy shifts of niche parties. Additionally, the estimates for the effects of the [*Mean shift − Party supporters*] variable (B_3) suggest that the observations do not support a finding that mainstream parties systematically respond to shifts in their supporters' positions (indeed, the coefficient is negative). Finally, although the coefficient, B_4, on the interaction variable [*Niche × Mean shift − All voters*] is not statistically significant, its sizeable negative estimate is suggestive that niche parties are less responsive to public opinion shifts than are mainstream parties.

6.4.3 Sensitivity analyses

The possibility of serially correlated errors within countries is also addressed. Given the structure of the data, the causal processes that generate the change in the policy position of a party at time t could also be operating during the prior inter-election period $t-1$. This concern is addressed by including the lagged version of the dependent variable [*Change in party position* $(t-1)$] in the core specification given in Equation 6.1 (see Beck and Katz 1995, 1996).[19]

Columns 3–5 in Table 6.1 report parameter estimates for pooled data analyses that control for additional factors that plausibly influence parties' policy positions, including the effects of past election results, party system convergence, and a full specification that accounts for all of the factors raised in the analysis.

Past election results: Column 3 reports estimates for a *past election results* model, which is identical to the basic model *except* that it controls for the possibility that parties adjust their Left–Right positions in response to the outcome of the previous election. Specifically, building on Budge's empirical finding (1994) that parties tend to shift their policies in the same direction as the last time if they gained votes at the previous election, and in the opposite direction if they lost votes (see also Adams et al. 2004; Somer-Topcu 2009; Budge et al. forthcoming), a variable [*Vote change* $(t − 1)$] is incorporated that denotes the party's vote gain or loss at the previous election, and the variable [*Vote change* $(t − 1) ×$ *Change in party position* $(t − 1)$] that interacts with the vote change variable with the party's Left–Right shift at the previous election. A positive coefficient estimate on this interactive variable will indicate that parties tend to shift their positions in the same direction as their previous policy shift if they gained votes at the previous election, and in the opposite direction if they lost votes. The parameter estimate on this

---

[19] The coefficient on the variable [*Change in party position* $(t − 1)$] is negative and statistically significant, which suggests that parties tend to shift policy in the opposite direction from their previous policy shift. This result is consistent with conclusions reported by Budge (1994) and Adams (2001).

variable that is reported in column 3 is indeed positive and statistically significant, which supports Budge's arguments. More importantly, the parameter estimates on the policy shifts of opinion leaders and other voters continue to support the General Electorate Hypothesis (H_1) and the Partisan Constituency Hypothesis (H_2).

Party system convergence: Previous studies by Adams and Somer-Topcu (2009), Ezrow (2007), and Keman and Pennings (2006) report results suggesting that parties tend to moderate their Left–Right positions over time, that is, Left-wing parties tend to shift to the Right while Right-wing parties shift leftward. To evaluate this hypothesis, a model was estimated that was identical to the basic model *except* that a [*Party ideology*] variable was incorporated that was scored at $+1$ for Left-wing parties, -1 for Right-wing parties, and zero for centrist parties.[20] Column 4 of Table 6.1 reports the parameter estimates for this *party moderation* model. The estimated coefficient on the [*Party ideology*] variable is positive and is not statistically significant. The inclusion of this variable does not alter the substantive conclusions: the parameter estimates for this model continue to support Hypotheses H_1 and H_2.

A fully specified model: Column 5 in Table 6.1 reports the parameter estimates for a *fully specified model*, which controls for both past election results and party system convergence. The coefficient estimates for this model continue to support H_1 and H_2.

Additional analyses: In addition to the results reported in Table 6.1 that control for country- and party-specific effects, the parameters were estimated for several additional pooled data specifications. First, the core model specification was re-estimated on a country-by-country basis, omitting one country at a time. The parameters of this model specification were re-estimated relaxing the definition of niche and mainstream parties.[21] In addition the likelihood of correlated errors among the parties competing in a particular election, a possibility arising from unobserved election-specific factors that could be influencing all of the parties' policy shifts, was addressed by estimating robust standard errors clustered by election (Rogers 1993; Williams 2000).[22] Finally, empirical analyses by Huber

---

[20] Parties are defined as Left-wing if the CMP classified the party as being a member of the Social Democratic party family, while Right-wing parties were those that the CMP classified as belonging to the Conservative or Christian Democratic party families. Parties were defined as centrist if they were classified as members of the Liberal party family. The parties' family designations are reported in Table A6.1.

[21] There are twenty-two observations from "regional" and "agrarian" party families that were omitted from the analyses because these parties are substantively different from niche and mainstream parties. Specifically, these parties do not compete on the Left–Right dimension. Nevertheless, it is reassuring that when they are included in the analyses classified as either niche or mainstream parties that the central findings remain unchanged.

[22] When parameters of this specification are estimated, it supports the finding of relative niche party responsiveness to their supporters (when compared to mainstream parties). However, the certainty decreases for a finding that would support absolute niche party responsiveness to their supporters.

(1989) suggest that with the exception of Belgium, Germany, and Ireland, the Eurobarometer respondents' Left–Right self-placements are comparable cross-nationally (i.e., respondents' self-placements are meaningfully related to the preferences along specific dimensions of policy debate). To account for this possibility, the parameters of the model specification in Equation 6.1 have been re-estimated excluding these countries, as well as those countries that were not members of the European Community at the time Huber completed his study. These additional analyses thus included observations from only Britain, Italy, Denmark, Portugal, France, Greece, Spain, the Netherlands, and Luxembourg. The parameter estimates for each of these model specifications described above support the substantive conclusions that are reported.

The possibility of collinearity between public opinion and supporter positions was also considered. If it were the case that these variables are highly collinear, then parsing out their effects would be difficult. This might be a problem especially for mainstream parties, where one could argue that supporters may be a more representative cross section of the public than is the case for niche parties. There is modest evidence of this: the correlation between public opinion changes and changes in the positions of party supporters is .25 for mainstream parties ($p <$ .01) and .01 for niche parties (not significant). However, for mainstream parties the correlation is not so high as to create severe collinearity. In quite a few cases (37.8%), changes in public opinion are in the opposite direction to those among mainstream party supporters. Moreover, columns 6 and 7 report parameter estimates for a *public opinion* model and a *party supporter* model, where the effects of <u>only</u> changes in public opinion and <u>only</u> changes in supporter positions were estimated. In each case, the results remain unchanged.

Endogeneity Analyses: Finally, two types of endogeneity are addressed. The first variant concerns the possible cueing of public opinion or supporters by parties. Although this chapter concentrates on the ideological *linkages* between parties and citizens rather than the direction in which ideological preferences are transmitted between these groups, cueing is nevertheless relevant. Indeed, it may be that citizens respond to parties, rather than the reverse, in which case the coefficients reported may be biased and inconsistent. Past studies that have explicitly addressed this issue of causality have found that any cue-giving effects by parties tend to be weaker than the corresponding cues that voters transmit to parties (see Carrubba 2001; Steenbergen et al. 2007). Nonetheless, a Durbin–Wu–Hausman test was performed in which public opinion and supporter positions were modeled as functions of their lagged values, computed the residuals, and entered these residuals into a model of parties' policy positions. If public opinion and supporter positions were endogenous with respect to party positions, then these positions would be reflected in the residuals; namely, the residuals would exert a significant effect on parties' Left–Right positions. There was no evidence of this for mainstream parties. For niche parties, there was evidence that the public opinion residual is significant.[23] The upshot is that the estimates reported in the tables are not marred by endogeneity. With the possible exception of the effect of public opinion on niche parties, these estimates are consistent.

In addition to the studies cited above by Carrubba (2001) and Steenbergen et al. (2007), the finding that mainstream parties in Western Europe respond to voters but that voters do not respond to parties is consistent with the results reported in recent studies by Hobolt and Klemmensen (2008), Adams et al. (2008), and Hellwig et al. (forthcoming). Hobolt and Klemmensen (2008) conclude that the range of voters' issue concerns moves, but is not significantly moved by, the issue diversity of party leaders' speeches. In addition, Adams et al. (2008) report cross-national results that suggest that voters do not systematically adjust their own Left–Right policy preferences when parties change their policy statements. Finally, Hellwig et al. (forthcoming) examine citizen perceptions of the diversity of policy offerings provided by the parties in their system and conclude that these perceptions are unconnected to objective measures of policy choices given by parties as measured in parties' policy statements. The central implication for all of these studies is that while it seems plausible for a small group of party elites in mainstream parties to respond to citizens' policy signals when producing their party platforms, voters appear less likely to respond systematically in kind to these policy platform changes.

The second type of endogeneity that could be present in the empirical analyses is that the results could inherently be tilted toward supporting the partisan constituency model of political representation. To the extent that this type of endogeneity is a problem, it should bias the statistical analyses in favor of the finding that parties respond to their supporters. For example, if a party shifts away from a segment of its constituency it should lose support from some of these voters. This policy shift should also produce a subsequent increase in support for the party by virtue of its moving toward a new set of voters. If this "party-switching" process were taking place, we would observe a pattern in which the mean Left–Right supporter position would shift in tandem with the party's policy shift even if none of the voters are actually shifting their ideological positions. Since this should bias the empirical findings toward a finding that *all* parties are responsive to their supporters, it cannot account for the observation that only niche parties are responding to their supporters. Given this unavoidable feature of the empirical analyses, it actually further strengthens the finding that mainstream parties respond to the mean voter position. Thus, to the extent that this second type of endogeneity is a "problem," it actually strengthens the substantive conclusion that mainstream parties are <u>not</u> disproportionately responsive to their supporters, since the statistical analyses may be biased in the opposite direction.

---

[23] For mainstream parties, the effect of the public opinion residuals yields $p = .941$, while the corresponding p-value for the supporter residuals is .261. For niche parties, the p-values are .376 for the supporter residual and .029 for the public opinion residual.

6.5 ELECTORAL SYSTEMS AND PARTY RESPONSIVENESS

A repeated point is that our understanding of policy linkages between citizens and parties can be enhanced by lowering the level of analysis from the country-level to the party-level. One does not necessarily need to know the precise type of electoral system in which a party competes; rather, the type of party family matters more for understanding these policy linkages. Of course, using the approach developed in this chapter (and the preceding chapters), this is an empirical question that can be addressed head on. Do electoral systems help determine whether parties respond to the mean voter position or to their core supporters? Theory leads to conflicting answers. One reasonable expectation is that

> Parties in disproportional systems are responsive to the mean voter position, and parties in proportional systems are responsive to their supporters.

The first argument that underlies this expectation is that less proportional voting systems – like plurality systems – plausibly motivate political parties to emphasize vote-seeking objectives, so that the parties competing in these systems can be expected to be more responsive to changes in the mean voter position. The reason that disproportional systems plausibly promote vote-seeking behavior by parties is because of the well-known fact that such voting systems tend to "punish" smaller parties and reward larger parties when national vote returns are converted into parliamentary seats (Cox 1997; see also Taagepera and Shugart 1989). Disproportional systems, for this reason, motivate parties to place a premium on gaining substantial vote shares, so that they can be among the large parties that benefit from this effect.

Jay Dow (2001) offers a related argument that in disproportional systems the major parties may reasonably aspire to win a single-party parliamentary majority, which gives these major parties added incentives to maximize votes. For instance, the plurality-based postwar elections held in Britain and New Zealand (the latter country featured plurality until its switch to proportional representation (PR) in 1996) returned single-party parliamentary majorities in over 80% of the cases.[24] Dow (2001) argues that this "winner-take-all" feature of disproportional, plurality-based elections motivates political parties to be highly responsive to voters' policy preferences.

By contrast, the lower effective seat thresholds associated with highly proportional voting systems plausibly motivate the parties in these systems to emphasize policy objectives and to thereby be more ideologically "rigid" in the face of mean voter shifts, because these parties are assured of at least some parliamentary

---

[24] Fifteen out of seventeen postwar British elections have returned single-party parliamentary majorities, while in New Zealand each of the postwar elections held under plurality through the mid-1990s returned parliamentary majorities.

representation when they are confident that their vote shares will exceed the relatively low national thresholds that are necessary to obtain legislative seats in highly proportional systems. Thus, parties in proportional systems are freer to respond to their core supporters' ideological preferences because they do not have to compete for marginal voters at the "Center" in order to gain representation in the legislature.

An additional set of considerations is that parties in PR systems – which should be smaller, on average, because there are more of them (see chapter 4) – should have more information about their supporters, and, furthermore, these parties are more flexible in terms of responding to shifts in their supporters' positions. In contrast, the large parties associated with electoral competition in disproportional systems should have more difficulty collecting information about their supporters, and their correspondingly larger organizational structures should make it more difficult to respond to their supporters' ideological shifts.[25]

While the above considerations suggest that the general electorate model applies to disproportional systems and that the partisan constituency model applies to proportional systems, there are another set of theoretical considerations that suggest the opposite holds; specifically, that

> Parties in disproportional systems are responsive to their supporters, and parties in proportional systems are responsive to the mean voter position.

Arguments on this side of the ledger refer to research on valence, party activists, and coalitions. The strategic implications of "valence" dimensions of party evaluation (i.e., dimensions related to voters' impressions of party elites' competence, honesty, or charisma) suggest that "valence-disadvantaged" parties in disproportional systems would not be oriented toward the mean voter position; instead, they have electoral incentives to differentiate themselves on policy grounds: if these parties present centrist policies that are similar to those advocated by valence-advantaged parties, then voters will choose based on the valence dimension – that is, they will choose parties that have superior valence images (Adams 1999; Schofield and Sened 2005, 2006; see also Macdonald and Rabinowitz 1998). To the extent that Schofield's argument captures real-world parties' electoral strategies, we should not expect all vote-seeking parties to appeal to the mean voter position. Even if plurality systems motivate parties to attach greater weight to vote-seeking, this will not in turn imply plurality elections motivate policy convergence.[26]

While the arguments in the paragraph above suggest that parties in plurality (or disproportional) systems are not responsive to the mean voter position, these

---

[25] The arguments in this paragraph are based on points raised by Gary Marks in conversation.

[26] Adams and Merrill (1999, 2000) present an alternative argument that voters' partisan loyalties can motivate vote-seeking parties to diverge from the Center, in the direction of the policies favored by the members of their partisan constituencies (see also Adams et al. 2005).

arguments however do not suggest that parties would be responsive to their core supporters. Miller and Schofield (2003), building on Aldrich (1983a, 1983b, 1995), develop a second, related, motivation for vote-seeking parties that revolves around strategic incentives related to *party activists*. The Miller–Schofield argument is that parties can enhance their vote shares by appealing to party activists who provide scarce campaign resources (i.e., time and money). Specifically, the authors argue that parties can use the added campaign resources they acquire via their policy appeals to activists to enhance their images along valence dimensions such as competence and integrity – and that this in turn will increase the parties' electoral support among rank-and-file voters. Given the above considerations on valence and activists, it would be reasonable to expect greater applicability of the partisan constituency model to disproportional systems than perhaps initially thought.

By contrast, party responsiveness to the mean voter position in proportional systems may not be so surprising if parties are concerned with maximizing their likelihood of being included in the governing coalition. If this is the case then appealing to the center may be a viable strategy. Schofield et al. (1998a) examine Dutch and German elections and determine that parties try to put themselves in good positions for the post-coalition negotiations. This entails presenting policies that are acceptable to potential coalition partners, which may provide incentives for policy moderation. If proportional systems motivate parties to present policies that are acceptable to coalition partners, then these parties may well present centrist positions. This finding is also in line with that of the other prominent coalition scholars who present theoretical and empirical results that support the claim that in proportional systems, gaining membership in the governing coalition is closely linked with centrist positioning (Axelrod 1970; Huber and Powell 1994; Laver and Shepsle 1996; Powell 2000). When facing the decision to respond to the core supporters or the mean voter, parties may choose the latter option with the expectation that this will enhance the possibility of joining the governing coalition after an election.

There is of course a third possibility: that is, that neither model of party responsiveness applies uniformly to either type of electoral system. The arguments above on party positioning incentives might counterbalance leading to the unremarkable yet plausible conclusion that sometimes parties respond to their core supporters, sometimes to the mean voter position, sometimes to both (if they shift in the same direction), and sometimes to neither – and that electoral systems do not apply incentives uniformly to the parties that compete within them.

Testing for Electoral System Effects: Of course, it is possible to test these claims using the framework established throughout the chapter (and indeed throughout the book) for fifteen Western European democracies over a thirty year period. Operationally, in order to evaluate the claims above, I estimate the parameter estimates of the fully specified model – from column 5 of Table 6.1 – that includes

TABLE 6.2 *Explaining parties' policy shifts across electoral systems*

	Electoral system effects (1)
Mean shift – All voters (t)	11.23*
	(6.02)
Mean shift – Party supporters (t)	.46
	(2.61)
Niche × Mean shift – All voters (t)	−5.71
	(7.82)
Niche × Mean shift – Party supporters (t)	8.72**
	(3.84)
Disproportionality × Mean shift – All voters (t)	**−.44**
	(.72)
Disproportionality × Mean shift – Party supporters (t)	**−.55**
	(.56)
Niche	−1.12
	(1.84)
Change in party position (t–1)	−.44***
	(.05)
Change in party position (t–1) × Vote change (t–1)	.024**
	(.012)
Vote change (t–1)	−.23*
	(.14)
Party ideology	.12
	(.80)
Intercept	1.83**
	(.73)
N	309
R^2	.21

Notes: Standard errors are in parentheses. The dependent variable is the change in a party's Left-Right policy position, based on the codings of parties' policy programs that are reported in the CD-ROM in Budge et al. (2001) and Klingemann et al. (2006). The model is estimated with country-specific intercepts, and disproportionality (t) drops out of the model because the estimates do not vary by country.

*p < .10, **p < .05, ***p < .01, two-tailed tests

two additional terms that interact the variables [*Mean shift − All voters (t)*] and [*Mean shift − Party supporters (t)*] with the [*Disproportionality (t)*] variable.[27]

Column 1 of Table 6.2 presents the results of estimating the parameter estimates of an electoral system effects model specification. With respect to the expectations raised above, if there is evidence that parties are relatively more sensitive to shifts

---

[27] The equation for the Gallagher Index of Disproportionality is $\sqrt{\frac{1}{2} \Sigma (v_i - s_i)^2}$, where v_i and s_i are the vote shares and subsequent seat shares for party i. This measure, based on a Gallagher (1991) study, is discussed at length in Chapter 3.

in the mean voter position in disproportional systems than in proportional systems, we would expect the coefficient on the [*Mean shift — All voters* (*t*) × *Disproportionality* (*t*)] variable to be positive and statistically significant. Alternatively, if the coefficient on the [*Mean shift — Party supporters* (*t*) × *Disproportionality* (*t*)] variable is positive and statistically significant, this would indicate that parties in less proportional systems are relatively more responsive to their supporters than parties in proportional systems.

With respect to the evidence on the mediating effects of electoral systems, the results are quite striking. The parameter estimates continue to support the General Electorate Result and Partisan Constituency Result that were reported earlier regarding mainstream and niche party responsiveness. However, the parameter estimates on the [*Mean shift — All voters* (*t*) × *Disproportionality* (*t*)] and [*Mean shift — Party supporters* (*t*) × *Disproportionality* (*t*)] variables are insignificant — which does not support a finding that electoral systems mediate how parties respond to citizen shifts.

6.6 CONCLUSION

How parties represent the policy preferences of citizens is the essence of political representation. In spite of the importance of understanding these linkages, there has been very little systematic cross-national empirical examination of the *dynamic* relationships that exist between parties, publics, and subconstituencies. This chapter hurdles some of the macro-level observational barriers that are required to analyze theories at the country- and party-levels. In so doing, two robust patterns or findings have been identified: the first finding is the *General Electorate Result*, which states that changes in the mean voter position cause corresponding shifts in mainstream parties' policy positions. This finding is relevant, as it demonstrates the exportability of the Stimson et al. (1995; see also Erikson et al. 2002) concept of dynamic representation to the mainstream parties in Western European democracies.

The second major finding is the *Partisan Constituency Result*, which states that while niche parties are unresponsive to shifts in the mean voter position, these "ideological" parties do appear responsive to the shifts in their supporters' positions. The central implication of this result is that the citizen–party linkage emphasized by Dalton (1985) and Wessels (1999) is particularly useful for understanding the policy shifts of niche parties in Western Europe. Taken together, these two results corroborate and extend the research that emphasizes the type of party (Meguid 2005, 2008; Adams et al. 2006; Ezrow 2008*a*; see also Calvo and Hellwig 2008) in spatial analyses of elections and political representation. Furthermore, these conclusions support the perspective of Laver (2005) and Fowler and Laver (2006), that it is worthwhile to model competition between sets of parties that employ different decision rules.

This chapter raises several interesting questions for future research. While the evidence suggests that there are indeed direct linkages between voter preferences and the policy positions that are on offer by parties in a political system, the explanations put forth in this chapter are only tentative. A comprehensive explanation requires *contextual* analyses of Western European parties: namely, of parties' organizational structures, of party elites, as well as of rank-and-file party supporters (see, e.g., Kitschelt 1988). An analysis of *why* different parties are apparently receiving different signals from different segments of the electorate, though outside the scope of this chapter, is necessary in order to reach a better understanding of how changes occur to the policy choices that political parties present to the electorate.

Nonetheless, the results of this analysis are relevant to our understanding of the democratic process and, specifically, to the dynamics between voter and party ideologies. Moreover, with the quotation at the outset of the chapter by Bernhard Wessels (1999) in mind, the key results of this chapter are perhaps refreshing for normative visions of democracy by demonstrating the existence of linkages between the policy preferences of citizens and parties.

Part IV

Conclusion

The Effects of Electoral Institutions

7.1 SUMMARY OF FINDINGS

The study has reached three general conclusions. First, electoral systems do not matter in the ways that are commonly accepted with respect to rewarding party policy centrism in elections and promoting party extremism (Chapters 2 and 3). Second, electoral systems do influence niche party competitiveness (Chapter 4). Finally, the existence of niche parties in turn has dramatic implications for the way in which representation works (Chapters 5 and 6). Thus, electoral systems matter because they influence the level of niche party competition.

Chapters 2 and 3 presented evidence that *democracies are similar* in important ways, which scholars have commonly overlooked. Across systems with different electoral rules there are common patterns of election outcomes and party positioning. Chapter 2 presented theoretical arguments and empirical analyses that support the hypothesis that moderate parties tend to gain greater vote shares than their distinctly noncentrist counterparts, and that this relationship holds across *all* multiparty systems, regardless of electoral laws.

In Chapter 3, I presented evidence that party policy distinctiveness is roughly the same across proportional and plurality-based party systems, a finding that runs counter to the conventional wisdom that proportional representation (PR)-based systems encourage radical party positioning. Moreover, the results in this chapter suggest that the electoral rewards for policy centrism are _not_ enhanced in disproportional systems, that is, in systems that reward large parties when votes are translated into seats in parliament.

In contrast to Chapters 2 and 3, which highlighted similarities across countries, Chapters 4–6 emphasized the dramatic differences in policy representation which result from the electoral rules. The main effect of these differences (reported in Chapter 4) is that PR systems encourage the formation of niche parties while plurality systems do not. Chapters 5 and 6 demonstrated the relevance of the niche or the mainstream party distinction for election outcomes (Chapter 5) and party positioning (Chapter 6). Chapter 5 revisited models of election outcomes (i.e., the party proximity model and the party distinctiveness model) and reported that mainstream parties' vote shares conform to expectations based on the party proximity model, namely, that mainstream parties benefit in national elections by occupying positions close to the mean voter position. By contrast, niche parties' vote shares are accurately characterized by the party distinctiveness model where more radical party positions are rewarded with votes in national elections.

Chapter 6 examined whether political parties respond to the ideological shifts of their supporters or to the shifts of the mean voter. Mainstream parties respond to shifts in the mean voter position (as opposed to shifts of their supporters), while niche parties are highly sensitive to shifts in the positions of their supporters (and not to shifts in the mean position). Thus, each model of representation is accurate at capturing parties' policy shifts, but the analyst must first specify the type of party being examined.

7.2 HOW ELECTORAL INSTITUTIONS MATTER

Let us return to the question posed in the title of this study about how electoral institutions matter for political representation. Several prominent studies classify electoral systems and address their consequences (e.g., Farrell 2001; Katz 1997; Lijphart 1994; Rae 1967; Taagepera and Shugart 1989). This well-developed literature catalogs trade-offs between disproportional and proportional systems.[1] Disproportional (or plurality) systems often return single-party majorities, rather than multiparty governing coalitions, in their lower house of parliament. Consequently, these systems are credited with greater government accountability, since it should be easier for citizens to reward and punish incumbents in these systems than for citizens who evaluate multiparty coalitions where several parties could be held responsible for governing outputs (Powell and Whitten 1993). Single-party governments are also considered less likely to dissolve (however, David Farrell (2001) reports that this expectation does not hold empirically).

On the other side, scholars attribute several advantages to PR systems. Proportional systems are associated with a greater number of viable parties, which is seen as beneficial because this offers more channels through which citizens' preferences may be expressed (Lijphart 1999; see also Chapter 4). PR systems generally have low vote thresholds and parties' representation in the legislature is roughly in line with their vote shares. Both of these features, low thresholds and proportional vote–seat translations, generate higher levels of sincere voting in these systems.

---

[1] Carey and Hix (2008) call into question the dichotomy of electoral systems – into plurality systems versus systems featuring proportional representation – and recognized trade-offs between the two. The authors are skeptical about this contention: "Is there a linear trade-off between representation and accountability? Or, is it possible to engineer electoral systems to approximate ideal levels of both?" (Carey and Hix 2008: 3).

TABLE 7.1 *Effects of electoral systems*

PR	Plurality
More parties	Fewer Parties
Less accountability	More accountability
Less stable (cf. Farrell 2001)	More stable
Enhance women's and minorities' representation	Representation of the majority ("majoritarian")
Higher citizen satisfaction	Less citizen satisfaction
Higher turnout	Lower turnout
Sincere voting	Strategic voting
Centrifugal incentives	Centripetal incentives
Niche party channels	Limited (if any) niche channels

Source: Lijphart (1999).

Additionally, proportional systems have higher levels of citizen satisfaction, voter turnout, and levels of political equality for women and minorities (Blais and Carty 1990; Anderson and Guillory 1997; Lijphart 1999; Franklin 2004).

Table 7.1 summarizes the consequences electoral systems help produce. The table also makes explicit where the current study fits in to this discussion. The penultimate entry notes that list PR systems encourage greater policy differentiation (i.e., that PR systems are associated with centrifugal incentives), which was questioned in Chapter 3. Moreover, this chapter reports a lack of evidence for the proposed causal mechanism, that is, centrist parties in plurality systems do not gain greater shares of the vote in comparison to their centrist counterparts in proportional systems. Hence, election rewards under plurality do not encourage more centrism and less extremism.

The second, central contribution of this study to our understanding of the consequences of electoral system design is to highlight the effect of electoral institutions on niche party competition. While there is some disagreement over the extent to which PR assists the electoral fortunes of any one type of niche party (e.g., extreme Right parties), the crucial observation from Chapter 4 is that disproportional systems do not exhibit niche party competition (or, at best, very little of it).

As a consequence, these disproportional systems are deprived of alternative channels of representation through which citizens may express their political preferences. Citizens in disproportional systems are unable to reward parties for policy distinctiveness. Moreover, parties in disproportional systems only respond to shifts in the mean voter position.

PR systems, like their disproportional counterparts, have mainstream parties that exhibit similar qualities. PR too rewards centrist parties and exhibits responsiveness to the mean voter position. However, proportional systems offer additional niche party outlets to their citizens: these parties' success in elections and policy responsiveness are characterized by the party distinctiveness and partisan constituency models. Thus, citizens in proportional systems have access to four models of political representation – the partisan constituency and general electorate models, and the party distinctiveness and party proximity models – while citizens in plurality systems have access to only two (the general electorate and party proximity models; see Figure 1.2).

7.3 WHERE DO WE GO FROM HERE?

These results invite further exploration. However, this study has natural limitations in terms of scope. It would be useful to conduct similar analyses along multiple political dimensions. Some of the challenges that will be faced in future investigations will be the statistical complexities associated with modeling elections on a multidimensional plane (Schofield 1997; Dow 2001). A more daunting task for cross-national studies will be to determine which are the salient dimensions of political competition, and how these change over time. In spite of these obstacles, the simple fact that I am able to cite authors in these areas leaves me with optimism.

Regarding breadth, although most Western European democracies have been covered in the previous chapters for a span of nearly thirty years which is significantly more than in similar studies, the analyses would benefit by expanding its scope to include even more democracies. Specifically, data collection on *emerging democracies* will make it possible to understand how the mechanics of representation change or remain unaltered as democracies age, by studying the causes and consequences of party policy positioning in these new democracies and comparing them to more stable and industrialized countries.[2] Glasgow, Golder, and Golder (2009) estimate the parameters of a mixed logit model to evaluate the factors that contribute toward becoming the prime ministerial party. They find that many of the dynamics that contribute to leading a governing coalition (e.g., party size) in older democracies operate similarly in younger ones.

In the previous chapters, a macro-level approach along the lines of Erikson et al. (2002; see also Bartle et al. 2007) has been adopted to address cross-national research questions. A preferred complementary approach would be to collect more information about each specific observation, and move toward filling the gap

---

[2] The analyses of OECD countries in Chapter 4 seem to sustain the observed relationship between the proportionality of election outcomes and party system size – and further, that proportionality encourages niche party competition, while disproportionality does not. As the temporal coverage of public opinion expands in these newer democracies, it will be rewarding for scholars who choose to study patterns of representation and particularly party responsiveness (e.g., Marks et al. 2006).

between inference and description. One possible route for adding this inference-laden description is to look systematically at specific party systems prior to, and after electoral rule changes. There are several cases that come to mind. One example would be to closely examine the differences that occurred within the French party system as the transition was made from the Fourth to the Fifth Republic in 1958 from a PR to a dual ballot system. More recent examples include the Italians' switch, caused by instability and scandal in 1993–94, from a PR to a mixed electoral system with three-fourth of the seats elected under single-member districts (SMD) and one-fourth under proportional electoral formulae. At approximately the same time, New Zealand changed from an electoral system with extremely disproportional outcomes with (SMD), to a mixed PR-plurality system in 1993 similar to the German system. For a brief period, the French returned to PR for the 1986 elections. The analyses here would benefit from complementary studies of quasi-experimental nature that would identify the causal effects of real changes to an existing set of electoral rules. The study by Robin Best (2009) represents a move in this direction where she examines the relationship between electoral rule changes and party system size. Relying on a series of error correction models, she is able to parse out existing short- and long-term effects of electoral rule changes on the number of effective parties that compete within a political system.[3]

7.4 NORMATIVE IMPLICATIONS

This study also has implications for how we conceive of choice and for our general evaluation of democracy. Section 7.3 suggests several alternatives for further empirical study. However, the most fascinating bit of potential research may be developing new ideas about how we conceive of "choice" in democracy. Prior studies suggest that having more party choices enhances citizen satisfaction by multiplying the number of expressive channels open to citizens. This is clear in the writings of Giovanni Sartori (1976: 27, italics original) who argues that "Parties are channels of expression. That is to say, parties belong, first and foremost, to the

---

[3] An additional feature of this study is that it examines the mediating role of state subventions, that is, state funding for political parties, on the relationship between electoral rules and party system size. She finds that increases in state subventions predictably expands party systems in the short term, presumably by offering potential parties financial incentives to compete in elections, but also finds that party systems then return to their long-term equilibrium. Best's emphasis on within country electoral rule changes is an excellent example of a complementary research design for examining the effects of electoral institutions. For another study of this genre on the 1993 switch to the Mixed Member Proportional system in New Zealand, see Vowles et al. (1998).

means of representation: They are an instrument, or an agency, for *representing* the people by *expressing* their demands."[4] In a recent paper, Ezrow and Xezonakis (forthcoming) build on Sartori's notion of choice by considering the representativeness of party choices and the consequences of representative choice for democracy. They report that while more parties matter for citizen satisfaction that, ceteris paribus, when these choices are more representative of the mean voter position, citizen satisfaction is enhanced.

The present study also addresses choice in the context of democracy through a slightly enhanced and nuanced lens. Rather than conceiving choice as the number of party policy offerings, this study has identified *choice in models* of political representation. In the previous chapters, four fundamentally different models of responsiveness and election outcomes have been identified and evaluated (i.e., the partisan constituency and general electorate models, and the party distinctiveness and party proximity models). Citizens in PR systems have access to all four of these models, and citizens in plurality systems to only two. The implication is that citizens are advantaged in systems that feature PR for the reasons cited above, but also because they have access to all four of these models rather than two. Put slightly differently, citizens in PR systems have access to mainstream and niche party competition (and their accompanying logics), while citizens in plurality systems have access only to mainstream party competition.

On balance, however, the study reflects well on the workings of *all* stable and developed democracies. Electorates' ideological preferences translate in systematic ways into election outcomes. Elections should link, in some fashion, the policy preferences of citizens to those of their elected representatives (Powell 2000). The previous chapters have demonstrated that this link exists and that the parties representing the greatest number of citizens' interests (i.e., the parties that are closer to the center of the underlying voter distribution) tend to receive more votes at election time. Groups of voters behave in a relatively sophisticated manner in Western European democracies, insofar as election outcomes reflect the average underlying ideological policy preference of citizens.[5] Participatory democracy is predicated on the notion that citizens are capable of expressing their policy interests in elections, and the aggregate patterns uncovered in the previous chapters reveal that this is indeed the case.

Furthermore, parties are responsive to the shifts in the ideological preferences of citizens over time. While PR systems appear to do better on this score because they have parties that respond to their supporters and parties that respond to the mean

---

[4] Furthermore, these systems may enhance satisfaction by minimizing the ideological distance between the governing position and the median citizen (Powell 2000; cf. Blais and Bodet 2006), and by narrowing gaps in satisfaction between winners and losers (Anderson and Guillory 1997).

[5] This finding is similar to the argument made in *The Rational Public* by Page and Shapiro (1992) about voters in the United States insofar as it implies that aggregates are more accurate at perceiving matters of representation than individuals.

voter, all systems do display responsiveness which is another crucial aspect of democracy.

Thus, this study concludes with a positive evaluation of democratic representation for the countries under review. While there are several pathways of representation and electoral systems vary in the number they offer, all democracies offer their citizens at least one mainstream channel. The contribution of this study has been to identify concrete manifestations of linkages between citizens and parties.

Appendix

Belgium

Belgian Communist Party (PCB)
Socialist Party-Flemish (SP)
Socialist Party-French (PS)
Ecologists (Ecolo/Agalev)
Francophone Front/Walloon Rally (FDF/RW)
People's Union (Volksunie)
Liberal Party-Flemish (PVV)
Liberal Reformation Party (PRL)
Flemish Christian Socialists (CVP)
French Christian Socialists (PSC)

Denmark

Socialist People's Party (Socialistisk Folkeparti)
Social Democratic Party (Socialdemokratiet)
Radical Liberal Party (Radikale)
Christian People's Party (Kristeligt Folkeparti)
Center Democrats (CD)
Liberal Party (Venstre)
Conservative Party (Konservative)
Progress Party (Fremkridtspartiet)

France

Communist (PCF)
Socialist (PSU)
Union for French Democracy (PR/UDF)
Gaullists – Rally for the Republic (RPR)
National Front (FN)

Germany

Greens (Grune)
German Social Democratic Party (SPD)
Free Democratic Party (FDP)
Christian Democratic Union/Christian Social
  Union (CDU/CSU)

Great Britain

Labour
Social and Liberal Democrats
Conservative

Greece

Left Coalition: Communist Party (KKE)
Panhellenic Socialist Movement Party
  (PASOK)
Democratic Renewal (Diana)
New Democracy (ND)

Ireland

Worker's Party
Labour
Green
Progressive Democrats
Republican Party (Fianna Fail)
United Ireland Party (Fine Gael)
Sinn Fein

Luxembourg

Communist Party of Luxembourg (KP/PC)
Green Alternative Party (GAP)
Socialist Workers Party (LSAP/POSL)
Democratic Party – Liberals (DP/PD)
National Movement (Bewegung)
Christian Social Party (CSV/PCS)

The Netherlands

Pacifist Socialist Party (PSP)
Radical Political Party (PPR)
Labor Party (PvdA)
Democrats'66 (D'66)
Christian Democratic Appeal (CDA)
People's Party for Freedom and Democracy
  (VVD)
Reformational Political Federation (RPF)
Reformed Political Union (GPV)
Political Reformed Party (SGP)
Center Party (CP)

Portugal

Communists (PCP)
Political Democratic Union (UDP)

Portuguese Democratic Movement
  (MDP/CDE)
Party of Democratic Renewal (PRD)
Socialist Party (PS)
Social Democratic Party (PSD)
People's Monarchy Party (PPM)
Christian Democratic Party (PDC)
Social Democratic Center (CDS)

Spain
Basque United People (HB)
United Left (IU)
Spanish Socialist Workers Party (PSOE)
Basque Nationalist Party (PNV)
Convergence and Union Party (CIU)
Democratic and Social Center (CDS)
Popular Coalition (CP)

Notes: Parties are ordered from "the left" to "the right" by country. The Castles–Mair survey does not place parties in Greece, Luxembourg, and Portugal. The citizen placements of parties contain the twelve existing European Community members at the time of the 1989 survey.

FIGURE A2.1 Underlying Ideological Distributions of Citizen Left–Right Preferences Across Western Europe Based on the Eurobarometer 31A (1989)

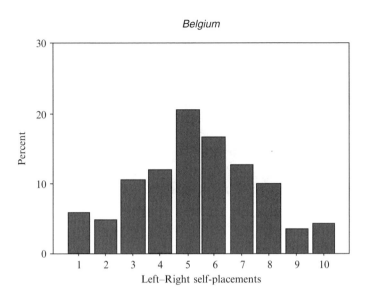

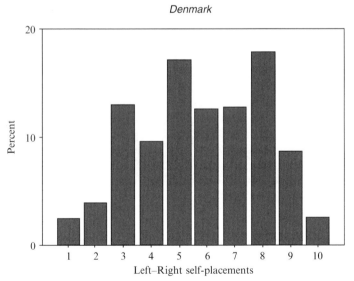

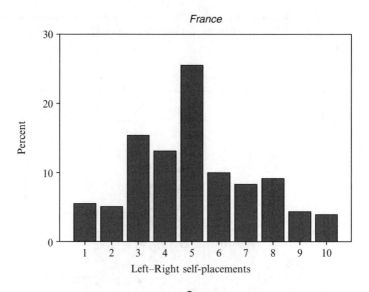

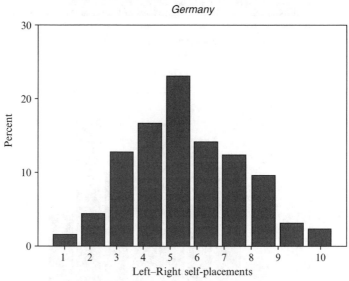

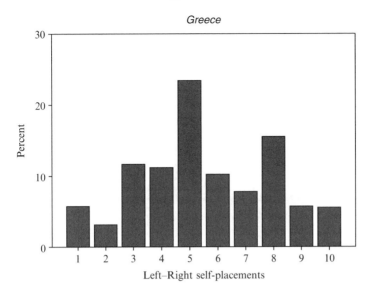

Greece

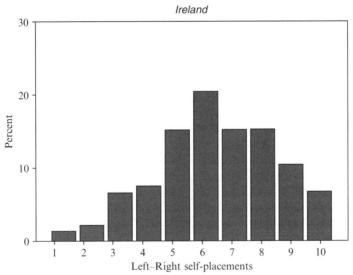

Ireland

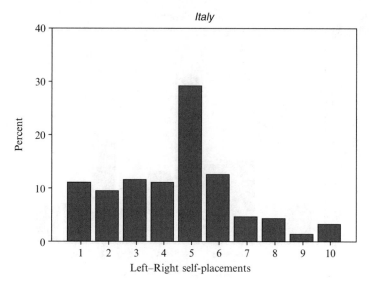

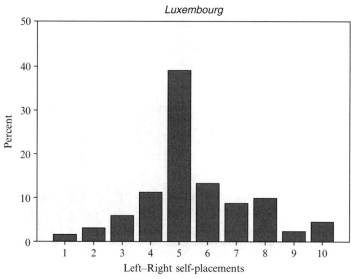

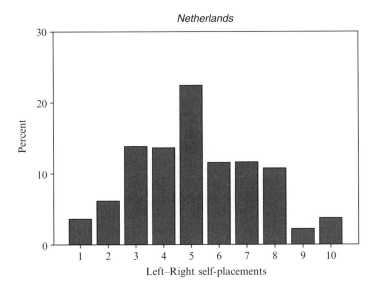

Netherlands

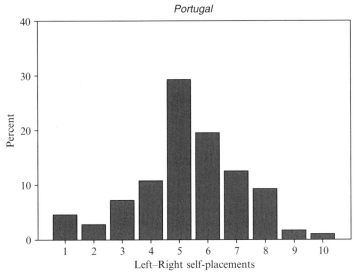

Portugal

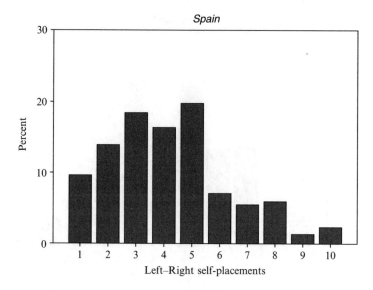

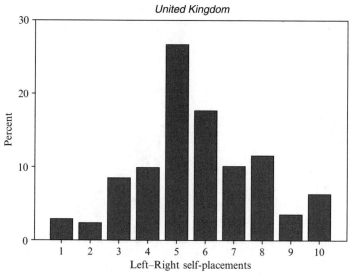

TABLE A3.1 *Data Points in the Empirical Analyses*

| Country | Source of parties' Left–Right placements | | | | | | Proportion-ality[c] | ENPP[d] |
| | Experts | | Citizens | | Manifestos | | | |
	WPE[a]	UPE[b]	WPE	UPE	WPE	UPE		
Australia	1.06	1.08	—	—	0.28	0.27	9.79	2.19
Belgium	0.74	0.75	0.71	0.70	0.31	0.28	16.85	5.49
Canada	0.44	0.57	—	—	0.30	0.34	7.78	2.35
Denmark	0.85	0.82	0.89	0.83	0.59	0.61	18.16	5.11
Finland	0.78	0.67	—	—	0.83	0.78	16.77	5.17
France	1.14	1.22	1.06	1.25	0.46	0.54	1.29	3.54
Germany	0.91	0.75	0.79	0.81	0.45	0.39	18.46	2.84
Greece	—	—	0.96	1.07	—	—	11.86	2.20
Ireland	0.45	0.87	0.75	1.13	0.65	0.88	16.74	2.76
Italy	0.82	0.91	0.91	0.76	0.33	0.37	16.12	5.22
Luxembourg	—	—	0.62	0.71	—	—	16.01	3.68
The Netherlands	0.67	0.71	0.81	0.91	0.31	0.26	18.65	4.68
Norway	0.94	0.95	—	—	0.41	0.52	15.24	3.61
Portugal	—	—	0.84	1.18	—	—	15.90	3.33
Spain	0.92	0.94	0.71	0.72	0.25	0.28	11.79	2.76
Sweden	0.80	0.79	—	—	0.37	0.39	18.17	3.52
UK	0.96	0.76	1.14	1.09	0.63	0.58	5.28	2.20
United States	0.42	0.42	—	—	0.47	0.47	4.34	2.41

Notes: Each parameter estimate reported in Tables 3.1 and 3.2 derives from these observations.

[a] WPE: Weighted measure of *average party policy extremism* (Equation 3.1).

[b] UPE: Unweighted measure of *average party policy extremism* (Equation 3.2).

[c] *Source*: "Index of Disproportionality" developed by Michael Gallagher (1991). The scale has been reversed so that higher scores now denote increased proportionality. The purpose of this transformation is to improve the substantive interpretation of the results.

[d] *Source*: Laakso and Taagepera (1979) measure of effective number of parliamentary parties (ENPP).

Appendix

TABLE A3.2 *Elections Included in the Empirical Analyses*

Country	Election	Included in empirical analyses based on the following
Australia	1983	Experts, manifestos
Belgium	1981	Experts, manifestos
Belgium	1987	Citizens
Canada	1980	Experts, manifestos
Denmark	1981	Experts, manifestos
Denmark	1988	Citizens
Finland	1983	Experts, manifestos
France	1981	Experts, manifestos
France	1988	Citizens
Germany	1983	Experts, manifestos
Germany	1990	Citizens
Greece	1989	Citizens
Ireland	1982	Experts, manifestos
Ireland	1989	Citizens
Italy	1983	Experts, manifestos
Italy	1987	Citizens
Luxembourg	1989	Citizens
The Netherlands	1982	Experts, manifestos
The Netherlands	1989	Citizens
Norway	1981	Experts, manifestos
Portugal	1987	Citizens
Spain	1982	Experts, manifestos
Spain	1987	Citizens
Sweden	1982	Experts, manifestos
United Kingdom	1983	Experts, manifestos
United Kingdom	1987	Citizens
United States	1980	Experts, manifestos

Notes: No country was observed more than once in any single set of statistical analyses.

TABLE A3.3 *Explaining Weighted Average Party Policy Extremism (WPE), Using a Dichotomous Measure of Electoral System Proportionality (Single-Member Districts (SMD) Versus Proportional Representation (PR))*

Left–Right party placements based on the following	Experts (1980–3)			Citizens (1987–90)			Manifestos (1980–3)		
Specification: Variable	Full	Bivariate	Bivariate	Full	Bivariate	Bivariate	Full	Bivariate	Bivariate
SMD/PR	−.06	−.02		−.30***	−.30***		−.007	.02	
	(.17)	(.12)		(.09)	(.08)		(.12)	(.09)	
Effective number of parliamentary parties	.03		.01	−.0001		−.03	.02		.02
	(.07)		(.05)	(.03)		(.04)	(.05)		(.04)
Constant	.74***	.80***	.75***	1.10***	1.10***	.98***	.38**	.43	.38**
	(.20)	(.10)	(.19)	(.11)	(.07)	(.14)	(.15)	(.08)	(.14)
N	15	15	15	12	12	12	15	15	15
Adjusted R²	−.15	−.08	−.07	.51	.56	−.02	−.15	−.07	−.06

Notes: Parameters are ordinary least squares (OLS) coefficients. Estimated standard errors are in parentheses. The dependent variable is the average party's policy distance from the Left–Right position of the mean voter weighted by its relative share of the vote, divided by the standard deviation of voter Left–Right self-placements (refer to Equation 3.1). *SMD/PR* is a dichotomous measure of electoral system proportionality that is equal to one when the district magnitude is greater than one.

$*p = .10$, $**p = .05$, $***p = .01$, two-tailed test

TABLE A3.4 *Explaining Unweighted Average Party Policy Extremism (UPE), Using a Dichotomous Measure of Electoral System Proportionality (Single-Member Districts (SMD) Versus Proportional Representation (PR))*

Left–Right party placements based on the following	Experts (1980–3)			Citizens (1987–90)			Manifestos (1980–3)		
Specification: Variable	Full	Bivariate	Bivariate	Full	Bivariate	Bivariate	Full	Bivariate	Bivariate
SMD/PR	-.01	-.001		-.23	-.28*		.04	.03	
	(.15)	(.11)		(.14)	(.14)		(.14)	(.11)	
Effective Number of Parliamentary Parties (ENPP)	.01		.02	-.06		-.09*	-.01		.004
	(.06)		(.06)	(.04)		(.05)	(.06)		(.04)
Constant	.79***	.81***	.82***	1.34***	1.17***	1.25***	.46**	.44***	.45**
	(.17)	(.09)	(.18)	(.18)	(.12)	(.18)	(.17)	(.09)	(.16)
N	15	15	15	12	12	12	15	15	15
Adjusted R²	-.17	-.08	-.14	.30	.24	.19	-.16	-.07	-.08

Notes: Parameters are ordinary least squares (OLS) coefficients. Estimated standard errors are in parentheses The dependent variable is the average party's policy distance from the Left–Right position of the mean voter, divided by the standard deviation of voter Left–Right self-placements (refer to Equation 3.2). *SMD/PR* is a dichotomous measure of electoral system proportionality that is equal to 1 when the district magnitude is greater than 1.

*p = .10, **p = .05, ***p = .01, two-tailed test

TABLE A3.5 *Explaining Weighted Average Party Policy Extremism (WPE), Using "Effective District Magnitude" to Measure Proportionality*

Left–Right party placements based on the following	Experts (1980–3)		Citizens (1987–90)			Manifestos (1980–3)		
Specification: Variable	Full	Bivariate	Full	Bivariate	Bivariate	Full	Bivariate	Bivariate
Effective district magnitude	−.002	−.001	−.0009	−.002		−.003	−.001	
	(.004)	(.003)	(.003)	(.002)		(.003)	(.002)	
Effective number of parliamentary parties (ENPP)	.03	.01	−.02		−.03	.04		.02
	(.06)	(.05)	(.05)		(.04)	(.04)		(.04)
Constant	.71***	.76***	.95***	.87***	.96***	.33**	.46***	.38**
	(.20)	(.19)	(.16)	(.06)	(.15)	(.15)	(.05)	(.14)
N	15	15	12	12	12	15	15	15
Adjusted R²	−.13	−.07	−.14	−.05	−.03	−.06	−.05	−.06

Notes: Parameters are ordinary least squares (OLS) coefficients. Estimated standard errors are in parentheses. The dependent variable is the average party's policy distance from the Left–Right position of the mean voter weighted by its relative share of the vote, divided by the standard deviation of voter Left–Right self-placements. *Effective district magnitude* is a measure developed in Taagepera and Shugart (1989, chapter 12), and it is computed by dividing the number of representatives by the number of districts.

*p = .10, **p = .05, ***p = .01, two-tailed test

TABLE A3.6 *Explaining Unweighted Average Party Policy Extremism (UPE), Using "Effective District Magnitude" to Measure Proportionality*

Left–Right party placements based on the following	Experts (1980–3)			Citizens (1987–90)			Manifestos (1980–3)		
Specification: Variable	Full	Bivariate	Bivariate	Full	Bivariate	Bivariate	Full	Bivariate	Bivariate
Effective district magnitude	−.002 (.003)	−.001 (.003)		−.00006 (.003)	−.003 (.003)		−.004 (.003)	−.003 (.003)	
Effective number of parliamentary parties (ENPP)	.02 (.05)		.002 (.04)	−.08 (.06)		−.08 (.05)	.04 (.05)		.006 (.04)
Constant	.76*** (.18)	.83*** (.06)	.80*** (.17)	1.23*** (.20)	.97*** (.08)	1.24*** (.18)	.38** (.17)	.49*** (.06)	.44** (.16)
N	15	15	15	12	12	12	15	15	15
Adjusted R²	−.13	−.06	−.08	.08	−.02	.17	−.05	−.008	−.08

Notes: Parameters are ordinary least squares (OLS) coefficients. Estimated standard errors are in parentheses. The dependent variable is the average party's policy distance from the Left–Right position of the mean voter, divided by the standard deviation of voter Left–Right self-placements (refer to Equation 3.2). *Effective district magnitude* is a measure developed in Taagepera and Shugart (1989, chapter 12), and it is computed by dividing the number of representatives by the number of districts.

*p = .10, **p = .05, ***p = .01, two-tailed test

TABLE A3.7 *Explaining Weighted Average Party Policy Extremism (WPE), Using Effective Thresholds to Measure Proportionality*

Left–Right party placements based on the following	Experts (1980–3)			Citizens (1987–90)			Manifestos (1980–3)		
Specification: Variable	Full	Bivariate	Bivariate	Full	Bivariate	Bivariate	Full	Bivariate	Bivariate
Effective threshold[a]	.0009	−.0003		.01***	.009***		.002	−.0002	
	(.006)	(.004)		(.003)	(.003)		(.005)	(.003)	
Effective number of parliamentary parties (ENPP)	.02		.01	.04		−.03	.03		.02
	(.08)		(.05)	(.03)		(.04)	(.06)		(.04)
Constant	.71*	.80***	.76***	.57***	.75***	.96***	.29	.44***	.38**
	(.36)	(.09)	(.19)	(.16)	(.04)	(.15)	(.27)	(.07)	(.14)
N	15	15	15	12	12	12	15	15	15
Adjusted R²	−.16	−.08	−.07	.49	.47	−.03	−.13	−.08	−.06

Notes: Parameters are ordinary least squares (OLS) coefficients. Estimated standard errors are in parentheses. The dependent variable is the average party's policy distance from the Left–Right position of the mean voter weighted by its relative share of the vote, divided by the standard deviation of voter Left–Right self-placements (refer to Equation 3.1).

[a]*Source:* Lijphart (1994: 27). *p= .10, **p = .05, ***p = .01, two-tailed test

TABLE A3.8 *Explaining Unweighted Average Party Policy Extremism (UPE), Using Effective Thresholds to Measure Proportionality*

Left–Right party placements based on the following	Experts (1980–3)		Citizens (1987–90)		Manifestos (1980–3)	
Specification: Variable	Full	Bivariate	Full	Bivariate	Full	Bivariate
Effective threshold[a]	.002	.0006	.01*	.01**	.002	.0005
	(.006)	(.004)	(.005)	(.004)	(.005)	(.004)
Effective number of parliamentary parties (ENPP)	.02	.002	−.02	−.08	.02	.006
	(.07)	(.04)	(.05)	(.05)	(.06)	(.04)
Constant	.71**	.80*** / .80***	.88***	.80*** / 1.24***	.37	.46*** / .44**
	(.31)	(.08) / (.17)	(.23)	(.06) / (.18)	(.30)	(.07) / (.16)
N	15	15 / 15	12	12 / 12	15	15 / 15
Adjusted R^2	−.16	−.07 / −.08	.38	.43 / .17	−.16	−.08 / −.08

Notes: Parameters are ordinary least squares (OLS) coefficients. Estimated standard errors are in parentheses. The dependent variable is the average party's policy distance from the Left–Right position of the mean voter, divided by the standard deviation of voter Left–Right self-placements (refer to Equation 3.2).

Source: Lijphart (1994: 27). *p= .10, **p = .05, ***p = .01, two-tailed test

[a]Source: Lijphart (1994: 27).

TABLE A3.9 *Explaining Weighted Average Party Policy Extremism (WPE), Using the Effective Number of Elective Parties (ENEP) to Measure the Number of Parties*

Left–Right party placements based on the following	Experts (1980–3)			Citizens (1987–90)			Manifestos (1980–3)		
Specification: Variable	Full	Bivariate	Bivariate	Full	Bivariate	Bivariate	Full	Bivariate	Bivariate
Degree of proportionality	−.008	−.004		−.02**	−.02**		.0009	.001	
	(.01)	(.01)		(.007)	(.006)		(.008)	(.008)	
ENEP	.03		.02	−.003		−.02	.005		.001
	(.04)		(.04)	(.02)		(.03)	(.03)		(.03)
Constant	.77***	.85***	.71***	1.13***	1.12***	.92***	.41**	.43***	.42***
	(.18)	(.15)	(.16)	(.12)	(.09)	(.13)	(.14)	(.11)	(.12)
N	15	15	15	12	12	12	15	15	15
Adjusted R^2	−.09	−.06	−.05	.38	.44	−.06	−.16	−.07	−.07

Notes: Parameters are ordinary least squares (OLS) coefficients. Estimated standard errors are in parentheses. The dependent variable is the average party's policy distance from the Left–Right position of the mean voter weighted by its relative share of the vote, divided by the standard deviation of voter Left–Right self-placements (refer to Equation 3.1). The definitions of the independent variables are given in the text. The ENEP measure is developed by Laakso and Taagepera (1979) and is calculated as $N = 1/\Sigma v_i^2$, where v_i is the proportion of votes of the *i*th party represented in the main legislative body.

$*p = .10$, $**p = .05$, $***p = .01$, two-tailed test

TABLE A3.10 *Explaining Unweighted Average Party Policy Extremism (UPE), Using the Effective Number of Elective Parties (ENEP) to Measure the Number of Parties*

Left–Right party placements based on the following	Experts (1980–3)		Citizens (1987–90)			Manifestos (1980–3)		
Specification: Variable	Full	Bivariate	Full	Bivariate	Bivariate	Full	Bivariate	Bivariate
Degree of proportionality	−.01	−.003	−.02	−.02*		.001	.0007	
	(.01)	(.01)	(.01)	(.01)		(.01)	(.009)	
ENEP	.02	.009	−.04		−.06	−.009		−.01
	(.04)	(.03)	(.03)		(.04)	(.04)		(.03)
Constant	.81***	.77***	1.34***	1.21***	1.15***	.48***	.45***	.49***
	(.16)	(.14)	(.18)	(.14)	(.16)	(.16)	(.13)	(.14)
N	15	15	12	12	12	15	15	15
Adjusted R²	−.13	−.07	.27	.24	.11	−.16	−.08	−.08

Notes: Parameters are ordinary least squares (OLS) coefficients. Estimated standard errors are in parentheses. The dependent variable is the average party's policy distance from the Left–Right position of the mean voter, divided by the standard deviation of voter Left–Right self-placements (refer to Equation 3.2). The ENEP measure is developed by Laakso and Taagepera (1979) and is calculated as $N = 1/\Sigma v_i^2$, where v_i is the proportion of votes of the *i*th party represented in the main legislative body.

*$p = .10$, **$p = .05$, ***$p = .01$, two-tailed test

TABLE A3.11 *Explaining Weighted Average Party Policy Extremism (WPE), Measuring the Number of Parties Based on 5% Thresholds*

Left–Right party placements based on the following

Specification: Variable	Experts (1980–3) Full	Experts (1980–3) Bivariate	Citizens (1987–90) Full	Citizens (1987–90) Bivariate	Manifestos (1980–3) Full	Manifestos (1980–3) Bivariate
Degree of proportionality	−.01	−.004	−.02**	−.02**	−.001	.001
	(.01)	(.01)	(.009)	(.006)	(.009)	(.008)
Number of parties based on a 5% threshold	.06	.04	−.02	−.02	.02	.02
	(.05)	(.04)	(.02)	(.03)	(.04)	(.03)
Constant	.68***	.85***	1.18***	1.12***	.36**	.43***
	(.18)	(.15)	(.13)	(.09)	(.15)	(.11)
		.62***		.96***		.35**
		(.17)		(.14)		(.13)
N	15	15	12	12	15	15
		15		12		15
Adjusted R²	.01	−.06	.40	.44	−.12	−.07
		.001		−.03		−.04

Notes: Parameters are ordinary least squares (OLS) coefficients. Estimated standard errors are in parentheses. The dependent variable is the average party's policy distance from the Left–Right position of the mean voter weighted by its relative share of the vote divided by the standard deviation of voter Left–Right self-placements (refer to Equation 3.1). The *number of parties based on a 5% threshold* is equal to the number of parties that received at least 5% of the national vote in an election.

*p = .10, **p = .05, ***p = .01, two-tailed test

TABLE A3.12 *Explaining Weighted Average Party Policy Extremism (UPE), Measuring the Number of Parties Based on 5% Thresholds*

Left–Right party placements based on the following

Specification: Variable	Experts (1980–3)			Citizens (1987–90)			Manifestos (1980–3)		
	Full	Bivariate	Bivariate	Full	Bivariate	Bivariate	Full	Bivariate	Bivariate
Degree of proportionality	−.007	−.003		−.02*	−.02*		−.0006	.0007	
	(.01)	(.01)		(.01)	(.01)		(.01)	(.009)	
Number of parties based on a 5% threshold	.03		.02	−.02		−.03	.01		.01
	(.04)		(.04)	(.04)		(.04)	(.04)		(.04)
Constant	.78***	.86***	.74***	1.29***	1.21***	1.06***	.43**	.45***	.42**
	(.17)	(.13)	(.16)	(.21)	(.14)	(.19)	(.17)	(.13)	(.15)
N	15	15	15	12	12	12	15	15	15
Adjusted R²	−.11	−.07	−.06	.18	.24	−.04	−.16	−.08	−.07

Notes: Parameters are ordinary least squares (OLS) coefficients. Estimated standard errors are in parentheses. The dependent variable is the average party's policy distance from the Left–Right position of the mean voter divided by the standard deviation of voter Left–Right self-placements (refer to Equation 3.2). The *number of parties based on a 5% threshold* is equal to the number of parties that received at least 5% of the national vote in an election.

*p = .10, **p = .05, ***p = .01, two-tailed test

Table A3.13 *Explaining Weighted Average Party Policy Extremism (WPE), Based on the Variances of Party Positions and Voters' Left–Right Self-placements*

Left–Right party placements based on the following	Experts (1980–3)			Citizens (1987–90)			Manifestos (1980–3)		
Specification: Variable	Full	Bivariate	Bivariate	Full	Bivariate	Bivariate	Full	Bivariate	Bivariate
Degree of proportionality	**−.02**	**−.01**		**−.04*****	**−.04*****		**.004**	**.01**	
	(.02)	**(.02)**		**(.01)**	**(.01)**		**(.01)**	**(.01)**	
Effective number of parliamentary parties (ENPP)	.09		.02	−.02		−.10	.02		.03
	(.09)		(.08)	(.05)		(.07)	(.07)		(.05)
Constant	.78**	.95***	.72***	1.53***	1.48***	1.28***	.19	.22	.20
	(.29)	(.22)	(.29)	(.20)	(.15)	(.26)	(.21)	(.15)	(.19)
N	15	15	15	12	12	12	15	15	15
Adjusted R²	−.05	−.03	−.07	.55	.58	.11	−.14	−.05	−.05

Notes: Parameters are ordinary least squares (OLS) coefficients. Estimated standard errors are in parentheses. The dependent variable is the average party's *squared* policy distance from the Left–Right position of the mean voter weighted by its relative share of the vote, divided by the *variance* of voter Left–Right self-placements (refer to Equation 3.1). The definitions of the independent variables are given in the text.

p = .10, **p* = .05, ***p* = .01, two-tailed test

TABLE A3.14 *Explaining Unweighted Average Party Policy Extremism (UPE), Based on the Variances of Party Positions and Voters' Left–Right Self-placements*

Left–Right party placements based on the following	Experts (1980–3)			Citizens (1987–90)			Manifestos (1980–3)		
Specification: Variable	Full	Bivariate	Bivariate	Full	Bivariate	Bivariate	Full	Bivariate	Bivariate
Degree of proportionality	**–.01**	**–.005**		**–.02**	**–.04**		**.007**	**.007**	
	(.02)	**(.02)**		**(.02)**	**(.02)**		**(.02)**	**(.01)**	
Effective number of parliamentary parties (ENPP)	.05		.02	–.13		–.18†	–.004		.02
	(.10)		(.08)	(.11)		(.10)	(.08)		(.06)
Constant	.85**	.95***	.81**	1.93***	1.62***	1.78***	.25	.24	.27
	(.31)	(.23)	(.29)	(.42)	(.33)	(.39)	(.24)	(.18)	(.23)
N	15	15	15	12	12	12	15	15	15
Adjusted R^2	–.13	–.07	–.07	.17	.13	.17	–.14	–.05	–.07

Notes: Parameters are ordinary least squares (OLS) coefficients. Estimated standard errors are in parentheses. The dependent variable is the average party's *squared* policy distance from the Left–Right position of the mean voter divided by the *variance* of voter Left–Right self-placements. The definitions of the independent variables are given in the text.

*$p = .10$, **$p = .05$, ***$p = .01$, two-tailed test; † $p = .103$

TABLE A3.15 *Explaining Weighted and Unweighted Average Party Policy Extremism (WPE and UPE), Relying on the Huber–Inglehart (1995) Survey of Experts*

	WPE			UPE		
Specification: Variable	Full	Bivariate	Bivariate	Full	Bivariate	Bivariate
Degree of proportionality	−.02	−.01		−.01	−.01	
	(.01)	**(.01)**		**(.01)**	**(.01)**	
Effective number of *parliamentary parties (ENPP)*	.07		.04	.07		.04
	(.05)		(.05)	(.05)		(.05)
Constant	.69***	.88***	.59**	.74***	.91***	.66***
	(.18)	(.15)	(.19)	(.19)	(.15)	(.19)
N	10	10	10	10	10	10
Adjusted R^2	.14	.003	−.04	.03	−.07	−.03

Notes: Parameters are ordinary least squares (OLS) coefficients. Estimated standard errors are in parentheses. The weighted version of the dependent variable is computed based on the average party's policy distance from the Left–Right position of the mean voter weighted by its relative share of the vote, divided by the standard deviation of voter Left–Right self-placements (refer to Equation 3.1). The unweighted version is calculated as the average party's policy distance from the Left–Right position of the mean voter, divided by the standard deviation of voter Left–Right self-placements (refer to Equation 3.2). The definitions of the independent variables are given in the text.

The number of observations is reduced to ten for this set of analyses, because the Huber and Inglehart study did not ask experts to place parties in Luxembourg and Greece; and Powell (2000) does not report the standard deviations of voters' Left–Right self-placements for the early 1990s.

*p = .10, **p = .05, ***p = .01, two-tailed test

Appendix

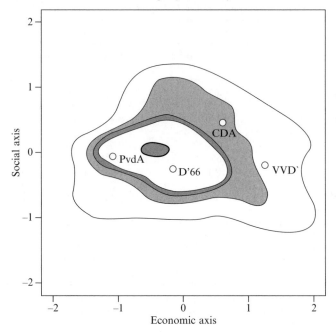

FIGURE A3.1a Spatial Mapping of Party Competition in the Netherlands
Source: Schofield and Sened (2006: 134).

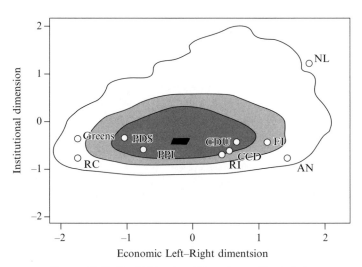

FIGURE A3.1b Spatial Mapping of Party Competition in Italy

Notes: Distribution of Italian voter ideal points and party positions in 1996. The contours give the 95%, 75%, 50%, and 10% highest density regions of the distribution.
Source: Schofield and Sened (2006: 116).

Multiparty democracy

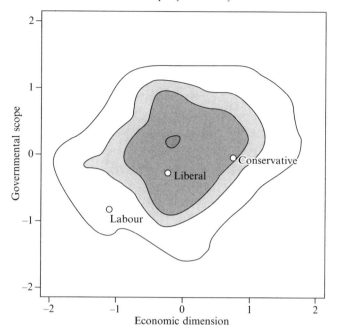

FIGURE A3.1c (2006) Spatial Mapping of Party Competition in Britain

Notes: Distribution of voter ideal points and party positions in Britain in the 1979 election, for a two-dimensional model, showing the highest density contours of the sample voter distribution at the 95%, 75%, 50%, and 10% levels.
Source: Schofield and Sened (2006: 152).

Political realignments in the United States

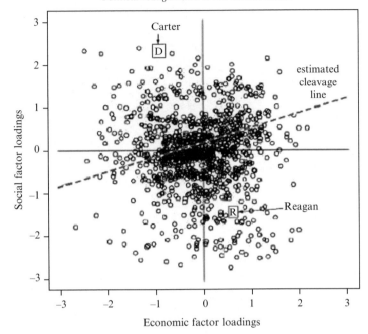

FIGURE A3.1d Spatial Mapping of Candidate Competition in the United States

Notes: The two-dimensional factor space, with voter positions and Carter's and Reagan's respective policy in1980, with linear estimated probability vote functions (log likelihood = -372).
Source: Schofield and Sened (2006: 187).

TABLE A4.1 *Disproportionality Scores and the Size and Number of Niche Parties, Stratified by Country and Election Year*

Country	Election year	Niche	Niche vote	Disproportionality[a]	EFFNv[b]	EffNs[c]
Australia	1977	0	0	14.93	3.11	2.46
Australia	1980	0	0	8.25	2.81	2.66
Australia	1983	0	0	10.31	2.67	2.24
Australia	1984	0	0	7.95	2.79	2.43
Australia	1987	0	0	10.42	2.9	2.28
Australia	1990	0	0	12.48	3.37	2.35
Australia	1993	0	0	8.12	2.91	2.39
Australia	1996	0	0	10.97	3.21	2.62
Australia	1998	0	0	10.87	3.44	2.48
Australia	2001	0	0	9.37	3.44	2.48
Austria	1979	0	0	0.93	2.27	2.22
Austria	1983	0	0	2.44	2.4	2.26
Austria	1986	1	4.82	0.93	2.72	2.63
Austria	1990	1	4.78	2.07	3.16	2.99
Austria	1994	1	7.31	1.03	3.87	3.73
Austria	1995	1	4.81	1.03	3.59	3.49
Austria	1999	1	7.4	3.53	3.82	3.41
Austria	2002	2	9.47	1.33	3.02	2.88
Belgium	1977	0	0	2.52	5.69	5.24
Belgium	1978	0	0	2.81	7.5	6.8
Belgium	1981	2	4.84	4.17	9.01	7.62
Belgium	1985	2	6.25	3.31	8.15	7
Belgium	1987	2	6.05	3.24	8.14	7.13
Belgium	1991	2	9.93	3.49	9.81	8.41
Belgium	1995	2	8.44	3.04	9.47	8.03
Belgium	1999	2	14.35	2.99	10.28	9.05
Belgium	2003	1	3.06	5.16	8.84	7.03
Canada	1979	0	0	10.41	3.09	2.45
Canada	1980	0	0	8.72	2.93	2.39
Canada	1984	0	0	20.91	2.74	1.69
Canada	1988	0	0	11.33	3.04	2.33
Canada	1993	0	0	17.67	3.93	2.35
Canada	1997	0	0	13.26	4.09	2.98
Canada	2000	0	0	13.56	3.77	2.54
Czech Republic	1990	1	13.2	11.54	3.5	2.22
Czech Republic	1992	2	19.99	8.57	7.31	4.8
Czech Republic	1996	2	18.34	5.55	5.33	4.15
Czech Republic	1998	2	11.03	5.7	4.69	3.71
Czech Republic	2002	1	18.51	5.73	4.82	3.67
Denmark	1977	3	10.23	0.41	5.23	5.17
Denmark	1979	3	12.43	1.49	4.99	4.83
Denmark	1981	3	10.07	1.57	5.76	5.47
Denmark	1984	3	14.86	1.38	5.24	5.04
Denmark	1987	2	16.74	2.11	5.82	5.31
Denmark	1988	1	13.01	2.34	5.83	5.31
Denmark	1990	1	8.3	2.62	4.85	4.36

(*continued*)

Appendix

TABLE A4.1 Continued

Country	Election year	Niche	Niche vote	Disproportionality[a]	EFFNv[b]	EffNs[c]
Denmark	1994	2	10.43	1.57	4.76	4.54
Denmark	1998	3	17.67	0.42	4.73	4.71
Denmark	2001	3	20.77	1.58	4.69	4.48
Finland	1979	1	17.9	2.68	5.75	5.21
Finland	1983	2	15.38	2.19	5.44	5.14
Finland	1987	1	17.67	4.98	6.13	4.93
Finland	1991	2	16.9	3.24	6.03	5.23
Finland	1995	2	17.68	3.81	5.82	4.88
Finland	1999	2	18.15	3.24	5.93	5.15
Finland	2003	2	17.94	3.16	5.65	4.93
France	1978	1	20.61	6.57	5.08	4.2
France	1981	1	16.13	16.04	4.13	2.68
France	1986	2	19.52	7.23	4.65	3.9
France	1988	2	20.96	11.84	4.4	3.07
France	1993	3	29.66	25.25	6.89	2.86
France	1997	4	31.08	17.69	6.56	3.54
France	2002	3	9.36	21.95	5.22	2.26
Germany	1976	0	0	0.59	2.91	2.85
Germany	1980	0	0	1.41	3.1	2.96
Germany	1983	1	5.57	0.5	3.22	3.16
Germany	1987	1	8.26	0.76	3.56	3.47
Germany	1990	2	3.63	4.63	3.75	3.17
Germany	1994	2	11.66	2.22	3.75	3.45
Germany	1998	2	11.8	3.15	3.78	3.31
Germany	2002	2	12.55	4.61	4.09	3.38
Great Britain	1979	0	0	11.58	2.87	2.15
Great Britain	1983	0	0	17.45	3.46	2.09
Great Britain	1987	0	0	14.95	3.33	2.17
Great Britain	1992	0	0	13.55	3.06	2.27
Great Britain	1997	1	0.41	16.51	3.22	2.13
Great Britain	2001	1	0.67	17.77	3.33	2.17
Great Britain	2005	0	0	16.73	3.59	2.46
Greece	1977	1	9.36	13.58	3.73	2.45
Greece	1981	1	10.94	8.4	2.69	2.09
Greece	1985	1	9.89	7.08	2.58	2.15
Greece	June, 1989	1	13.13	4.37	2.73	2.4
Greece	November, 1989	1	10.97	3.94	2.56	2.32
Greece	1990	1	10.28	3.97	2.63	2.37
Greece	1993	1	4.54	7.57	2.63	2.17
Greece	1996	2	10.73	9.45	3.07	2.36
Greece	2000	2	8.73	6.78	2.64	2.21
Hungary	1990	0	0	13.75	7.05	3.77
Hungary	1994	0	0	16.18	5.74	2.9
Hungary	1998	1	5.57	10.88	5.18	3.45
Hungary	2002	0	0	8.2	2.94	2.21

Country	Election year	Niche	Niche vote	Disproportionality[a]	EFFNv[b]	EffNs[c]
Iceland	1978	1	22.87	3.39	4.21	3.85
Iceland	1979	1	19.72	2.67	3.89	3.79
Iceland	1983	1	17.24	3.72	4.26	4.06
Iceland	1987	1	13.35	2.31	5.77	5.34
Iceland	1991	1	14.39	2.79	4.23	3.78
Iceland	1995	1	14.3	1.98	4.3	3.95
Iceland	1999	1	9.12	1.06	3.55	3.45
Iceland	2003	1	8.82	1.85	3.94	3.71
Ireland	1977	0	0	4.91	2.75	2.36
Ireland	1981	1	1.72	2.73	2.87	2.62
Ireland	February, 1982	1	2.18	1.69	2.69	2.53
Ireland	November, 1982	1	3.25	2.74	2.72	2.52
Ireland	1987	1	3.79	5.14	3.47	2.89
Ireland	1989	2	6.47	3.85	3.38	2.94
Ireland	1992	2	4.18	3.1	3.94	3.46
Ireland	1997	2	5.27	6.55	4.03	3
Ireland	2002	1	3.85	6.62	4.13	3.38
Italy	1976	3	41.25	2.75	3.53	3.16
Italy	1979	3	37.02	2.69	3.91	3.47
Italy	1983	4	38.16	2.57	4.52	4.02
Italy	1987	4	36.68	2.52	4.62	4.07
Italy	1992	5	38.55	2.51	6.63	5.71
Italy	1994	5	51.2	7.81	7.58	7.67
Italy	1996	5	57.9	6.91	7.17	6.09
Italy	2001	6	41.4	10.22	6.32	5.3
Japan	1976	1	10.38	7.44	4.07	3.18
Japan	1979	1	10.42	4	3.79	3.3
Japan	1980	1	9.83	6.59	3.45	2.74
Japan	1983	1	9.34	4.27	3.67	3.24
Japan	1986	1	8.79	7.22	3.38	2.58
Japan	1990	1	7.96	6.73	3.48	2.71
Japan	1993	1	7.7	6.36	5.29	4.2
Japan	1996	1	13.08	10.67	4.12	2.94
Japan	2000	1	11.23	11.49	4.56	3.17
Japan	2003	1	7.76	8.52	3.26	2.59
Luxembourg	1979	1	4.9	5.17	4.17	3.46
Luxembourg	1984	2	8.6	2.99	3.56	3.23
Luxembourg	1989	3	11.82	5.03	4.65	3.77
Luxembourg	1994	1	9.9	4.67	4.71	3.9
Luxembourg	1999	1	9.6	3.22	4.71	4.34
The Netherlands	1977	0	0	1.52	3.96	3.7
The Netherlands	1981	0	0	1.3	4.56	4.29
The Netherlands	1982	0	0	1.16	4.24	4.01
The Netherlands	1986	0	0	1.67	3.77	3.49
The Netherlands	1989	1	4.07	0.9	3.9	3.75

(*continued*)

TABLE A4.1 Continued

Country	Election year	Niche	Niche vote	Disproportionality[a]	EFFNv[b]	EffNs[c]
The Netherlands	1994	2	4.79	1.08	5.72	5.42
The Netherlands	1998	2	10.8	1.28	5.15	4.81
The Netherlands	2002	3	29.85	0.88	6.04	5.79
The Netherlands	2003	3	17.17	1.05	4.99	4.74
New Zealand	1978	0	0	15.55	2.87	2.01
New Zealand	1981	0	0	16.63	2.9	2.08
New Zealand	1984	0	0	15.4	2.99	1.98
New Zealand	1987	0	0	8.89	2.34	1.94
New Zealand	1990	0	0	17.24	2.77	1.74
New Zealand	1993	0	0	18.19	3.52	2.16
New Zealand	1996	0	0	3.43	4.27	3.76
New Zealand	1999	1	5.16	2.97	3.86	3.45
New Zealand	2002	1	7	2.37	4.17	3.76
Norway	1977	1	4.18	5.93	3.76	2.97
Norway	1981	1	4.94	4.94	3.87	3.19
Norway	1985	1	5.46	4.75	3.63	3.09
Norway	1989	1	10.08	3.68	4.84	4.23
Norway	1993	1	7.91	3.95	4.73	4.04
Norway	1997	1	6.01	3.44	4.94	4.36
Norway	2001	1	12.55	3.22	6.19	5.35
Poland	1991	3	7.74	3.62	13.82	10.86
Poland	1993	1	5.77	17.81	9.81	3.88
Poland	1997	0	0	10.63	4.59	2.95
Poland	2001	0	0	6.33	4.5	3.6
Portugal	1976	3	17.64	3.68	3.99	3.43
Portugal	1979	3	22.29	3.74	3	2.61
Portugal	1980	3	20.07	3.93	2.89	2.5
Portugal	1983	3	18.4	3.04	3.73	3.34
Portugal	1985	3	16.02	3.63	4.78	4.19
Portugal	1987	4	12.57	6.12	2.98	2.37
Portugal	1991	2	8.96	6.09	2.79	2.23
Portugal	1995	2	8.74	4.6	2.97	2.55
Portugal	1999	3	11.58	4.9	3.13	2.61
Portugal	2002	2	9.87	4.64	3.03	2.5
Slovakia	1990	2	16.43	3.54	5.81	4.98
Slovakia	1992	2	45.19	11.15	5.36	3.19
Slovakia	1994	4	47.72	5.94	5.81	4.41
Slovakia	1998	2	36.07	2.9	5.33	4.75
Slovakia	2002	2	25.88	6.97	8.87	6.12
Spain	1977	1	9.27	10.05	4.3	2.91
Spain	1979	1	10.8	10.56	4.25	2.81
Spain	1982	1	4.13	8.02	3.19	2.34
Spain	1986	1	3.83	7.19	3.59	2.68
Spain	1989	1	9.13	9.35	4.13	2.85
Spain	1993	1	9.63	7.08	3.52	2.67
Spain	1996	1	10.54	5.36	3.21	2.72

Country	Election year	Niche	Niche vote	Disproportionality[a]	EFFNv[b]	EffNs[c]
Spain	2000	1	5.45	6.1	3.12	2.48
Sweden	1976	1	4.75	1.23	3.57	3.45
Sweden	1979	1	5.61	1.27	3.63	3.48
Sweden	1982	1	5.56	2.4	3.39	3.13
Sweden	1985	1	5.36	1.35	3.52	3.39
Sweden	1988	2	11.37	2.45	3.92	3.67
Sweden	1991	2	7.89	2.86	4.57	4.19
Sweden	1994	2	11.19	1.18	3.65	3.5
Sweden	1998	2	16.49	0.97	4.55	4.29
Sweden	2002	2	13.04	1.52	4.51	4.23
Switzerland	1979	2	1.92	1.73	5.51	5.14
Switzerland	1983	2	4.7	2.94	6.04	5.31
Switzerland	1987	2	7.94	3.78	6.82	5.74
Switzerland	1991	4	11.16	2.6	7.38	6.7
Switzerland	1995	4	10.74	4.37	6.79	5.6
Switzerland	1999	4	9.02	3.17	5.87	5.16
Switzerland	2003	4	10.4	2.47	5.44	5.01
United States	1976	0	0	9.67	2.02	1.79
United States	1980	0	0	4.59	2.06	1.97
United States	1984	0	0	5.39	2.03	1.95
United States	1988	0	0	5.55	2.03	1.93
United States	1992	0	0	7.08	2.14	1.94
United States	1996	0	0	3.21	2.18	2
United States	2000	0	0	3.15	2.25	2.02
United States	2004	0	0	2.99	2.18	2

[a] *Source*: "Index of Disproportionality" developed by Michael Gallagher (1991). Gallagher and Mitchell (2008) report election year estimates in appendix B.

[b] *Source*: Laakso and Taagepera (1979) measures of the effective number of elective parties.

[c] *Source*: Laakso and Taagepera (1979) measure of the effective number of parliamentary parties.

Appendix

TABLE A5.1 *Niche Parties Included in the Empirical Analyses for Chapter 5*

Country	Niche party
Belgium	PCB (Communist)
	Ecologie (Green)
	Agalev (Green)
Denmark	Socialistisk Folkeparti (Communist)
France	PCF (Communist)
	FN (National)
Germany	Grune (Green)
Greece	K.K.E (Communist)
Ireland	Workers' Party (Communist)
	Green
Italy	PCI (Communist)
	DP (Communist)
	Verdi (Green)
	AN (National)
Luxembourg	KP/PC (Communist)
Portugal	PCP (Communist)
	UDP (Communist)
	PPM (National)
Spain	IU (Communist)

Notes: The Comparative Manifesto Project (CMP) designates to which "party family" a party belongs in their published CD-ROM. Approximately 1,000 respondents per country were asked to place their national political parties, including these niche parties, on a 1–10 Left–Right scale in the Eurobarometer 31A survey (1989).

TABLE A6.1 *List of Countries, Inter-Election Periods, Parties, Party Families, and Mean Left–Right Party Supporter Positions Included in the Empirical Analyses*

Country	Party	Party family	Mean Left–Right party supporter position
Inter-election period			
Austria			
1995–9; 1999–2003	Austrian Peoples' Party (ÖVP)	Conservative	5.84
	League of the Independents, later named Freedom Movement (VdU/FPÖ)	Liberal	6.63
	Social Democratic Party (SPÖ)	Social Democratic	4.33
	Green Alternative (GA)	Green	4.79
Belgium	Christian Social Party (PSC)	Christian Democratic	6.43
1974–7; 1977–8; 1979–81; 1985–7; 1987–91; 1991–5; 1995–9	Christian People's Party (CVP)	Christian Democratic	6.89
	Liberal Reformation Party (PRL)	Liberal	6.47
	Liberal Reformation Party – Francophone Democratic Front (PRL–FDF)	Liberal	6.22
	Flemish Liberals and Democrats (VLD)	Liberal	6.37
	Francophone Socialist Party (PS)	Social Democratic	3.94
	Flemish Socialist Party (SP)	Social Democratic	4.34
	AGALEV	Green	4.45
	ECOLA	Green	4.58
	Flemish Bloc (VB)	Nationalist	6.36
Denmark	Conservative People's Party (KF)	Conservative	7.33
1977–9; 1979–81; 1981–4; 1984–7; 1987–8; 1988–90; 1990–4; 1994–8; 1998–2001	Radical Party (RV)	Liberal	5.42
	Liberals (V)	Liberal	
	Social Democratic Party (SD)	Social Democratic	6.86
	Center Democrats (CD)	Social Democratic	4.95
	Socialist People's Party (SF)	Communist	6.42

(continued)

TABLE A6.1 Continued

Country	Party	Party family	Mean Left–Right party supporter position
	Progress Party (FP)	Nationalist	3.48
Finland	National Rally (KOK)	Conservative	7.91
1995–9; 1999–2003	Finnish Center (KESK)	Liberal	6.46
	Finnish Social Democrats (SSDP)	Social Democratic	4.48
	Left Wing Alliance (VL)	Communist	3.01
	Green Union (VL)	Green	5.23
France	Gaullists	Conservative	7.14
1978–81; 1981–6; 1986–8; 1988–93; 1993–7; 1997–2002	Rally for the Republic (RPR)	Conservative	7.18
	Union for French Democracy (UDF)	Conservative	6.43
	Socialist Party (PS)	Social Democratic	3.66
	French Communist Party (PCF)	Communist	2.59
Germany	Christian Democratic Party/Christian Social Union (CDU/CSU)	Christian Democratic	6.43
1976–80; 1980–3; 1983–7; 1987–90; 1990–4; 1994–8; 1998–2002	Free Democratic Party (FDP)	Liberal	5.86
	Social Democratic Party (SDP)	Social Democratic	4.40
	Party of German Socialism (PDS)	Communist	4.23
Greece	New Democracy (ND)	Christian Democratic	8.14
1981–5; 1985–9 (Jun); 1989 (June)–89 (Nov); 1989–90; 1990–3; 1993–6; 1996–2000	Panhellenic Socialist Movement (PASOK)	Social Democratic	4.59
	Communist Party of Greece (KKE)	Communist	2.12
	Progressive Left Coalition (SAP)	Communist	2.69

Country	Party	Party family	Mean Left–Right party supporter position
Ireland	Fianna Fail	Conservative	6.56
1977–81; 1981–2 (February); 1982 (February)–82 (November); 1982–7; 1987–9; 1989–92; 1992–7; 1997–2002	Fine Gail	Christian Democratic	6.37
	Progressive Democrats (PD)	Liberal	6.15
	Labour Party (LP)	Social Democratic	4.88
Italy	Italian Social Movement (AN)	Nationalist	8.26
1976–9; 1979–83; 1987–92; 1992–4; 1994–6; 1996–2001	Northern League (LN)	Nationalist	6.10
	Go Italy (FI)	Conservative	7.01
	Italian People's Party (PPI)	Christian Democratic	5.70
	Republican Party (PRI)	Liberal	4.95
	Italian Democratic Socialist Party (PSDI)	Social Democratic	4.50
	Socialist Party (PSI)	Social Democratic	3.62
	Newly Founded Communists (RC)	Communist	2.06
	Democrats of the Left (DS)	Communist	2.48
Luxembourg	Christian Social People's Party (PCS/CSV)	Christian Democratic	6.82
1979–84; 1984–9; 1989–94; 1994–9	Patriotic and Democratic Group (PD/DP)	Liberal	5.76
	Socialist Workers' Party (POSL/LSAP)	Social Democratic	4.20
	Communist Party (PCL/KPL)	Communist	3.14

(continued)

TABLE A6.1 Continued

Country	Party	Party family	Mean Left–Right party supporter position
The Netherlands 1977–81; 1981–2; 1982–6; 1986–9; 1989–94; 1994–8; 1998–2002	Christian Democratic Appeal (CDA)	Christian Democratic	6.67
	People's Party for Freedom and Democracy (VVD)	Liberal	6.84
	Labour Party (PvdA)	Social Democratic	3.76
	Democrats 66 (D'66)	Social Democratic	4.75
	Green Left (GL)	Green	3.34
Portugal 1987–91; 1991–5; 1995–9	Center Social Democrats (CDS/PP)	Conservative	7.37
	Popular Democratic Party (PPD/PSD)	Social Democratic	6.95
	Portuguese Socialist Party (PSP)	Social Democratic	4.63
	Unified Democratic Coalition, (CDU)	Communist	2.64
Spain 1986–9; 1989–93; 1993–6; 1996–2000	Popular Alliance (AP/PP)	Conservative	7.29
	Convergence and Union (CiU)	Conservative	5.33
	Spanish Socialist Workers' Party (PSOE)	Social Democratic	3.54
	Communist Party (IU)	Communist	2.74
Sweden 1994–8; 1998–2002	Moderate Coalition Party (MSP)	Conservative	7.80
	Christian Democratic Community Party (KdS)	Christian Democratic	6.48
	People's Party (FP)	Liberal	6.23
	Center Party (CP)	Liberal	5.90

Country	Party	Party family	Mean Left–Right party supporter position
	Social Democratic Labour Party (SdsP)	Social Democratic	4.18
	Communist Party (VP)	Communist	2.90
	Green Party	Green	4.63
United Kingdom	Conservative Party	Conservative	6.97
1979–83; 1983–7; 1987–92; 1992–7; 1997–2001	Liberal Democrats (LD)	Liberal	5.39
	Labour Party	Social Democratic	4.26

Notes: Parties are observed in at least three successive elections. The mean Left–Right party supporter position is calculated as the average of the mean party supporter positions for all of the elections in which the party is included in the empirical analysis.

TABLE A6.2 Citizen Mean Left–Right Self-Placements (Stratified by Year and Country)

Election year

Country	1973	1974	1975	1976	1977	1978	1979	1980	1981	1982	1983	1984	1985	1986	1987	1988	1989	1990	1991	1992	1993	1994	1995	1996	1997	1998	1999	2000	2001	2002
Belgium	5.67	5.76	—	6.00	6.02	6.03	5.82	6.39	5.75	5.83	5.79	5.74	5.71	5.71	5.50	5.62	5.53	5.50	5.55	5.42	5.38	5.15	5.36	5.36	5.29	5.33	5.10	5.20	5.17	5.20
Denmark	5.41	—	5.43	5.45	5.36	5.53	5.60	5.48	5.66	5.63	5.87	5.64	5.62	5.66	5.69	6.04	5.78	5.60	5.70	5.69	5.58	5.54	5.57	5.54	5.67	5.63	5.65	5.68	5.61	5.56
France	5.05	—	—	4.88	4.90	4.87	4.83	5.36	4.79	4.98	5.11	5.23	5.32	5.18	4.94	4.95	4.85	4.95	4.83	4.95	4.97	4.86	4.93	4.65	4.76	4.81	4.71	4.67	4.69	4.98
Germany	5.63	—	—	5.92	5.96	5.82	5.75	5.80	5.56	5.53	5.45	5.39	5.48	5.38	5.45	5.32	5.33	5.39	5.45	5.37	5.17	5.21	5.21	5.21	5.19	5.14	5.26	5.23	5.11	5.27
Ireland	6.30	—	—	5.99	6.42	6.22	6.11	5.84	6.25	6.19	5.99	6.25	6.18	6.08	6.22	6.22	6.05	5.69	5.66	5.64	5.57	5.72	4.78	5.61	5.53	5.60	5.60	5.60	5.53	5.57
Italy	4.69	—	—	4.39	4.40	4.42	4.31	4.52	4.51	4.62	4.63	4.62	4.68	4.69	4.70	4.82	4.65	4.63	4.76	4.77	4.73	5.11	5.04	5.02	5.20	5.17	5.33	5.30	5.25	5.35
Luxembourg	5.43	5.52	—	5.70	6.01	5.77	5.83	5.55	5.59	5.56	5.79	5.66	5.78	5.86	5.71	5.75	5.48	5.47	5.30	5.21	5.10	5.34	5.18	5.22	5.26	5.02	4.99	4.91	4.95	4.94
The Netherlands	5.80	—	—	5.92	5.72	5.43	5.53	5.55	5.59	5.46	5.50	5.30	5.37	5.26	5.29	5.33	5.31	5.22	5.39	5.40	5.40	5.33	5.39	5.23	5.17	5.23	5.20	5.10	5.06	5.25
Great Britain	5.37	5.57	—	5.97	5.89	5.72	5.79	5.72	5.59	5.74	5.72	5.74	5.79	5.62	5.83	5.77	5.57	5.40	5.59	5.54	5.39	5.23	5.23	5.20	5.05	5.15	5.03	5.16	5.08	4.96
Greece	—	—	—	—	—	—	—	5.15	5.68	4.95	5.16	5.21	5.11	5.44	5.48	5.43	5.57	5.68	5.77	5.80	5.57	5.68	5.51	5.52	5.34	5.55	5.69	5.77	5.25	5.62
Portugal	—	—	—	—	—	—	—	—	—	—	—	—	5.54	5.44	5.79	5.44	5.41	5.50	5.49	5.54	5.45	5.20	5.27	5.29	5.26	5.11	5.20	5.30	5.20	5.31
Spain	—	—	—	—	—	—	—	—	—	—	—	—	5.00	4.78	4.55	4.50	4.38	4.43	4.27	4.52	4.62	4.82	4.75	4.70	4.66	4.77	4.69	4.86	4.66	4.62
Finland	—	—	—	—	—	—	—	—	—	—	—	—	—	—	—	—	—	—	—	—	—	—	5.79	5.78	5.74	5.78	5.78	5.67	5.49	5.57
Sweden	—	—	—	—	—	—	—	—	—	—	—	—	—	—	—	—	—	—	—	—	—	—	5.29	5.24	5.32	5.38	5.43	5.19	5.32	5.24
Austria	—	—	—	—	—	—	—	—	—	—	—	—	—	—	—	—	—	—	—	—	—	—	5.27	5.14	4.78	4.75	5.12	4.88	5.16	4.93

Notes: The table entries represent the mean citizen Left–Right (1–10) self-placements, based on the Eurobarometer surveys from 1973 to 2002. Bold type denotes an election year. The four observations in 1974 and 1975 have been interpolated based on the 1973 and 1976 data (because the self-placement item is omitted from these survey years). The conclusions do not depend on the inclusion of these observations. The administration of the Eurobarometer surveys begins in Greece, Portugal, Spain, Finland, Sweden, and Austria at roughly the same time that these countries joined the European Union.

Bibliography

Abedi, Amir. 2002. "Challenges to Established Parties: The Effects of Party System Features on the Electoral Fortunes of Anti-Political-Establishment Parties." *European Journal of Political Research* 41: 551–83.

Achen, Christopher. 1977. "Measuring Representation: Perils of the Correlation Coefficient." *American Journal of Political Science* 21(4): 805–15.

——1978. "Measuring Representation." *American Journal of Political Science* 22(3): 475–510.

Adams, James. 1999. "Policy Divergence in Multiparty Probabilistic Spatial Voting." *Public Choice* 100: 103–22.

——2001. *Party Competition and Responsible Party Government: A Theory of Spatial Competition Based upon Insights from Behavioral Voting Research.* Ann Arbor, MI: University of Michigan Press.

——and Samuel Merrill, III. 1999. "Party Policy Equilibrium for Alternative Spatial Voting Models: An Application to the Norwegian Storting." *European Journal of Political Research* 36(October): 35–55.

————2000. "Spatial Models of Candidate Competition and the 1988 French Presidential Election: Are Presidential Candidates Vote-Maximizers?" *Journal of Politics* 62: 729–56.

————2005. "Parties' Policy Platforms and Elections Outcomes: The Three Faces of Policy Representation." *European Journal of Political Research* 44(6): 899–918.

————2009. "Policy-Seeking Parties in a Parliamentary Democracy with Proportional Representation: A Valence-Uncertainty Model." *British Journal of Political Science* 39 (3): 539–58.

——and Zeynep Somer-Topcu. 2009. "Moderate Now, Win Votes Later: The Electoral Consequences of Parties' Policy Shifts in Twenty-Five Postwar Democracies." *Journal of Politics* 71(2): 678–92.

————Forthcoming. "Do Parties Adjust Their Policies in Response to Rival Parties' Policy Shifts? Spatial Theory and the Dynamics of Party Competition in Twenty-Five Postwar Democracies." *British Journal of Political Science.*

——Ben Bishin, and Jay Dow. 2004. "Representation in Congressional Campaigns: Evidence for Directional/Discounting in U.S. Senate Elections." *Journal of Politics* 66: 348–73.

——Samuel Merrill, III, and Bernard Grofman. 2005. *A Unified Theory of Party Competition: A Cross-National Analysis Integrating Spatial and Behavioral Factors.* Cambridge, England: Cambridge University Press.

——Lawrence Ezrow, and Zeynep Somer-Topcu. 2008. *Is Anybody Listening? Evidence that Voters Do Not Respond to European Parties' Policy Programmes.* Presented at the 'Politics of Change' Workshop at the Vrije Universiteit, Amsterdam, June 13–14.

Adams, James. and Michael Clark, Lawrence Ezrow, and Garrett Glasgow. 2004. "Understanding Change and Stability in Party Ideologies: Do Parties Respond to Public Opinion or Past Election Results?" *British Journal of Political Science* 34: 589–610.

Adams, James, and Michael Clark, Lawrence Ezrow, and Garrett Glasgow. 2006. "Are Niche Parties Fundamentally Different from Mainstream Parties?: The Causes and Electoral Consequences of Western European Parties' Policy Shifts, 1976–1998." *American Journal of Political Science* 50(3): 513–29.

Aldrich, John. 1983*a*. "A Downsian Spatial Model with Party Activists." *American Political Science Review* 77: 974–90.

—— 1983*b*. "A Spatial Model with Party Activists: Implications for Electoral Dynamics." *Public Choice* 41: 63–100.

—— 1995. *Why Parties?*. Chicago, IL: University of Chicago Press.

Alesina and Rosenthal. 1995. *Partisan Politics, Divided Government, and the Economy.* Cambridge: Cambridge University Press. Chapters 1–4.

Alvarez, R. Michael and Jonathan Nagler. 1995. "Economics, Issues and the Perot Candidacy: Voter Choice in the 1992 Presidential Election." *American Journal of Political Science* 39: 714–44.

———— 1998. "When Politics and Models Collide: Estimating Models of Multiparty Elections." *American Journal of Political Science* 42: 55–96.

———— 2001. "Economic Voting in the United States: Methodological Issues and Research Agendas." Typescript.

———— 2004. "Party System Compactness: Consequences and Measures." *Political Analysis* 12: 46–62.

———— and Shaun Bowler. 2000*a*. "Issues, Economics, and the Dynamics of Multiparty Elections: The 1997 British General Election." *American Political Science Review* 42: 55–96.

———— and Jennifer Niemann. 2000*b*. "Measuring the Relative Impact of Issues and the Economy in Democratic Elections." *Electoral Studies* 19: 237–53.

Anderson, Christopher J. and Christine A. Guillory. 1997. "Political Institutions and Satisfaction with Democracy: A Cross-National Analysis of Consensus and Majoritarian Systems." *American Political Science Review* 91(1): 66–82.

Anderson, Simon and Gerhard Glomm. 1992. "Alienation, Indifference, and the Choice of Ideological Position." *Social Choice and Welfare* 9: 17–31.

Andrews, Josephine and Robert Jackman. 2008. "If Winning Isn't Everything, Why Do They Keep Score? Consequences of Electoral Performance for Party Leaders." *British Journal of Political Science* 38: 657–75.

—— and Jeannette Money. 2005. "Champions and Challengers: Ideology and the Success of Non-Established Parties in Established Party Systems." Typescript.

———— Forthcoming. "The Spatial Structure of Party Competition: Party Dispersion Within a Finite Policy Space." *British Journal of Political Science*.

Ansolabahere, Steve and James Snyder. 2000. "Valence Politics and Equilibrium in Spatial Election Models." *Public Choice* 103: 327–36.

Ansolabehere, Stephen, James Snyder, and Charles Stewart. 2001. "Candidate Positioning in U.S. House Elections." *American Journal of Political Science* 45: 136–59.

Arzeimer, Kai. 2009. "Contextual Factors and the Extreme Right Vote in Western Europe, 1980–2002." *American Journal of Political Science* 53(2): 259–75.

Austen-Smith, David and Jeffrey Banks. 1988. "Elections, Coalitions, and Legislative Outcomes." *American Political Science Review* 82: 405–22.

Axelrod, Robert. 1970. *Conflict of Interest*. Chicago, lll: Markhan.

Bartle, John, Sebastion Dellepiane, and James A. Stimson. 2007. "The Moving Centre." Paper prepared for the meetings of the European Consortium for Political Research, Pisa, Italy, September 6.

Beck, Nathaniel and Jonathan N. Katz. 1995. "What To Do (and What Not To Do) With Time-Series – Cross-Section Data." *American Political Science Review* 89: 634–47.

—— and Jonathan Katz. 1996. "Nuisance vs. Substance: Specifying and Estimating Time-Series-Cross-Section Models." *Political Analysis* 6: 1–36.

Benoit, Kenneth. 2006. "Duverger's Law and the Study of Electoral Systems." *French Politics* 4(1): 69–83.

—— Michael Laver, and Slava Mikhaylov. 2009. "Treating Words as Data with Error: Uncertainty in Text Statements of Policy Positions." *American Journal of Political Science* 53(2): 495–513.

Best, Robin. 2009. "Electoral Institutions and the Dynamics of Party System Size in Western Democracies, 1950–2005." Typescript.

Blais, Andre. 2000. *To Vote or Not to Vote: The Merits and Limits of Rational Choice Theory.* Pittsburgh, PA: University of Pittsburgh Press.

—— and Marc Andre Bodet. 2006. "Does Proportional Representation Foster Closer Congruence Between Citizens and Policy Makers?" *Comparative Political Studies* 39 (10): 1243–62.

—— and R. Kenneth Carty. 1990. "Does Proportional Representation Foster Voter Turnout?" *European Journal of Political Research* 18: 167–81.

Brambor, Thomas, William R. Clark, and Matthew Golder. 2006. "Understanding Interaction Models: Improving Empirical Analyses." *Political Analysis* 14(1): 63–82.

Braumoeller, Bear F. "Hypothesis Testing and Multiplicative Interaction Terms." *International Organization* 58: 807–20.

Brody, Richard A. and Benjamin I. Page. 1972. "Comment: The Assessment of Policy Voting." *American Political Science Review* 66(2): 450–8.

Budge, Ian. 1994. "A New Theory of Party Competition: Uncertainty, Ideology, and Policy Equilibria Viewed Temporally and Comparatively." *British Journal of Political Science* 24: 443–67.

—— and Michael McDonald. 2006. "Choices Parties Define: Policy Alternatives in Representative Elections – 17 Countries 1945–1998." *Party Politics* 12(4): 451–66.

—— David Robertsen, and Derek J. Hearl, eds. 1987. *Ideology, Strategy, and Party Change: Spatial Analyses of Post-War Election Programmes in 19 Democracies.* Cambridge: Cambridge University Press.

—— Lawrence Ezrow, and Michael M. McDonald. Forthcoming. "Ideology, Party Factionalism and Policy Change: An Integrated Dynamic Theory." *British Journal of Political Science.*

—— Hans-Dieter Klingemann, Andrea Volkens, Judith Bara, and Eric Tanenbaum. 2001. *Mapping Policy Preferences: Estimates for Parties, Electors, and Governments 1945–1998.* Oxford: Oxford University Press.

Burden, Barry. 2001. *Choices and Echoes in U.S. House Elections.* Presented at the Annual meeting of the Public Choice Society, San Antonio, TX, March 9–11.

Burden, Barry, and David Kimball. 1998. "A New Approach to the Study of Ticket-Splitting." *American Political Science Review* 92: 533–44.

Burt, Gordon. 1997. "Party Policy: Decision Rule or Chance? A Note on Budge's New Spatial Theory of Party Competition." *British Journal of Political Science* 27(4): 647–58.

Calvo, Ernesto and Timothy Hellwig. 2008. "Centripetal and Centrifugal Incentives Under Majoritarian Electoral Rules." Paper prepared for the "Analyzing European Politics in the 21st Century" Conference hosted by the European Union Center of Excellence at Texas A&M University, July 28–29.

Canes-Wrone, Brandice, David W. Brady, and John F. Cogan. 2002. "Out of Step, Out of Office: Electoral Accountability and House Members' Voting." *American Political Science Review* 96: 127–40.

Carey, John and Simon Hix. 2008. "The Electoral Sweet Spot: Low Magnitude Proportional Electoral Systems." Typescript.

Carrubba, Clifford. 2001. "The Electoral Connection in European Union Politics." *Journal of Politics* 63(1): 141–58.

Carter, Elisabeth. 2004. "Does PR Promote Political Extremism? Evidence from the West European Parties of the Extreme Right." *Representation* 40: 82–100.

Castles, Francis and Peter Mair. 1984. "Left-Right Political Scales: Some Expert Judgments." *European Journal of Political Research* 12: 73–88.

Converse, Philip. 1964. "The Nature of Belief Systems in Mass Publics." In *Ideology and Discontent*, ed. D. Apter. New York: Free Press, pp. 206–61.

—— and Roy Pierce. 1993. "Comment on Fleury and Lewis-Beck." *Journal of Politics* 55: 1110–17.

Cox, Gary. 1987. "Electoral Equilibrium Under Alternative Voting Institutions." *American Journal of Political Science* 31: 82–108.

—— 1990. "Centripetal and Centrifugal Incentives in Electoral Systems." *American Journal of Political Science* 34: 905–35.

—— 1997. *Making Votes Count*. Cambridge: Cambridge University Press.

D'Alimonte, Roberto. 1999. "Party Behavior in a Polarized System: The Italian Communist Party and the Historic Compromise." In *Policy, Office, or Votes? How Political Parties in Western Europe Make Hard Decisions*, eds. Wolfgang Muller and Kaare Strom. Cambridge: Cambridge University Press, pp. 141–71.

Dalton, Russell. 1985. "Political Parties and Political Representation." *Comparative Political Studies* 17(3): 267–99.

—— 1996. *Citizen Politics* (second edition). Chatham, NJ: Chatham House Publishers.

—— 2002. *Citizen Politics* (third edition). Chatham, NJ: Chatham House Publishers.

De Palma, André, Gap-Seon Hong, and Jacques-François Thisse. 1990. "Equilibria in Multiparty Competition Under Uncertainty." *Social Choice and Welfare* 7: 247–59.

Dow, Jay K. 1997. "Voter Choice and Strategies in French Presidential Elections: The 1995 First Ballot Election." Paper presented at the annual meeting of the Midwest Political Science Association.

—— 1998. "A Spatial Analysis of Candidate Competition in Dual Member Districts: The 1989 Chilean Senatorial Elections." *Public Choice* 97: 451–74.

—— 2001. "A Comparative Spatial Analysis of Majoritarian and Proportional Elections." *Electoral Studies* 20(1): 109–25.

Downs, Anthony. 1957. *An Economic Theory of Democracy*. New York: Harper.

Duverger, Maurice. 1954. *Political Parties*. New York: Wiley.

—— 1986. "Duverger's Law: Forty Years Later." In *Electoral Laws and Their Political Consequences*, eds. B. Grofman and A. Lijphart. New York: Agathon Press, pp. 69–84.

Eaton, B. Curtis and Richard G. Lipsey. 1975. "The Principle of Minimum Differentiation Reconsidered: Some New Developments in the Theory of Spatial Competition." *Review of Economic Studies* 42: 27–49.

Enelow, James and Melvin Hinich. 1982. "Non-Spatial Candidate Characteristics and Electoral Competition." *Journal of Politics* 44: 115–30.

—————— 1984. *The Spatial Theory of Voting*. Cambridge: Cambridge University Press.

Erikson, Robert and Gerald Wright. 1993. "Voters, Candidates, and Issues in Congressional Elections." In *Congress Reconsidered*, fifth edition, eds. Lawrence Dodd and Bruce Oppenheimer. Washington, DC: Congressional Quarterly Press.

—————— 1997. "Voters, Candidates, and Issues in Congressional Elections." In *Congress Reconsidered*, sixth edition, eds. Lawrence Dodd and Bruce Oppenheimer. Washington, DC: Congressional Quarterly Press.

—— Michael MacKuen, and James Stimson. 2002. *The Macro Polity*. Cambridge: Cambridge University Press.

—— and David Romero. 1990. "Candidate Equilibrium and the Behavioral Model of the Vote." *American Political Science Review* 84: 1103–26.

Ezrow, Lawrence. 2005. "Are Moderate Parties Rewarded in Multiparty Systems? A Pooled Analysis of Western European Elections, 1984–1998." *European Journal of Political Research* 44(6): 881–98.

—— 2007. "The Variance Matters: How Party Systems Represent the Preferences of Voters." *Journal of Politics* 69(1): 182–92.

—— 2008*a*. "On the Inverse Relationship Between Votes and Proximity for Niche Parties." *European Journal of Political Research* 47(2): 206–20.

—— 2008*b*. "Parties' Policy Programmes and the Dog that Didn't Bark: No Evidence that Proportional Systems Promote Extreme Party Positioning." *British Journal of Political Science* 38(3): 479–97.

—— and Giorgios Xezonakis. Forthcoming. "Citizen Satisfaction with Democracy and Parties' Policy offerings: A Cross-National Analysis of Twelve European Party Systems, 1976–2003." *Comparative Political Studies*.

—— Catherine E. De Vries, Marco Steenberger, and Erica E. Edwards Forthcoming "Mean Voter Representation and Partisan Constituency Representation: Do Parties Respond to the Mean Voter Position or to their Supporters?" *Party Politics*.

Farrell, David. 2001. *Electoral Systems: A Comparative Introduction*. Basingstoke, United Kingdom: Palgrave.

Feddersen, Timothy J., Itai Sened, and Stephen G. Wright. 1990. "Rational Voting and Candidate Entry Under Plurality Rule." *American Journal of Political Science* 34: 1005–16.

Fleury, Christopher and Michael Lewis-Beck. 1993. "Anchoring the French Voter: Ideology Versus Party." *Journal of Politics* 55: 1100–9.

Fowler, James H. and Michael Laver. 2006. *A Tournament of Party Decision Rules*. Presented at the annual meeting of the American Political Science Association, Philadelphia.

Franklin, Mark N. 2004. *Voter Turnout and the Dynamics of Electoral Competition in Established Democracies Since 1945*. Cambridge: Cambridge University Press.

Gabel, Matthew and John Huber. 2000. "Putting Parties in Their Place: Inferring Party Left-Right Ideological Positions from Party Manifesto Data." *American Journal of Political Science* 44(1): 94–103.

Gallagher, Michael. 1991. "Proportionality, Disproportionality and Electoral Systems." *Electoral Studies* 10: 33–51.

—— and Paul Mitchell, eds. 2008. *The Politics of Electoral Systems*. Oxford: Oxford University Press.

Giannetti, Daniela and Itai Sened. 2004. "Party Competition and Coalition Formation: Italy 1994–96." *Journal of Theoretical Politics* 16: 483–515.

Givens, Terri E. 2004. "The Radical Right Gender Gap." *Comparative Political Studies* 37(1): 30–54.

Glasgow, Garrett. 2001. "Mixed Logit Models for Multiparty Elections." *Political Analysis* 9: 116–36.

—— and R. Michael Alvarez. 2005. "Voting Behavior and the Electoral Context of Government Formation." *Electoral Studies* 24: 245–64.

—— Matt Golder, and Sona N. Golder. 2009. "Who 'Wins'? Determining the Party of the Prime Minister." Typescript.

Golder, Matt. 2003*a*. "Electoral Institutions, Unemployment and Extreme Right Parties: A Correction." *British Journal of Political Science* 33(3): 525–34.

—— 2003*b*. "Explaining Variation in the Success of Extreme Right Parties in Western Europe." *Comparative Political Studies* 36(4): 432–66.

Green, Donald and Ian Shapiro. 1994. *Pathologies of Rational Choice Theory: A Critique of Applications in Political Science*. New Haven, CT: Yale University Press.

—— Soo Yeon Kim, and David H. Yoon. 2001. "Dirty Pool." *International Organization* 55(2): 441–68.

Grofman, Bernard. 1985. "The Neglected Role of the Status Quo in Models of Issue Voting." *Journal of Politics* 45: 230–37.

Groseclose, Tim. 2001. "A Model of Candidate Location When One Candidate Has a Valence Advantage." *American Journal of Political Science* 45: 862–86.

Grumm, John. 1958. "Theories of Electoral Systems." *Midwest Journal of Political Science* 2: 357–76.

Harmel, Robert and Kenneth Janda. 1982. *Parties and Their Environments*. New York: Longman.

Hearl, Derek. 2001. "Checking the Party Policy Estimates: Reliability." In *Mapping Policy Preferences: Estimates for Parties, Electors, and Governments 1945–1998*, eds. Ian Budge, Hans-Dieter Klingemann, Andrea Volkens, Judith Bara, and Eric Tanenbaum. Oxford: Oxford University Press, pp. 111–25.

Hellwig, Timothy. 2009. "Explaining the Salience of Left-Right Ideology in Postindustrial Democracies: The Role of Structural Economic Change." *European Journal of Political Research* 46(6): 687–709.

—— Anna Mikulska, and Burcu Gezgor. Forthcoming. "Perceptions of Policy Choice in Contemporary Democracies." *European Journal of Political Research*.

Hermens, Ferdinand A. 1941. *Democracy or Anarchy?*. Notre Dame, IN: University of Notre Dame Press.

Hinich, Melvin and Peter Ordeshook. 1970. "Plurality Maximization vs. Vote Maximization: A Spatial Analysis with Variable Participation." *American Political Science Review* 64: 772–91.

—— Christian Henning, and Susumu Shikano. 2004. *Proximity Versus Directional Models of Voting: Different Results but One Theory.* Presented at the annual meeting of the Public Choice Society, March 11–14, Baltimore, MD.

Hoag, Clarence G. and George H. Hallet Jr. 1926. *Proportional Representation.* New York: MacMillan.

Hobolt, Sara B. and Robert Klemmensen. 2008. "One for All, All for One: Issue Competition in Party Leader Rhetoric." Paper prepared for the annual meeting of the Midwest Political Science Association.

Hsiao, Cheng. 2003. *Analysis of Panel Data*, second edition, Cambridge: Cambridge University Press.

Huber, John. 1989. "Values and Partisanship in Left-Right Orientations: Measuring Ideology." *European Journal of Political Research* 17(5): 599–621.

—— and G. Bingham Powell Jr. 1994. "Congruence Between Citizens and Policymakers in Two Visions of Liberal Democracy." *World Politics* 46(3): 291–326.

—— and Ronald Inglehart. 1995. "Expert Interpretations of Party Space and Party Locations in 42 Societies." *Party Politics* 1: 73–111.

Hug, Simon. 1995. "Third Parties in Equilibrium." *Public Choice* 82: 159–80.

Iversen, Torben. 1994*a*. "Political Leadership and Representation in West European Democracies: A Test of Three Models of Voting." *American Journal of Political Science* 38(1) 45–74.

—— 1994*b*. "The Logics of Electoral Politics." *Comparative Political Studies* 27(2): 155–89.

Jackman, Robert and Karin Volpert. 1996. "Conditions Favouring Parties of the Extreme Right." *British Journal of Political Science* 26: 501–22.

Jennings, Kent and Richard Niemi. 1981. *Generations and Politics.* Princeton, NJ: Princeton University Press.

Kam, Cindy and Robert Franzese, Jr. 2005. *Modeling and Interpreting Interactive Hypotheses in Regression Analyses: A Refresher and Some Practical Advice.* Typescript.

Katz, Jonathan N. and Gary King. 1999. "A Statistical Model for Multiparty Electoral Data." *American Political Science Review* 93: 15–32.

Katz, Richard. 1997. *Democracy and Elections.* Oxford: Oxford University Press.

Kedar, Orit. 2002. *Balancing the Seesaw: Rationality and Menu-Dependence in Voting Behavior.* Presented at the annual meeting of the Midwest Political Science Association, Chicago, IL, April 25–28.

—— 2004. "The Micro Foundations of (Vertically) Divided Government: Evidence from Germany." Paper presented at the annual meeting of the American Political Science Association, Chicago, IL, September 2–5.

—— 2005. "When Moderate Voters Prefer Extreme Parties: Policy Balancing in Parliamentary Elections." *American Political Science Review* 99(2): 185–99.

Keman, Hans and Paul Pennings. 2006. "Competition and Coalescence in European Party Systems: Social Democracy and Christian Democracy Moving into the 21st Century." *Swiss Political Science Review* 12(2): 95–126.

Kirchheimer, Otto. 1966. "The Transformation of Western European Party Systems." In *Political Parties and Political Development*, eds. Joseph La Palombara and Myron Weiner. Princeton, NJ: Princeton University Press, pp. 177–200.

Kitschelt, Herbert. 1988. "Organization and Strategy of Belgian and West German Ecology Parties: A New Dynamic of Party Politics in Western Europe?" *Comparative Politics* 20 (2): 127–54.

—— 1994. *The Transformation of European Social Democracy*. New York: Cambridge University Press.

—— 1997. "European Party Systems: Continuity and Change." In *Developments in West European Politics*, eds. Martin Rhodes, Paul Heywood, and Vincent Wright. New York: St. Martin's Press, pp. 131–50.

—— with Anthony J. McGann. 1995. *The Radical Right in Western Europe: A Comparative Analysis*. Ann Arbor, MI: University of Michigan Press.

Klingemann, Hans-Dieter, Andrea Volkens, Judith Bara, Ian Budge, and Michael D. McDonald. 2006. *Mapping Policy Preferences II: Estimates for Parties, Electors and Governments in Central and Eastern Europe, European Union and OECD 1990–2003*. Oxford: Oxford University Press.

Kollman, Ken, John H. Miller, and Scott E. Page. 1998. "Political Parties and Electoral Landscapes." *British Journal of Political Science* 28: 139–58.

Laakso, Markku and Rein Taagepera. 1979. "'Effective' Number of Parties: A Measure with Application to West Europe." *Comparative Political Studies* 12: 3–27.

Lacy, Dean and Phil Paolino. 1998. "Downsian Voting and the Separation of Powers." *American Journal of Political Science* 42(4): 1180–99.

—— —— 2001. *Downsian Voting and Separation of Powers in the 1998 Texas and Ohio Gubernatorial Elections*. Presented at the Annual Meeting of the Midwest Political Science Association, Chicago, IL, April.

Laver, Michael. 2005. "Policy and the Dynamics of Political Competition." *American Political Science Review* 99(2): 263–81.

—— and John Garry. 2000. "Estimating Policy Positions from Political Texts." *American Journal of Political Science* 44: 619–34.

—— and Norman Schofield. 1990. *Multiparty Government: The Politics of Coalition in Europe*. Oxford: Oxford University Press.

—— and Kenneth Shepsle. 1996. *Making and Breaking Governments*. Cambridge: Cambridge University Press.

—— Kenneth Benoit, and John Garry. 2003. "Extracting Policy Positions from Political Texts Using Words as Data." *American Political Science Review* 97(2): 311–31.

Lewis, Jeffrey B. and Gary King. 2000. "No Evidence on Directional vs. Proximity Voting." *Political Analysis* 8(1): 21–33.

Lewis-Beck, Michael. 1988. *Economics and Elections*. Ann Arbor, MI: University of Michigan Press.

Lijphart, Arend. 1984. *Democracies: Patterns of Majoritarian and Consensus Government in Twenty-One Countries*. New Haven, CT: Yale University Press.

—— 1994. *Electoral Systems and Party Systems: A Study of Twenty-Seven Democracies*. Oxford, New York: Oxford University Press.

—— 1999. *Patterns of Democracy: Government Forms and Performance in Thirty-Six Countries*. New Haven, CT: Yale University Press.

Lin, Tse-Min, Yun-Han Chu, and Melvin J. Hinich. 1996. "Conflict Displacement and Regime Transition in Taiwan: A Spatial Analysis." *World Politics* 43: 453–81.

—— James Enelow, and Han Dorussen. 1999. "Equilibrium in Multicandidate Probabilistic Spatial Voting." *Public Choice* 98(1–2): 59–82.

Lipset, Seymur Martin and Stein Rokkan, eds. 1967. *Party Systems and Voter Alignments.* New York: Free Press.

Lomborg, Bjorn. 1996. "Adaptive Parties in a Multiparty, Multidimensional System with Imperfect Information." Typescript.

Londregan, John and Thomas Romer. 1993. "Polarization, Incumbency, and the Personal Vote." In *Political Economy: Institutions, Competition, and Representation*, eds. William A. Barnett, Melvin Hinich, and Norman Schofield. New York: Cambridge University Press.

Macdonald, Stuart Elaine and George Rabinowitz. 1998. "Solving the Paradox of Nonconvergence: Valence, Position, and Direction in Democratic Politics." *Electoral Studies* 17: 281–300.

———— and Ola Listhaug. 1998. "On Attempting to Rehabilitate the Proximity Model: Sometimes the Patient Just Can't Be Helped." *Journal of Politics* 60(3): 653–90.

Mackie, Thomas T. and Richard Rose. 1991. *The International Almanac of Electoral History.* Washington, DC: Congressional Quarterly Inc.

———— 1997. *A Decade of Election Results: Updating the International Almanac.* Glasgow: Center for the Study of Public Policy, University of Strathclyde.

Marks, Gary (ed.). 2007. "Special Symposium: Comparing Measures of Party Positioning: Expert, Manifesto, and Survey Data." *Electoral Studies* 26: 1–141.

—— Liesbet Hooghe, Moira Nelson, and Erica Edwards. 2006. "Party Competition and European Integration in the East and West: Different Structure, Same Causality." *Comparative Political Studies* 39(2): 155–75.

McCarty, Nolan, Keith T. Poole, and Howard Rosenthal. 2006. *Polarized America: The Dance of Ideology and Unequal Riches.* Cambridge, MA: MIT Press.

———— 2009. "Does Gerrymandering Cause Polarization?" *American Journal of Political Science* 53(3): 666–80.

McDonald, Michael and Ian Budge. 2005. *Elections, Parties, and Democracy: Conferring the Median Mandate.* Oxford: Oxford University Press.

—— and Sylvia Mendes. 2001. "Checking the Party Policy Estimates: Convergent Validity." In *Mapping Policy Preferences: Estimates for Parties, Electors, and Governments 1945–1998*, eds. Ian Budge, Hans-Dieter Klingemann, Andrea Volkens, Judith Bara, and Eric Tanenbaum. Oxford: Oxford University Press, pp. 127–42.

—— Sylvia Mendes, and Ian Budge. 2004. "What Are Elections For? Conferring the Median Mandate." *British Journal of Political Science* 34(1): 1–26.

Meguid, Bonnie. 2005. "Competition Between Unequals: The Role of Mainstream Party Strategy and Niche Party Success." *American Political Science Review* 99(3): 347–60.

—— 2008. *Party Competition Between Unequals.* Cambridge: Cambridge University Press.

Merrill, Samuel III and James Adams. 2002. "Centripetal Incentives in Multicandidate Elections." *Journal of Theoretical Politics* 14(3): 275–300.

—— and Bernard Grofman. 1999. *A Unified Theory of Voting: Directional and Proximity Models.* Cambridge: Cambridge University Press.

Merrill, Samuel III, Bernard Grofman. and James Adams. 2001. "Assimilation and Contrast Effects in Voter Projections of Party Locations: Evidence from Norway, France, and the U.S.A." *European Journal of Political Research* 40: 199–221.

Mikhaylov, Slava, Michael Laver, and Kenneth Benoit. 2008. "Coder Reliability and Misclassification in Comparative Manifesto Project Codings." Paper presented at the annual meetings of the Midwest Political Science Association.

Mill, John S. 1861. *Considerations on Representative Government*. New York: Harper and Brothers.

Miller, Gary and Norman Schofield. 2003. "Activists and Partisan Realignment in the United States." *American Political Science Review* 97(2): 245–60.

Müller, Wolfgang C. and Kaare Strøm, eds. 1999. *Policy, Office, or Votes? How Political Parties in Western Europe Make Hard Decisions*. Cambridge: Cambridge University Press.

Myagkov, Mikhail and Peter Ordeshook. 1999. "The Spatial Character of Russia's New Democracy." *Public Choice* 97: 491–523.

Nagel, Jack. 2001. *Center-Party Strength and Major-Party Polarization in Britain*. Presented at the Annual Meeting of the American Political Science Association, San Francisco, CA, August 30–September 2.

Nagel, Jack, and Christopher Wlezien. Forthcoming. "Centre-Party Strength and Major-Party Divergence in Britain, 1945–2005." *British Journal of Political Science*.

Norris, Pippa. 2005. *Radical Right: Voters and Parties in the Electoral Market*. Cambridge: Cambridge University Press.

North, Douglass C. 1990. *Institutions, Institutional Change and Economic Performance*. Cambridge: Cambridge University Press.

Ordeshook, Peter C. and Olga Shvetsova. 1994. "Ethnic Heterogeneity, District Magnitude, and the Number of Parties." *American Journal of Political Science* 38: 100–23.

Page, Benjamin and Robert Shapiro. 1992. *The Rational Public*. Chicago, IL: The University of Chicago Press.

Paldam, Martin. 1991. "How Robust Is the Vote Function? A Study of Seventeen Nations over Four Decades." In *The Economics of Politics: The Calculus of Support*, ed. Helmut Norpoth, Michael S., Lewis-Beck, and Jean-Dominique Lafay. Ann Arbor, MI: University of Michigan Press, pp. 9–31.

Pelizzo, Riccardo. 2003. "Party Position or Party Direction? An Analysis of Party Manifesto Data." *West European Politics* 26(2): 67–89.

Pitkin, Hanna. 1967. *The Concept of Representation*. Berkeley, CA: University of California Press.

Powell, G. Bingham. 2000. *Elections as Instruments of Democracy. Majoritarian and Proportional Visions*. New Haven, CT: Yale University Press.

—— 2008. *Changing Party System Polarization, Election Rules, and Ideological Congruence*. Presented at the Annual Meeting of the American Political Science Association.

—— and Georg S. Vanberg. 2000. "Election Laws, Disproportionality, and Median Correspondence: Implications for Two Visions of Democracy." *British Journal of Political Science* 30: 383–411.

—— and Guy D. Whitten. 1993. "A Cross-National Analysis of Economic Voting: Taking Account of Political Context." *American Journal of Political Science* 37: 391–414.

Przeworski, Adam and John Sprague. 1986. *Paper Stones: A History of Electoral Socialism*. Chicago, IL: University of Chicago Press.

Quinn, Kevin and Andrew Martin. 2002. "An Integrated Computational Model of Multiparty Electoral Competition." *Statistical Science* 17: 405–19.

Rabinowitz, George and Stuart Elaine Macdonald. 1989. "A Directional Theory of Issue Voting." *American Political Science Review* 83(1): 93–121.

Rae, Douglas. 1967. *The Political Consequences of Electoral Laws*. New Haven, CT: Yale University Press.

Riker, William H. 1982. "The Two-Party System and Duverger's Law: An Essay on the History of Political Science." *American Political Science Review* 76: 753–66.

—— 1986. "Duverger's Law Revisited." In *Electoral Laws and Their Political Consequences*, eds. B. Grofman and A. Lijphart. New York: Agathon Press, pp. 19–42.

Robertson, David. 1976. *A Theory of Party Competition*. London: Wiley.

Rogers, William H. 1993. "Regression Standard Errors in Clustered Samples." *Stata Technical Bulletin* 13:19–23.

Rovny, Jan and Erica E. Edwards. 2009. "Struggle over Dimensionality: Party Competition in Europe." Typescript.

Sartori, Giovanni. 1976. *Parties and Party Systems*. New York: Cambridge University Press.

Schmitt, Herman and Evi Scholz. 2005. The Mannheim Eurobarometer Trend File, 1970–2002 [Computer file].

Schofield, Norman. 1993. "Political Competition and Multiparty Coalition Government." *European Journal of Political Research* 23: 574–94.

—— 1997. *A Comparison of Majoritarian and Proportional Electoral Systems Based on Spatial Modeling and "Rational" Politicians*. Presented at the Conference on Constitutional Issues in Modern Democracies, Messina, Italy, 25–27 September.

—— 2001. "Constitutions, Voting and Democracy: A Review." *Social Choice and Welfare* 18: 571–600.

—— 2003. "Valence Competition in the Spatial Stochastic Model." *Journal of Theoretical Politics* 15: 371–83.

—— and Itai Sened. 2005. "Multiparty Competition in Israel: 1992–1996." *British Journal of Political Science* 35: 635–63.

—— —— 2006. *Multiparty Democracy: Parties, Elections, and Legislative Politics*. Cambridge: Cambridge University Press.

—— —— and David Nixon. 1998a. "Nash Equilibrium in Multiparty Competition with 'Stochastic' Voters." *Annals of Operations Research* 84: 3–27.

—— Andrew Martin, Kevin Quinn, and David Nixon. 1998b. "Multiparty Electoral Competition in the Netherlands and Germany: A Model Based on Multinomial Probit." *Public Choice* 97(3); 257–93.

Somer-Topcu, Zeynep. 2009. "Timely Decisions: The Effects of Past National Elections on Party Policy Change." *Journal of Politics* 71(1): 238–48.

Soroka, Stuart and Christopher Wlezien. 2010. *Degrees of Democracy: Politics, Public Opinion, Policy*. Cambridge: Cambridge University Press.

Spoon, Jae-Jae. 2010. "Balancing Preferences: A Theory of small Party Survival." Typescript.

Sprague, John. 1980. "On Duverger's Sociological Law: The Connection Between Electoral Laws and Party Systems." Political Science Paper 48. Saint Louis, MO: Washington University.

Steenbergen, Marco, Erica E. Edwards, and Catherine E. De Vries. 2007. "Who's Cueing Whom? Mass-Elite Linkages and the Future of European Integration." *European Union Politics* 8(1):13–35.

Stimson, James, Michael MacKuen, and Robert Erikson. 1995. "Dynamic Representation." *American Political Science Review* 89(3): 543–65.

Stokes, Donald. 1963. "Spatial Models of Party Competition." *American Political Science Review* 57: 368–77.

Stokes, Susan. 1999. "What Do Policy Switches Tell Us About Democracy?" In *Democracy, Accountability, and Representation*, eds. Adam Przeworski, Susan Stokes, and Bernard Manin. Cambridge: Cambridge University Press.

Taagepera, Rein and Matthew Shugart. 1989. *Seats and Votes: The Effects and Determinants of Electoral Systems*. New Haven, CT: Yale University Press.

Taggart, Paul. 1996. *The New Populism and New Politics: New Protest Parties in Sweden in Comparative Perspective*. London: MacMillan.

Tarrow, Sidney. 1989. *Democracy and Disorder*. Oxford: Clarendon Press.

Van Kersbergen, Kees. 1999. "Contemporary Christian Democracy and the Demise of the Politics of Mediation." In *Continuity and Change in Contemporary Capitalism*, eds. Herbert Kitschelt, Peter Lange, Gary Marks, and John D. Stephens. Cambridge: Cambridge University Press, pp. 346–70.

Vowles, Jack, Peter Aimer, Susan Banducci, and Jeffrey Karp. 1998. *Voters' Victory? New Zealand's First Election Under Proportional Representation*. Auckland: Auckland University Press.

Wagner, Markus. 2010. "Defining and Measuring the Niche Party Concent." Typescript.

Weissberg, Robert. 1978. "Collective vs. Dyadic Representation in Congress." *American Political Science Review* 72: 535–47.

Wessels, Bernhard. 1999. "System Characteristics Matter. Empirical Evidence from Ten Representation Studies." In *Policy Representation in Western Democracies*, eds. Warren Miller, Sören Holmberg, and Roy Pierce. Oxford: Oxford University Press, pp. 137–61.

Westholm, Anders. 1997. "Distance Versus Direction: The Illusory Defeat of Proximity Theory." *American Political Science Review* 91: 865–83.

—— 2001. "Distance, Direction, and the Problem of Causal Order: A Dynamic Solution to a Static Controversy." Typescript.

Williams, Rick L. 2000. "A Note on Robust Variance Estimation for Cluster-Correlated Data." *Biometrics* 56(2): 645–6.

Wittman, Donald. 1973. "Parties as Utility Maximizers." *American Political Science Review* 67: 490–98.

—— 1977. "Candidates with Policy Preferences: A Dynamic Model." *Journal of Economic Theory* 14: 180–9.

—— 1983. "Candidate Motivation: A Synthesis of Alternatives." *American Political Science Review* 77: 142–57.

Index

Abedi, A. 81
accountability 120, 121
activists 42, 62, 63, 98, 112, 113
Adams, J. 4, 13, 24, 103, 104
Adams, J. and Merrill, S. 24, 25 n.4, 27,
    32, 63 n.20, 87 n.10, 97, 112 n.26
Adams, J. and Somer-Topcu, Z. 108
Adams, J. et al. 14, 83, 85, 92, 93, 96,
    98, 110
Adams, J., Merrill, S. and Grofman, B.
    25 n.4, 29 n.10, 98
Aldrich, J. 63, 113
Alvarez, R. M. and Nagler, J. 27, 29, 51,
    52 n.14
Anderson, C. and Guillory, C. 121
Andrews, J. and Money, J. 92
Arzeimer, K. 69
Australia, niche parties 71, 77
Austria, niche parties 71
average party policy extremism 49–58, 64,
    see also party system size hypothesis

Bartle, J. et al. 122
Beck, N. and Katz, J. N. 33 n.16
Belgium 27, 30, 109
    niche parties in 71
    proportional electoral system in 59
Benoit, K. 68–9
Best, R. 123
Blair, T. 23, 41
Blais, A. 62
Britain 8, 27, 30, 64, 109
    disproportional electoral system in 48,
        59, 68
    General Election (1983) 10 n.8, 52–4
    mean voter position and 68 n.1
    New Labour party in 23
    niche parties in 71, 75, 77
    parliamentary majorities in 46
    party responsiveness and 111
    policy centrism and 41, 52–4

vote losses due to proximity in 36 n.21
vote share in 68 n.1
Brody, R. A. and Page, B. I. 27 n.8
Budge, I. 26, 30, 72, 103, 104, 107
Budge, I. and McDonald, M. 44
Burt. G. 103 n.12

Canada 8, 27
    disproportional electoral system in 48
    niche parties in 71, 77
Carey, J. and Hix, S. 9 n.7
Carrillo, S. 82
Carrubba, C. 110
Castles-Mair (1984) study 30, 31
centrifugal policy incentives 45–6, 47, 58,
    121
centripetal policy incentives 45, 58, 121
centrist policy positioning 4, 5, 9, 13, 14,
    16, 17, 28, 47, 58, 92–3, 113, 119
    Britain and 41, 52–4
    disproportional electoral systems and 119
    electoral success and 23–5
    nonpolicy-related advantages and 36
    plurality systems and 41
    PR systems and 42, *see also* party policy
        convergence
Christian Democratic parties 4, 12, 24, 95
Clinton, B. 23
CMP (Comparative Manifesto Project) 35
    n.19, 72, 77, 100, 104, 106 n.15
coalitions 26, 28, 42, 62, 63, 112, 113
collinearity 109
Communist parties 4, 11, 12, 82, 83, 95, 98
competition 16, 41, 44, 46, 47, 62–3, 64,
    83–6
    niche party 67, 70, 74, 81, 119, 121,
        see also spatial models of electoral
        competition
congruence 5, 17, 26, 95
Conservative parties 4, 12, 52–4, 95
costly policy moderation result 93